No. 1473
$19.95

THE
MICROCOMPUTER BUILDER'S BIBLE

BY CHRIS JOHNSTON

TAB TAB BOOKS Inc.
BLUE RIDGE SUMMIT, PA. 17214

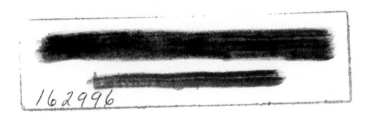

FIRST EDITION

FOURTH PRINTING

Printed in the United States of America

Library of Congress Cataloging in Publication Data

Johnston, Chris, 1955-
    The microcomputer builder's bible.

    Includes index.
    1. Microcomputers—Amateurs' manuals. I. Title.
TK9969.J63 1982   621.3819′582   82-5920
ISBN 0-8306-2473-2   AACR2
ISBN 0-8306-1473-7 (pbk.)

Contents

Introduction

Building your own computer can be a very rewarding experience. You can certainly save a lot of money by "doing it yourself," but there are even greater benefits than lower cost.

One of the greatest advantages to building your own system is that it allows you to combine the best features of several different products into a computer that will serve *your* needs better than a commercial one. You can expand your system as your interests grow and as finances become available. You can add more memory, for example, or a printer or disk drive.

All along the line there are decisions to be made such as should you build from scratch or from a kit, or should you purchase an addition already assembled and tested? That is part of the reason why I have written so much about the various products on the market—their capabilities and the differences between similar boards.

Building a computer is something that should be thought out carefully before you start. I have tried to provide enough information to allow you to make reasonable choices.

My first system was built about six years ago and I have continually expanded it, adding memory, a printer, etc. At the present time I am interested in graphics hardware and software and am adding such equipment to my system.

Some of the schematic diagrams in this book are taken directly from equipment in use in my machine. Some circuits were recently designed and are just now being tested.

There is a great feeling of accomplishment when you look at and use a computer that you have built yourself, something that will do what you want because you planned it that way.

This book is dedicated to my parents, who typed, photocopied, trimmed, criticized, and generally made the whole thing possible.

How to Size Your Computer Needs

Whether you are a businessman who wants to keep inventory records, an engineer who needs to do repetitive calculations, or a hobbyist looking for a home computer, you have to decide how much computing equipment you will need and what kind will best fulfill your requirements. You will also have to decide whether you would be better off building or buying your computer equipment. In order to help you decide, I will discuss several different types of computers in this chapter. The build/buy decision is put off until the next chapter.

To determine what equipment you will need you must first evaluate what "minimums" you require. That is really asking the question "What do I *have* to have to let me do what I want?" You want to avoid, of course, getting equipment that either will not fulfill your needs or has more capability than you can use. In either case you would be unhappy with your computer system.

For example, a business that has to keep track of 10,000 customer accounts, payroll for fifty people, and a 5000-item inventory will hardly be happy with a personal computer that has one 5¼-inch disk drive! On the other hand, a person who purchases a $50,000 minicomputer to handle the inventory of a small store with a staff of three would be spending a lot more than necessary.

This disparity is common in the construction or purchase of home (hobbyist) computers. An individual who wants a small computer because he enjoys playing with his friend's $5,000 home-built system will be disappointed if he buys a $200 computer and discov-

1

ers that it cannot be expanded to do all the "neat" things he has seen. Similarly, it would be a waste of money to spend $5,000 on a computer and use it only to play games.

It *is* important to have a computer that can be expanded later if your needs and interests change. Once you have your own computer, it will be very easy to find things to do with it that you hadn't even thought of at the time you obtained it. Expandability is therefore, of prime importance.

Acquiring a computer for the rather vague reason that "the kids will have to know something about them" really *does* make good sense. People once received their first computer experience (if they ever got any) in college. As computers became more common in high schools, students began entering college with some (sometimes quite extensive) computer experience. As the home (appliance) computer field expands (and the systems drop in price), younger children are being exposed to the computer in their homes. A child that has had exposure to a small, friendly computer since he was two or three years old, will *enter* school with a firm footing in the basics of computer science.

In my experience I've found that a good many older people who have never been exposed to computers are afraid of them. The computer, to many of them, is the machine that makes mistakes in their monthly bills. This unfortunate, if understandable, attitude has prevented many from understanding the strengths as well as the weaknesses of computers. Until recently computers *were* big nasty machines and the people who used them tended never to speak English when they talked about them.

How many times have you heard "computer error" used to explain a problem? Many people do not realize that most of the time this error was committed by a *person* entering wrong data or a program—developed by a *person*—that wasn't properly tested. (The computer merely does what it's told to do!)

A small computer can also be a powerful creative tool. Obvious areas are computer-generated art and music. However, writing and testing a computer program is an equally great opportunity to create something that is the unique product of your own mind. Many people enjoy small computers for this reason. Writing a program is the ultimate crossword puzzle and rivals any conventional game. Before you start to play the game, however, you need the tools.

PROGRAMMABLE CALCULATORS

The programmable calculator links the world of hand-held

calculators to the world of computers. If you need a pocket-sized portable computer, this is really your only choice. Example of modern programmable calculations are the Texas Instruments TI-59 and the Hewlett-Packard HP-41C (Fig. 1-1). THe HP-41C calculator, with an LCD alphanumeric display, has options including memory modules, a card reader, printer, cassette program recorder, and bar code scanner.

Programmable calculators are designed for high precision mathematical calculations. Because they can be programmed, they are good for repetitive calculations. Very few small computers can handle mathematics with the facility of a calculator. Programmable calculators normally have built-in capability to do trigonometric calculations, summations, coordinate conversions, and similar functions that are often not found in small computers. They are also small and light, making them usable anywhere when on their internal battery pack.

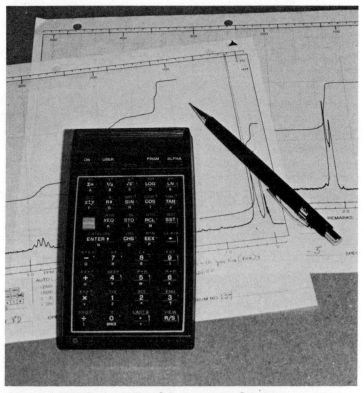

Fig. 1-1. Hewlett Packard HP-41C Programmable Calculator.

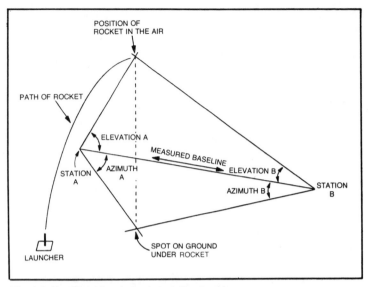

Fig. 1-2. Tracking triangle for two-station tracking.

One type of program for which a programmable calculator is ideally suited is the calculation of model rocket altitudes using standard two-station tracking. In this procedure, two trackers capable of measuring azimuth and elevation angles are set up a known distance apart (Fig. 1-2). Measurement of a model rocket's position at apogee by the two trackers will result in two sets of angles. Application of the formulas in Fig. 1-3 will allow the calculation of two altitudes. If both altitudes are within 10 percent of the average of the two, the data is considered good. This fairly simple set of calculations should be done on the flying field and may have to be repeated one hundred times in an afternoon in the course of a meet. This is an ideal application for a small battery-powered programmable calculator.

These calculators do, however, have several drawbacks. They are, first of all, very slow. They take minutes or hours to do what a computer does in seconds or minutes. Generally they have only the most limited of alphabetic display capability. One line (or part of one line) is all that is available for display at any time. They have essentially no capability outside of mathematical calculations.

Programming mathematical calculators is generally similar to programming in assembly language on a computer—the programs can be very complex and quite cryptic. This programming problem has been attacked by several manufacturers. Radio Shack and Sharp have produced "pocket computers." These are slightly larger than a normal calculator and programmed in BASIC, but they have a limited amount of internal memory.

If your computing requirements are limited to a lot of mathematical calculations (especially repetitive calculation) a small portable device, then you should look seriously at a programmable calculator.

MICROCOMPUTERS

The microcomputer is really at the heart of the "computer revolution." The development of the inexpensive, single-chip microprocessor, and the simultaneous development of high capacity and inexpensive memory chips, has made computers affordable by the average person.

The current microcomputer industry is an outgrowth of interest shown by electronic hobbyists in the new (at that time) microprocessor chips. The first real microcomputers were developed by hobbyists, and small businesses (often operated by these computer hobbyists) sprang up to service the growing market.

The hobby market was distributed among a small group of systems. The first (and oldest) were built around the 100-pin bus defined by MITS, Inc. for their Altair 8800. The major event that shaped the future of the microcomputer was the IMS Associates' decision to use the same system in their IMSAI 8080 computer. As

$$A = \frac{\text{Baseline}}{\text{Sin } 180 - (\text{Azimuth A} + \text{Azimuth B})}$$

Alt 1 = A Sin (Azimuth B) Tan (Elevation A)
Alt 2 = A Sin (Azimuth A) Tan (Elevation B)

$$\text{Avg Alt} = \frac{(\text{Alt 1}) + (\text{Alt 2})}{2}$$

If Alt 1 and Alt 2 are both within ± 10% of Avg Alt:
Then track closes; Else tracking error.

Fig. 1-3. Tracking equation.

more and more manufacturers jumped to this design, the Standard 100 (S-100) bus was born.

At the same time, Southwest Technical Products introduced their SWTPC 6800. This computer, built around the Motorola 6800 microprocessor, used a 50-pin bus for memory and a small one for peripherals. This became known as the SS-50 bus. The Digital Group, Inc. also brought out a line of very nice computers based on their own bus design. A large number of single-board computers were introduced, some of which (like the KIM-1) became very popular.

Several interesting things happened at this point. Some of the older, original manufacturers left the scene. MITS was bought by Pertec, and the IMSAI slowly faded away. There were enough new companies building products for the S-100 bus that the absence of the original manufacturers had little effect. The Digital Group also went out of business, killing the Digital Group bus as a result since they were essentially the only ones supporting it.

Several new microcomputer giants developed. Apple Computer Company, riding the phenomenal success of their APPLE II computer, became one of the industry leaders. Radio Shack and its TRS-80 surprised everyone (especially themselves) with their popularity. Radio Shack is now, in fact, the most popular manufacturer in terms of units sold. Texas Instruments, Heath, and Atari have all entered the market. In the recent past the "real" computer corporations also have entered the micro market—DEC, IBM, and Xerox.

Much of this expansion is a result of the discovery that small businesses could put these computers to work. There was initial disappointment for some of these smaller businesses when they discovered how small their computers were and how large their small businesses!

The microcomputer is a good answer to nearly any small computing project, but there are major difficulties in their use. While much faster than programmable calculators, microprocessors tend to be much slower than minicomputers and larger systems.

Their total amount of disk storage is also more limited than that in larger computers. One inventory management system advertised for a microcomputer requires six 5¼-inch disk drives for storage of about 4800 items in inventory. Six disk drives is a lot for any small system (probably over $3000 just for disk drives!). This is really pushing the capabilities of a small computer. If, then, you needed to keep inventory records on 7000 items, you wouldn't want to try it on a small computer using 5¼-inch diskettes! This case would require a hard disk or multiple double density 8-inch diskette drives, all of which are discussed and explained in Chapter 9.

If you need to do a lot of high speed numerical calculations, then a microcomputer isn't right for you either.

But, there are many cases where a microcomputer *is* the right choice. If you want a small computer because you are interested in learning how to write programs, then having a micro at home is ideal. There is a great advantage in being able to use the computer whenever it is convenient for you, and for as long as you want. Once the computer is complete all that is required is to keep it in electricity and diskettes or cassettes!

If you are interested in computer hardware, then a microcomputer is for you also, especially since you may gain more pleasure and knowledge by building it yourself. The microcomputer really shines as a word processor. A microcomputer, two double-sided, double-density 8-inch diskettes and a letter-quality printer can be purchased for less than half the price of commercial word-processing systems. When you are not composing letters or documents, you have a general-purpose computer to work (and play) with. The decision-making power of a small computer is also of great value in many industrial, scientific, and home applications where control or monitoring is necessary.

Keep in mind, however, that there are operations better suited to a computer larger than a micro. It is as a home computer that the microprocessor is of greatest value. It is an affordable, understandable tool for use at home.

If you are considering the investment in a computer, get out and talk to people. Talk to sales representatives, people at the computer stores, and, especially, talk to other users. There is no better recommendation for any computer than a large group of satisfied users.

MINI AND LARGER COMPUTERS

The minicomputer—generally with a sixteen-bit word size— has been around much longer than the micro. Recent advances in microcomputer hardware now have somewhat blurred the traditional distinction between "minis" and "micros." The minicomputer tends, in general, to be built up out of many smaller circuits. While this greatly increases the computer's complexity, it also increases its speed. They are available with diskettes or hard-disk storage and are generally comparable to microcomputers in that respect.

7

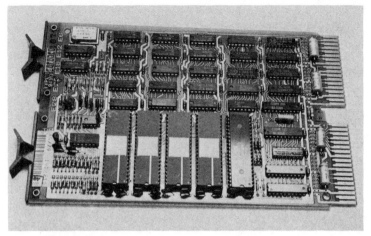
Fig. 1-4. The Digital Equipment LSI 11/2 processor card.

Digitial Equipment Corporation makes a line of computers that range from the LSI-11/2 computer (Fig. 1-4) to the large PDP 11/70. The instruction sets (the list of operations built into the computer) are upward compatible within the series. This means that programs written for the LSI-11/2 in principle, can be run on the PDP 11/70.

Because of their greater expense, most users of home computers will not consider purchasing minicomputers. The one exception is probably the DEC LSI-11. Heath sells their H-11 system, and LSI-11, in their own enclosure. Also, an experienced hobbyist can build up an "11" piece by piece, using equipment from a variety of manufacturers.

There are areas to which "large" computers will always be best suited. Handling huge address spaces and running extremely large complex programs will always be the territory of the large computer. One, the Cray Research Cray-I can perform *one hundred million 64-bit floating point mathematical operations per second.* It costs, by the way, between ten and fifteen million dollars, depending on options!

Microcomputers are encroaching on the larger ones in many situations where the prospective user needs some intermediate size computing facilities. Networks of small computers can often be used to replace one larger central computer. Determining the size of the computer that you need can be a complex problem.

For home use and for many small businesses the microcomputer provides the needed computing power at a reasonable cost.

Word processors are especially vulnerable to replacement by micro systems both because of cost and the utility of the system when it is not word processing. For businesses with several hundred to a couple of thousand items in inventory, or who need payroll for a fairly small number of employees, the microcomputer is often the right size.

Build or Buy?

Once you decide that you want a microcomputer, you must decide which one you want. No matter whose computer you might buy you are stuck with the choices that the designer made when the computer was originally planned. While you can never get completely away from having to make compromises, you can minimize them if you build your own system. Because you are providing the labor yourself you can also save money—or get more computer for your money.

If you don't want to build the entire computer, purchase one that will be expandable as your interest grows. Then do the expansion yourself. Many specialized uses require hardware that is not commercially available, at least not at an affordable price. There is also a satisfaction involved in building your own system that you just don't obtain by buying one already assembled. But even with all the advantages associated with building your own system there are sometimes circumstances that call for purchasing it instead.

DO COMMERCIAL COMPUTERS FILL YOUR NEEDS?

A strong argument for building your own microcomputer is that the computer to do exactly what you want is usually not available. If you do find a computer on the market that seems just right, then the advantages of purchasing it must be considered. A computer purchased fully assembled will generally work right the first time that it is plugged in. This is not necessarily true of a home-built computer!

One way you can really get an idea of what a computer can do is to study the manufacturer's manual *first*—before you make a decision. If you decide after studying the manual that the computer will do everything you want *now,* is it expandable to do things in the future that you might not even be thinking of now? Never assume, for example, that because you can get along with 16K bytes of memory now, you will always be able to tolerate a 16K system. Can the system be expanded? Most microprocessors can address up to 64K bytes of memory, so any computer you might consider should be able to address up to at least 48K bytes.

Can you purchase accessories for the computer from companies other than the manufacturer? You certainly don't want to invest in a system and have it become an orphan if the manufacturer folds up some day. You also don't want to be stuck paying inflated prices because the manufacturer is the only place you can obtain accessories.

Purchasing some systems really isn't a bad idea. For example, the Quasar Data Products QDP—100 computer (Figs. 2-1 and 2-2) is built around the S-100 bus and is complete with CPU card, disk controller, 64K memory, disk drives and power supply. This system, built around a standard bus (the S-100), is working when you get it and yet has provisions for easy expansion.

DO COMMERCIAL COMPUTERS FIT YOUR BUDGET?

The question whether to build or buy a computer is really a decision involving a trade-off between time and money. For most computers used in business the trade-off will come down heavily on the side of time. Having someone custom build your computer can easily prove to be more expensive, in terms of both time and money, than buying an assembled system.

Most home computerists work on a limited budget. Since you are providing your own labor (and people who charge themselves labor are quite rare!) the total cost of the home-built system should be much less than an assembled unit.

Remember throughout this book that you don't have to get the ultimate system all at once! There is no reason why you cannot build your own system slowly. I've been building my system (Fig. 2-3) for the last five years. It started with about $600 worth of equipment that was purchased over about a year. The same $600 would buy a lot more computer now than it did when this project was started.

Fig. 2-1. Quasar QDP 100 computer (courtesy Tony Zirngibl).

When figuring the cost of building a computer, you must allow for the cost of getting the computer running after it is built, as this is sometimes an area of difficulty.

DO YOU KNOW ANYTHING ABOUT ELECTRONICS?

A complete beginner in electronics should probably not try to build a computer. If you have no electronics construction experience then you would be better off either buying the computer outright or buying some simple electronics assembly kits to get experience. Many of the Heathkit kits are suitable for a first construction project. Their instructions are legendary and the kits are usually quite simple to construct.

If you can afford to, build an oscilloscope or (better yet) the Heath H-19 terminal (Fig. 2-4). This will give you good electronics assembly experience and something to use with your computer.

If you have some electronics assembly experience but have no theoretical background in electronics, then consider the many computer kits available. These are available as kits or as bare boards. You may find that the instructions (documentation) are less detailed: for example, "solder in all of the resistors and capacitors", rather than the Heathkit style "solder in resistor R-101 (brown, black, white)." Building up a bare board is more of a challenge than building a kit, but it offers you a greater opportunity to save money. You get the printed circuit board and some documentation. It is up to you to buy sockets and all necessary parts to complete the board.

If you have some theoretical (and practical!) background, you can design and build your own boards. There are some items (CPU card, for example) that you should probably not try to design until you have had a lot more experience. You cannot appreciate the complexity of a CPU card until you try to repair it. To design and build a computer circuit means that *you* take on the responsibility of making sure that it is designed correctly *and* making sure that it is well constructed.

Some single-board computers are available both as kits and as bareboards. For example, the Romac Computer Company has a

Fig. 2-2. Another view of Quasar QDP 100 (courtesy of Tony Zirngibl).

13

Fig. 2-3. The author's S-100 system, including Heath H-19 terminal.

single-board Z-80 system and a video terminal available as bareboards or kits.

If you have considerable experience in electronics, construction of a microcomputer will allow you to use some of that experi-

Fig. 2-4. Interior of Heath H-19 terminal.

ence. It will also, undoubtedly, force you to learn a lot of new things. In the end you will wind up with a better computer than you could get by purchasing one—and it will be suited directly to your interests.

DO YOU HURT YOURSELF WITH SIMPLE TOOLS?

Building a computer or add-on devices for a computer does require some mechanical dexterity. You should have a well-lighted work area; and, since somewhere within the computer power supply there will be 110 Vac line voltage present, you will need to treat the power supply with proper respect.

You will need to have (and know how to use) a small 25-watt fine-tipped soldering iron. Because most boards require a lot of soldering (a *minimum* of thirty-two 16-pin sockets on the average memory board) you will need a roll of fine rosin core solder and a tip-cleaning sponge. You will also need simple tools like wire cutters, pliers, etc., many of which you may already have.

Your computer will need some sort of enclosure—if only to keep you from dropping things into it. Most home-built computers have home-built cabinets. This will require some proficiency with an electric drill and similar tools. Knowledge of the operation of tools like a lathe, bandsaw and drill press also can't hurt. If you have experience (any at all) with, and access to, a milling machine you should be really set. You don't absolutely need anything more than a saw and an electric drill, but anything else will help.

One of the best things about building your own computer is being able to show it off to people. It is especially nice if your computer is neatly and competently constructed. People who don't know anything about computers tend to be more impressed by the enclosure and wiring than by the fact that you might have the fastest, most advanced microprocessor available, along with 250K of memory!

Choice of Processor

The microprocessor, usually a single chip, is the heart of any small computer. This one device contains all of the circuitry needed to read, decode, and execute instructions in memory; and to write to memory or to the input/output devices.

Among the microprocessor-based computers, any one of them is capable of doing nearly anything that any other can do. The user normally doesn't care what microprocessor runs his computer as long as the job gets done. However, the details of *how* the computer does what it does will differ from one type of microprocessor to another.

What the computer does is defined by the software and by hardware external to the microprocessor. The high resolution graphics capability of an APPLE II, for example, is not a function of the 6502 microprocessor inside it—but of the software written for it and the hardware interfaced to it. It would be possible to build a computer that "acted" just like an APPLE II but ran with a Z-80 microprocessor.

To illustrate: The Radio Shack TRS-80, the Heath H-89, and nearly any new S-100 bus computer all run with a Z-80 microprocessor. While the instructions that each of these computers executes are identical, the differences in their hardware make them incompatible. In this case, the hardware interfaced to the microprocessor is different enough to make them mutually exclusive. (The H-89 has, by the way, now been modified so that it is compatible with most of the S-100 CP/M world.)

There are three areas in which the choice of a specific micro-processor is important—assembly programming, interface details and word width.

Assembly Language Programming. Each different type of microprocessor uses somewhat different instructions, and the details of the assembly language differ from one type to another. Some micros have instruction sets that are "slanted" toward a particular type of applicaton. For example, although a set of programs can be written for different microprocessors that take the same input data and generate the same output data, the ease of programming will not be the same for each. This is the direct result of the differences in instruction sets.

Interface Details. Each microprocessor is unique in its hardware requirements. Some need more than one power supply voltage while others can use just +5V. Some require two-phase clock signals; some only a single phase. Some will allow direct connection to a crystal to generate the clock signal.

Details of the interface and CPU card circuitry are determined by the requirements of the processor. Some of these details may also show up as programming differences. For example, 6800- and 6502-based systems reserve a part of their memory space for I/O devices, where 8080 and Z-80-based systems have I/O ports separate from memory space and special instructions to handle them.

The specifics of the processor define the amount and type of registers available for fast internal storage. Many processors have instructions that use (or assume the use of) a particular register. Most processors have at least one accumulator, which is a register for performing mathematics and logical functions. For example, an exclusive OR operation using an 8080 will XOR the contents of the accumulator with a byte of data obtained from another register, from memory, or from the coded instruction. The result ends up in the accumulator.

Width. The last area of differences among processors involves word width. Most of the common microprocessors are designed to use 8-bit words. The instructions for a 6502, for instance, are eight bits wide. Some instructions may require an additional data byte or two additional address bytes, but the basic instruction is read from memory in one gulp.

A jump instruction taking up three bytes in memory (as shown in Fig. 3-1) is read in three pieces. First, the processor executes an instruction fetch which gets the first byte from memory. The instruction byte is decoded within the microprocessor. As a result of

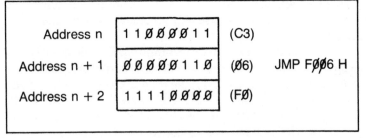

Address n	1 1 Ø Ø Ø Ø 1 1	(C3)	
Address n + 1	Ø Ø Ø Ø Ø 1 1 Ø	(Ø6)	JMP FØØ6 H
Address n + 2	1 1 1 1 Ø Ø Ø Ø	(FØ)	

Fig. 3-1. An 8080/Z-80 JUMP instruction in three consecutive memory locations.

this decoding, the processor determines that it must fetch two additional bytes from memory to serve as the address of the jump.

A processor with an 8-bit-wide instruction set is limited to only 256 different instructions. Some 8-bit processors extend this by defining a "prefix" byte. This approach is used in the Z-80 where two prefixes are used. The prefix byte tells the processor that the next byte is to be used as an instruction but it will be decoded differently than normal. Figure 3-2 illustrates this process for a hypothetical 3-bit microprocessor. If the instruction fetched is 011 (instruction 3), it tells the processor to fetch another word and treat it as an instruction *but* to use the alternate instruction table for decoding. If in normal operation the instruction fetched is 010 (2), then the word in the accumulator is added to itself. If the instruction is 011 (3), and the next instruction fetched is 010(2), then the word in the accumulator is subtracted from itself.

A processor with 16-bit-wide instructions can have 65,536 different instructions. No real processor requires that many instructions so the extra width of the word can be used for data. For example, if nine bits are used for instruction decoding, then seven are left for data. A relative jump instruction could be written using the lower seven bits as an offset.

The wider word size allows more instructions and therefore a more powerful processor. Most of the new 16-bit processors have "multiply" instructions built-in—a feature missing from the 8-bit processors. Some of the 16-bit processors can address more than 64K of memory by using special memory management hardware.

The Intel 8088 8-bit processor is actually a 16-bit processor (the 8086) with special bus hardware built in to read data eight bits at a time rather than sixteen at a time. This was done in order to make integration easier with existing 8-bit wide peripheral and memory chips. It looks like a 16-bit processor on the inside and an 8-bit machine on the outside.

8-BIT PROCESSORS

Following is a comparison of several of the common 8-bit processors.

8080

The 8080 developed by Intel was a successor to the 8008, which was originally meant to be a machine-controller IC. Much of the 8080 design philosophy was borrowed directly from the 8008. Intel did not foresee the use of these devices as personal, general-purpose computers. It was first picked up by hobbyists who built simple computers, and the rest is, as they say, history.

The 8080 has an accumulator and a flag register along with a set of six general purpose registers (see Fig. 3-3). The 8080 is stack-oriented, meaning that a set of instructions is included to manage part of memory as a last-in, first-out (LIFO) memory. This stack is used for temporary storage without the need for keeping track of addresses.

When the processor executes a "CALL" instruction the program counter (the 16-bit register holding the address of the next instruction to execute) contents are pushed onto the stack. The stack pointer which holds the address of the next available stack is decremented by two, and a jump to the subroutine occurs. When processing is complete the last instruction executed is a RETURN. This pops the return address off the stack and execution continues.

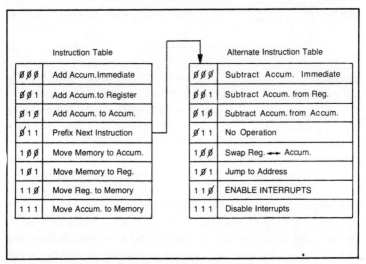

Fig. 3-2. An illustration of the use of a prefix byte in an instruction.

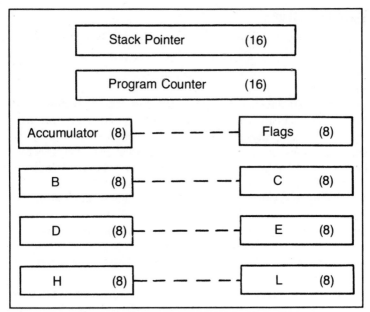

Fig. 3-3. The 8080 register set.

8080 Characteristics

Power Supplies   +5, +12, −5 volts

Clock   Nonoverlapping two-phase clock at +12 volts. Maximum frequency 2MHz

Registers   Accumulator, flag register, six general-purpose 8-bit registers combinable to three 16-bit registers, stack pointer and program counter (Fig. 3-3)

Interrupts   Single maskable interrupt

I/O Space   256 ports

Memory Space   64K bytes normally; 128K using stack status — 64K stack memory/64K program memory

8085

The 8085 is an improved version of the 8080. From the perspective of the programmer, the 8085 is nearly identical to the 8080 with two additional instructions to handle the built-in interrupt extensions. The pinout and structure is different, with the data bits and lower eight address bits being multiplexed onto a common bus. This frees up enough pins to allow several additional interrupt inputs. The clock driver required by the 8080 has been built in, allowing direct connection to a crystal. A serial I/O port is also built in.

8085 Characteristics

Power Supplies	+5 volts
Clock	No clock inputs. Provision for direct connection to a crystal. Some versions have maximum frequencies up to 5 MHz.
Registers	Accumulator, flag register, six general-purpose 8-bit registers combinable into three 16-bit registers, interrupt mask register, stack pointer, program counter (Fig. 3-4)
Interrupts	One maskable interrupt, three maskable restart interrupts, one nonmaskable TRAP interrupt
I/O Space	256 ports, one onboard serial I/O port
Memory Space	64K normally; 128K using stack status line—64K stack memory/ 64K program memory

Z-80

The Z-80, brought out by Zilog (and second-sourced by Mostek and NEC), was developed to be a new-generation 8080. Most of the unused 8080 opcodes were utilized to expand the instruction set of the Z-80. A set of index registers was added. This allowed the use of instructions which will, for example, load the accumulator with the contents of the memory location whose address is stored in the index register (plus or minus an offset). This is a powerful method for managing lists or tables. A set of block move instructions was included to facilitate movement of data from one place in memory to another.

An expanded interrupt system was added, allowing for several types of responses to interrupts. A duplicate set of main registers was also included; these registers are not available simultaneously with the standard set, but they can be exchanged—making the reserve set current and reserving the other set.

Best of all, the Z-80 is almost completely compatible with software written for the 8080. In fact, most programs written for the 8080 will run with no problems on a Z-80. The only exceptions involve the flag register (Fig. 3-5).

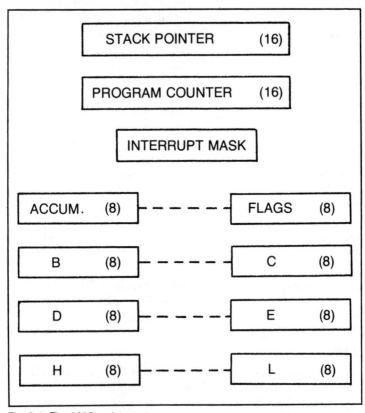

Fig. 3-4. The 8085 register set.

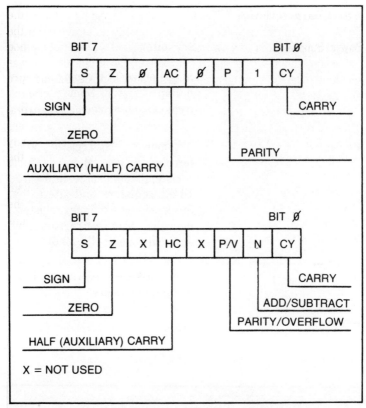

Fig. 3-5. Comparison of the 8080 and Z-80 flag registers.

The 8080 flag register has five active bits while the Z-80 has six. The flags are identical with two exceptions. First, the 8080 parity flag (bit two of the flag register) reflects the parity resulting from an operation. The same flag in the Z-80 serves as a parity flag for logical operations and as an overflow flag for arithmetic operations. This is the major source of problems encountered when running programs written for the 8080 on a Z-80. While it doesn't occur frequently, there are some programs which are notorious for this problem. Because of this, the original Altair Basic would not run on Z-80s. The newer versions of Microsoft Basic have corrected this, of course.

The second flag discrepancy occurs in bit position one. This bit is always set (a one) in the 8080 but serves as an add/subtract flag in the Z-80. This is internally used for BCD operations and is not testable through a normal instruction.

Z-80 Characteristics

Power Supplies   +5 volts

Clock   Single phase TTL compatible with pullup resistor. Some versions have clock frequencies of 6 MHz.

Registers   Accumulator, flag register and alternates, six general-purpose 8-bit registers combinable into three 16-bit registers and alternates. Stack pointer, two index registers, interrupt and refresh registers, and program counter (Fig. 3-6)

Interrupts   One maskable, one nonmaskable using three modes.

I/O Space   256 ports

Memory Space   64K

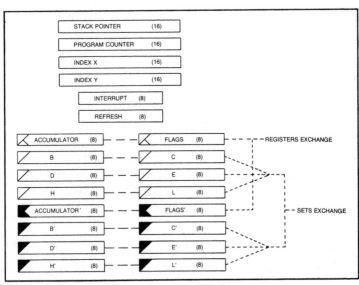

Fig. 3-6. The Z80 register set.

6502

The MOS Technology 6502 microprocessor, used in the APPLE II, Atari and OSI Superboard computer, is similar to the 6800. The 6502 runs on a single +5V power supply and has an onboard crystal oscillator. The crystal can be attached directly to the chip. The 6502 is designed around 256 word "pages" of memory. There are instructions that will work only with data in page 0 and the stack is similarly limited. The stack pointer is only eight bits wide (in contrast to the 8080 or 6800 sixteen bit stack pointer) which limits the stack to a single page in memory.

In general, the 6502 has a great number of addressing modes but is severely limited by the width of its registers. The two index registers (X and Y) are also only eight bits wide. There are no general-purpose registers other than the accumulator. A common complaint about the 6502 concerns the exceptions in its instruction set—some instructions can be used with only one index register or the other! All in all, however, it is efficient and quite fast. Basic interpreters written for the 6502 tend to be faster than similar programs on the other microprocessors.

6502 Characteristics

Power Supply	Single +5V supply
Clock	Internal oscillator requires only an external crystal; some versions operate up to 2 MHz.
Registers	8-bit accumulator, two 8-bit index registers, status register, 8-bit stack pointer, 16-bit program counter (Fig. 3-7)
Interrupts	One maskable, one nonmaskable interrupt
I/O Space	Uses memory mapped I/O
Memory Space	64K of addressable space.

6800

The 6800 is Motorola's first-generation microprocessor. It operates on a single +5 volt power supply and, like the 8080,

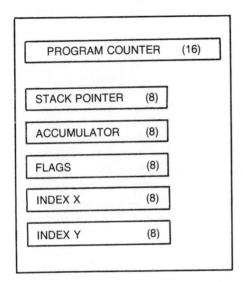

Fig. 3-7. The 6502 register set.

Inside the figure:

PROGRAM COUNTER (16)

STACK POINTER (8)

ACCUMULATOR (8)

FLAGS (8)

INDEX X (8)

INDEX Y (8)

requires a two-phase clock. The 6800 contains two 8-bit accumulators, an advantage when a lot of numerical or logical computation is required. It has a 16-bit register with an indexed addressing mode, a 16-bit stack pointer, and a status register.

The interrupt response of the 6800 is interesting: While the 8080/Z-80 interrupt saves the return address (the address at the time of the interrupt) on the stack, the 6800 saves *everything*— return address, status registers, accumulators and index register on the stack. Considerable processor work is thus eliminated.

While the 8080 begins execution at address 0 after a reset, the 6800 reads the start address from locations FFFE and FFFF. This eliminates the need for extensive power-on-jump circuitry. The interrupt response locations are stored, in a similar manner, in the six bytes from FFF8 to FFFD.

6800 Characteristics

Power Supply	Single +5V supply
Clock	Two-phase some versions operate up to 2 MHz.
Registers	Two 8-bit accumulators, flag register, a 16-bit index register, stack pointer, and program counter (Fig. 3-8)

Interrupts	One maskable, one nonmaskable
I/O Space	Memory mapped I/O
Memory Space	Total addressing space of 64K bytes.

Other 8-Bit Processors

There are several other 8-bit processors which have either not become popular, or are new and not yet widely used.

RCA's 1802 processor is the only CMOS microprocessor. It features extremely low power consumption. The major advantage of the 1802 is that it can be easily battery powered. This is an important factor in the development of lightweight portable equipment. It is constructed around a set of general-purpose registers.

The older Fairchild F8 is not so much a general-purpose microprocessor as it is a flexible, programmable controller. It is not a single chip device and may require several chips depending on the application.

Among the newer devices is the Motorola 6809 microprocessor. This is an upgrade of the 6800's capabilities, including a larger and more versatile instruction set. There is an additional index register available as well as another stack pointer. This two-stack system allows control over stack usage; for example it separates passing data on the stack from return addresses. An additional

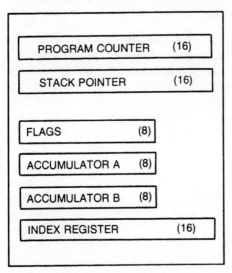

Fig. 3-8. The 6800 register set.

27

register, the Direct Page register, has also been added in the 6809. The direct (page 0) instructions of the 6800 are now used in conjunction with this new register. The 6809 Direct Page register holds the upper byte of a memory address (the page address), and the direct addressing instructions address the page in this register rather than only page 0 as in the 6800.

Another of the newer processors is the Zilog Z8. One member of this Z8 microprocessors family is the Z8671. This contains 2K of ROM programmed with a BASIC interpreter/debugger. This chip also contains 144 8-bit registers. The bottom four serve as I/O ports, the next 124 are general-purpose registers. The upper sixteen registers handle the stack, the interrupt system, the port programming, an internal counter/timer, and have register numbers from 240 to 255. Registers numbered between 128 and 239 (inclusive) are not available. The I/O ports include a serial port and three 8-bit parallel ports. This processor is ideal for dedicated applications where a full computer system isn't practical. You don't really need a 64K dual-disk system with a printer to control your furnace!

16-BIT PROCESSORS

As integrated circuit technology developed and it became possible to pack more transistors on a chip, and more powerful processors were designed. The biggest move has been toward 16-bit processors; and the movement continues toward 32-bit single-chip processors.

One of the first 16-bit processors was the Texas Instruments TMS 9900—it remained nearly alone until Intel announced its 8086. Then in quick succession Zilog introduced the Z8000 series and Motorola the MC68000. The long lag before the 68000 was available had an interesting effect on the microprocessor market. The 8086 was available first and gathered a respectable market. The superior Z8000 came out next and began to attract part of the market. The 68000 is superior to the Z8000 and far superior to the 8086, but the interesting effect is that the market seems to be dividing between the 8086 and the 68000. The 8086 has been available long enough to have a sizable software base and the 68000 is so far superior to the others that it is gaining support. Users have been choosing the inferior 8086 over the Z8000, mainly because of the market lead. Each of these microprocessors has its own strengths and weaknesses.

TMS 9900

The Texas Instruments TMS 9900 is described as having a "memory-to-memory architecture." This type of microprocessor architecture makes use of memory instead of internal registers. In fact, the only registers available to the programmer are the program counter, the status register, and a workspace pointer. The workspace pointer register holds the address of a sixteen word block of memory. This block of memory is used by the processor as if it were a set of internal registers. An advantage of this arrangement is the possibility of doing a "context switch." If a program being executed is interrupted and its status register saved, the program and workspace pointer can be modified to point at a different program and its attendant workspace. Return to the original program involves only saving the status register, changing the program counter and workspace pointer registers, and restoring the original status register contents. This allows the interrupted program to proceed as if it were never interrupted.

The 9900 requires +5V, +12V and −5V power supplies. The processor requires a four-phase, nonoverlapping clock. The 9900 itself is housed in a 64-pin DIP package. This large package is required because the processor maintains separate data and address buses (it does not multiplex these onto one set of pins). It is interesting to note that there are only fifteen address bits available. While 64K bytes of memory are available, there are only 32K of words.

The instruction set is, of course, based on the workspace register and includes multiply and divide instructions.

9900 Characteristics:

Power Supply	+5V, +12V, −5V
Clock	Nonoverlapping four-phase clock; some versions operate up to 4 MHz.
Registers	16-bit program counter, status register, and workspace pointer (Fig. 3-9)
Interrupts	Built-in vectored interrupt capability.

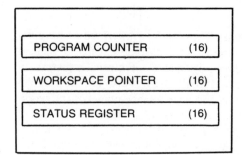

Fig. 3-9. The TMS 9900 register set.

I/O Space	Memory mapped I/O
Memory Space	32K word addressability

8086/8088

The Intel 8086/8088 microprocessor was the first of the "new" 16-bit processors. Unlike the older TMS9900, the 8086 uses multiplexed address and data lines to reduce the package size. The 8086 is contained in a standard 40-pin DIP package. It addresses up to one megabyte of memory, which can be logically separated into code, stack, data, and extra data areas. This allows some insulation between programs, stack, and data areas. Properly managed, this prevents a program from inadvertently overwriting the stack.

The interrupt system of the 8086 provides for a nonmaskable interrupt and maskable interrupts, working something like the Z-80 Mode 2 interrupt. It has a set of byte instructions allowing manipulations of half words, a feature common to most 16-bit processors. Multiply and divide instructions are included, as are a set of string manipulation instructions.

The 8088 is nearly identical to the 8086 except it has an 8-bit bus interface. The processors are identical from the programmer's point of view, having the same instruction and register sets. Because of the 8-bit interface the 8088 must do more work in transferring data with the result that execution is slower. It has the same one megabyte addressing range and will, like the 8086, address up to 64K of I/O ports.

8086/8088 Characteristics:

Power Supply	+5 volts
Clock	33% duty cycle single phase. Some versions operate up to 10 MHz

Registers	16-bit accumulator, three 16-bit registers, 16-bit status register, four 16-bit segment registers, 16-bit instructions, stack and base pointers, 16-bit source and destination index registers (Fig. 3-10).
Interrupts	Nonmaskable and maskable (vectorable) interrupts
I/O Space	64K I/O ports
Memory Space	One megabyte total

Z8000

The Zilog Z8000 family of microprocessors (second-source by AMD) consists of two main processors. The Z8001 is the "segmented" version housed in a 48-pin DIP package, directly addressing eight megabytes *per address space*. The Z8002 is the

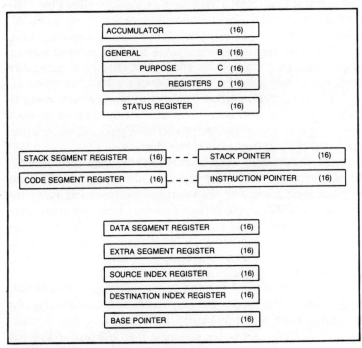

Fig. 3-10. The 8086/8088 register set.

"nonsegmented" version housed in a 40-pin DIP package, addressing 64K *per address space.*

The *"per address space"* clause can be important. Both a "system" and a "normal" mode are defined for the processor. This definition allows the physical separation of operating system memory areas from user memory areas, decreasing the chance of a malfunctioning program overwriting the operating system.

Each mode (normal or system) is further subdivided into stack, code (program), and data spaces. This also protects the operating system by minimizing the chance of a program attempting to execute data or corrupt the stack. Fully expanded each of these address spaces can be eight megabytes long in the Z8001 or 64K long in the Z8002. This brings the total memory addressing capability up to 48 megabytes in the Z8001 and 384K in the Z8002.

The Z8001 was identified as the "segmented" version of the processor. This means that it has a 7-bit segment address bus available. Memory can then be separated into 128 segments each 64K long.

The Z8001 is designed to be used with the Z8010 Memory Management Unit (MMU) This memory manager allows the 64K-long segments to be addressed nearly anywhere in the 24-bit addressing range. The Memory Management Unit is programmed like an I/O port by the processor and takes the 7-bit segment number and the upper eight bits of the address (or offset) and, using data programmed into it by the CPU, generates a 24-bit address.

The unit provides memory protection by allowing memory to be write protected, system mode access only, instruction fetch mode only, etc. This allows the protection of pieces of memory (the operating system) from inadvertent changes.

The Z8000 family has a nonmaskable interrupt and a nonvectored interrupt, both of which supply an identifying word from the external logic generating the interrupt. Vectored interrupts are available with 256 usable service routines. There are traps (synchronous interrupts) that occur, for instance, when a user (normal mode) program attempts to use a "privileged" instruction (system mode). An error picked up from the MMU (a write protect violation, for example) also produces a trap.

The instruction set is quite varied, allowing nybble (4-bit), byte (8-bit), word (16-bit) and long word (32-bit) addressing. An interesting point is that I/O instructions are only legal in system mode. The Z8000 instruction set some Z-80 I/O instructions but with advanced design enhancements. There is a wide variety of addressing modes, including a kind of page 0 mode and auto-increment mode. The auto-increment mode will automatically add *two* to a register used as a pointer to a list in memory so that no explicit instructions need to be used to point at the next array element.

Z8001/Z8002 Characteristics:

Power Supply   +5 volts

Clock   Single phase

Registers   **Z8001**—sixteen 16-bit general-purpose registers R0-R15; registers R0-R7 usable as pairs of 8-bit registers; R14 and R15 used as 32-bit normal mode stack pointer. Alternate registers R14′ and R15′ used as 32-bit system stack pointer. Registers R1-R15 usable as index registers. Registers also usable as pairs for 32-bit operations and quads for 64-bit operation; 16-bit flag control registers, 16-bit program counter offset register and seven bits of program counter segment number, and upper offset register for New Program Status Area Pointer (Fig. 3-11).

Z8002—sixteen 16-bit general-purpose registers R0-R15; registers R0 through R7 usable as pairs of 8-bit registers; R15 used as a 16-bit normal mode stack pointer. Alternate register R15′ used as 16-bit system mode pointer. Registers R1-R15 usable as index registers. Registers available as pairs for 32-bit operations and as quads for 64-bit operations. 16-flag control, program counter, and refresh registers. Upper pointer register for new program status area pointer (Fig. 3-12).

Interrupts

Nonmaskable and nonvectored interrupts supply 16-bit identifier word. Vectored interrupts supply a 16-bit identifier word whose low-order byte is an 8-bit vector to one of 256 service routines. Z8001 generates service routine address with segment data.

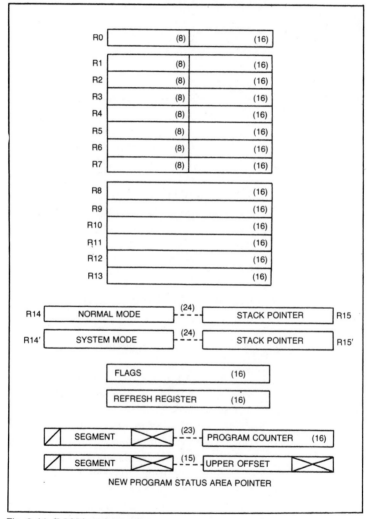

Fig. 3-11. Z-8001 register set.

I/O Space	64K of I/O ports. I/O ports only accessible from system mode.
Memory	**Z8001**—eight megabytes directly; 42 megabytes with system/normal and code/data/stack decoding.
	Z8002—64K directly; 384K with system/normal and code/data/stack decoding.

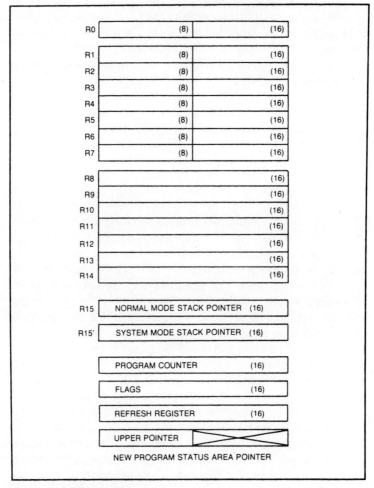

Fig. 3-12. Z-8002 register set.

68000

The Motorola 68000 microprocessor is the newest and most capable of the 16-bit processors. It is packaged in a 64-pin package eliminating the necessity of multiplexing signals to obtain all functions. This is a different strategy than the Z8000 or 8086 which are packaged in smaller (40- and 48-pin) packages. The multiplexed microprocessors are slightly easier to handle (sockets are more easily available, for instance) but require external logic to latch and demultiplex the signals. The 68000 trades the packaging advantage for a more straightforward design and fewer external parts.

The 68000 uses a 24-bit address bus, allowing a 16 megabyte addressing range. If the function codes are also decoded, then a total of 64 megabytes can be addressed, divided into 16-megabyte user data, user program, supervisor data, and supervisor program areas.

The 68000, like the Z8000, has a supervisor or system mode with special privileged instructions. The supervisor mode is designed for use with the operating system (which has full instruction privileges) while the user mode is for programs running under the operating system. Unlike the Z8000, the 68000 uses memory mapped I/O. (I/O devices are addressed the same as memory locations rather than as special I/O ports separate from memory.)

The 68000's direct addressing capability makes a device like the Z8010 MMU unnecessary. One disadvantage is that there is no "built-in" capability to qualify memory accesses such as READ ONLY. Without function code decoding there seems to be no separation between supervisor and user memory areas, which could allow supervisor programs to be accessed by a user program. To enforce the operating system/user separation the function code decoding must be done. This places system and user memory in physically different memory arrays. There is no way for a user mode program to get into supervisor mode memory without the operating system "knowing about it".

The interrupt system of the 68000 is part of the larger subject of "exception processing". An exception occurs with an interrupt or when several other conditions are met. An illegal instruction fetch, for example, generates a trap. A bus error signal is available and is used to signal the processor that something is wrong. Bus accesses can be repeated if necessary. There is a trace mode, where execution of each program statement generates a trap to a preprogrammed location. This is useful with a debugger program where control is returned to the debugger after each instruction is executed.

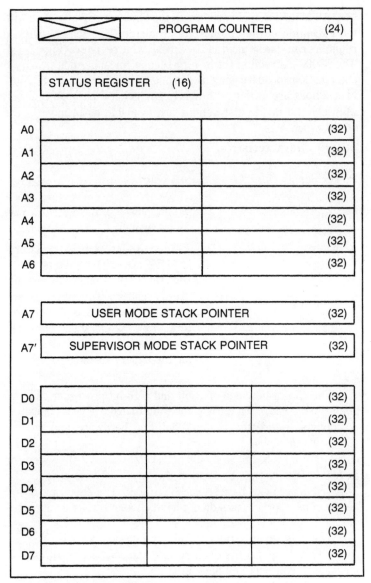

Fig. 3-13. The 68000 register set.

There are seven interrupt priority levels, level seven being highest in priority and nonmaskable. The interrupting device can provide a response vector which selects an entry in an interrupt service table.

All of the internal registers in the 68000 are 32 bits wide with the exception of the 16-bit status register. The general-purpose registers can also be used as 16- or 8-bit wide registers (Figs. 3-13). The 68000 instruction set is very regular, meaning that nearly all combinations of addressing modes and instructions are legal. Most instructions are usable with nearly any general purpose register. Multiply and divide instructions are available as in most of the 16-bit processors.

68000 Characteristics:

Power Supply	+5 volt
Clock	Single phase; 4,6 and 8 MHz versions available.
Registers	Fifteen 32-bit general registers. D0-D17 are data registers while registers A0 through A6 are address registers. The data registers are usable as 32, 16, or 8-bit registers. Two 32-bit stack pointers, one for the user mode stack and one for the supervisor mode stack.

The choice between an 8-bit and a 16-bit processor chip depends, in the end, upon the use you want to make of your computer. A hobbyist interested in both building hardware and writing software can choose any microprocessor. A person who needs a computer for his business should get a CP/M based Z-80 system, or an 8086/8088 system, because of the large software base for the Z-80 and the growing base for the 8086/8088. The Z8000 and 68000 series of microprocessors do not have enough software support—yet.

There is great variety in microprocessor designs. You can surely find a chip that fits the hardware and software requirements for whatever project you have in mind.

The S-100 Bus

A bus-oriented computer system is built of a number of circuit cards connected together. The bus is not just a function of the type of connections or the connector to be used. To specify a bus you must define:

- Type of connector and number of pins.
- Size, shape, and spacing of the boards.
- Characteristics of each signal on each pin.
- Timing relationships among the signals.

The bus is a concept, an ordering of signals. The S-100 (Standard-100) bus is a collection of 100 signals whose positions and definitions are standardized. A motherboard with 100 pin sockets is *not* the S-100 bus. The bus is composed of the definitions of each of these 100 lines and the definitions of the timing relationship between the signals on these 100 lines. You could design a perfectly reasonable computer system using S-100 prototype boards and an S-100 motherboard that would *not* be an S-100 system.

ADVANTAGES AND DISADVANTAGES

The S-100 is a very popular bus system for microcomputers. The editor of one of the popular computer magazines estimated that there are 500,000 existing S-100 systems, most of them built into industrial equipment. The bus enjoys widespread support with many manufacturers making boards for the S-100.

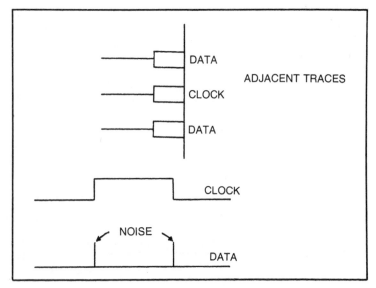

Fig. 4-1. Adjacent signal lines can allow noise to propagate.

One of the disadvantages of the S-100 is that, as originally developed, the signals on the bus were a reflection of the pinout of the 8080 CPU chip. The control and status lines available on the 8080 are available on the bus. Unfortunately, most other CPU chips do not make the same information available.

The bus also was set up with two unidirectional data buses instead of one bidirectional data bus. This was apparently done because it was cheaper and easier to implement than a bidirectional bus.

Another common complaint about the S-100 bus involves the physical placement of signal lines on the bus. In many cases high speed signals are placed next to or across from other signals whose functions are critical to the operation of the computer. Noise will propagate from one line to another causing glitches and bad data. (Fig. 4-1) It would be nice if the high-speed signals could be ground-isolated from other signals on the bus. (Fig. 4-2)

One other problem was the practice of many manufacturers redefining signals on the bus to suit their own convenience. This was widespread at first but slackened as manufacturers realized that incompatibility would remove all the advantages of a "standard" bus. There is now an IEEE standard proposal for the S-100 bus, and many manufacturers are bringing their products into line with it.

The bus is fairly simple to understand, which makes it easy to design add-on boards. It now has options for 24-bit addressing, 16-bit data transfers, a 16-bit I/O bus, and several uncommitted lines for expansion.

The S-100 bus is, despite its faults, a good and reasonably reliable system that has excellent industry support. It is an excellent choice for the small computer user.

SIGNAL DESCRIPTIONS

The S-100 bus can be broken into groups of logically similar signals. These groups include data and address lines, status lines, strobe or timing signals, power supplies, and miscellaneous signals.

Special handshaking protocols allow smooth transitions between permanent and temporary bus masters (DMA controllers for instance) and selectable 8- or 16-bit data transfers. A normal 8-bit data transfer uses the Data-Out bus if data is coming from the CPU and the Data-In bus if data is moving to the CPU card. CPU cards that have 16-bit processors can request a 16-bit transfer. Along both the Address and Status lines the 16-bit data transfer request line (sXTRQ*) is activated. If the selected memory board is equipped to permit 16-bit transfers, the 16-bit Acknowledge (SIXTN*) signal is activated, and the Data In and Data Out buses are used as a 16-bit wide bidirectional data bus.

There are several *types* of signals on the bus. These include master signals generated by the bus master device (usually the

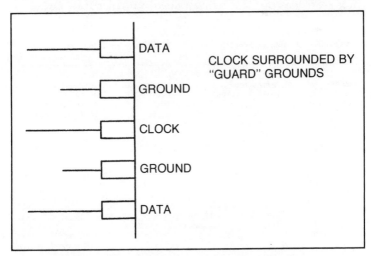

DATA

GROUND

CLOCK

GROUND

DATA

CLOCK SURROUNDED BY "GUARD" GROUNDS

Fig. 4-2. Ground isolation of signal lines can protect against noise.

S-100 BUS BY FUNCTION

16- bit address bus

NAME	NUMBER		NAME	NUMBER	
A0	79	least significant	A8	84	
A1	80		A9	34	
A2	81		A10	37	
A3	31		A11	87	
A4	30		A12	33	
A5	29		A13	85	
A6	82		A14	86	
A7	83		A15	32	Most sig. of 16 bit address bits

Extended Address bus

A16	16	Least sig. ext. bit	A20	61	
A17	17		A21	62	
A18	15		A22	63	
A19	59		A23	64	Most sig. ext. bit

Data IN bus

Data OUT bus

DI0	95	least sig. bit	DO0	36	Most sig. bit
DI1	94		DO1	35	
DI2	41		DO2	88	
DI3	42		DO3	89	
DI4	91		DO4	38	
DI5	92		DO5	39	
DI6	93		DO6	40	
DI7	43		DO7	90	

FOR 16-BIT TRANSFERS DO0 IS THE LEAST SIGNIFICANT BIT, DI7 THE MOST.

Data transfer status signals

Data transfer strobe signals

sMEMR	47	Memory read	pDBIN	78	Data bus IN
sWO*	97	Write or Output	pWR*	77	Write
sINP	46	INPUT cycle	MWRT	68	Memory write
sOUT	45	OUTPUT cycle	SIXTN*	60	16 Acknowledge
sXTRQ	58	16 request			
PHANTOM*	67	Overlay memory			

Interrupt system

NAME	NUMBER	
INT*	73	Interrupt input to processor
NMI*	12	Non-Maskable interrupt input to processor
VI0*	4	Highest priority Vectored Interrupt
VI1*	5	
VI2*	6	
VI3*	7	
VI4*	8	

```
VI5*     9
VI6*     10
VI7*     11       Lowest priority Vectored Interrupt
sINTA    96       Interrupt acknowledge from processor
```

Control Status signals			TMA (or DMA) system	

---

sM1	44	M1 cycle	HOLD*	74	Requests HOLD state
sHLTA	48	HALT Acknowledge	TMA0*	55	TMA
			TMA1*	56	request
			TMA2*	57	priority
Control Strobe signals			TMA3*	14	code
			~ADSB*	22	Address Disable
			DODSB*	23	Data OUT disable
pSYNC	76	Processor SYNC	SDSB*	18	Status Disable
pSTVAL	25	Status valid	CDSB*	19	Control Out bus disable
		was phase 1 clock			
pHLDA	26	HOLD Acknowledge			
RDY	72	Requests a Wait state			
		when LOW			
XRDY	3	Requests a Wait state			
		when low			

Other Signals

```
POC*     99       Power-ON-Clear
RESET*   75       Reset system
SLAVE
 CLR*    54       Reset slaves (not the CPU card)
         24       Master system clock
CLOCK    49       2 MHz clock signal
ERROR*   98       system error trap
PWRFAIL* 13       Power failure signal

+8       1,51     +8 Volt unregulated supply
+16      2        +16 Volt unregulated supply
-16      52       -16 Volt unregulated supply
GROUND   50,100   ground
         20,53,70          also ground

NDEF     66,65,21 Not Defined    66 is commonly REFRESH*
RFU      71,69,28,27 Reserved for future use
                 27 was pWAIT
```

Fig. 4-3. S-100 Bus, by function.

CPU card), slave signals produced by slave devices (memory and I/O boards), and bus signals which need to be generated somewhere in the system.

Master Signals

Master signals are generated by the CPU board and are necessary for the operation of the computer. They include the following:

Address Lines. There are 16 address lines and 8 extended address lines. Any CPU board will use the lower 16 lines, yielding an addressing range of 2^{16} or 65,536 bytes. If the card uses the 8 extended address bits the addressing range would be 2^{24} or 16,777,216 bytes.

Data Out Lines. There are 8 data lines out from the processor board. If a 16-bit data transfer is underway (an option for new processors as provided for in the standard) then these lines are the low-order byte to be transferred.

Status Lines. These lines tell the rest of the system what the processor is doing at a particular time. The SM1 signal, for instance, tells the rest of the system that an instruction fetch (M1 cycle) is in progress.

Strobe Lines. Strobe lines instruct the rest of the system *when* to do things. For example, the pSTVAL signal (STATUS VALID) enables the other components of the computer to figure out when the status lines are valid. They are also commonly used to tell the memory boards when there is valid data on the Data Out line.

Slave Signals

The signals generated by the slave device either transfer data to the processor or inform the processor of special conditions.

Data In Lines. There are eight lines that carry data to be input to the processor. For 16-bit transfers these lines carry the high-order byte of the word to be processed.

Interrupt Lines. These 10 lines include eight *vectored* interrupt lines, the processor interrupt line, and the nonmaskable interrupt line. The latter two signals feed directly into the processor card, causing it to respond to the interrupt. Vectored interrupt lines normally enter a special priority interrupt controller which then interrupts the processor, using the processor interrupt line. Interrupts force the processor to attend to important events occurring in the system. A further discussion of interrupts is given in Chapter 13.

Strobe Signals. These signals generally request the processor to enter a special mode of operation. The most familiar are xRDY and pRDY. When these are high they tell the processor that the system is **"ready"** and that normal processing may continue. If either one is low they force the processor into a **"wait state."** This effectively freezes the bus until it becomes ready again. This capability is used when a memory or I/O device can't respond to a read or write request fast enough for the data to be captured when the CPU expects it. For instance, a Z-80A processor running at 4 MHz it requires memory that has an access time of no more than 250 ns.

This is because about 250 ns after the processor addresses the memory chip it wants to read data from it. If your computer is filled with 450 ns memory it must use one of the ready lines to cause the processor to hold the address and status lines for an extra clock cycle so that there is sufficient time for the memory to respond.

Signal lines are available for another board to use to temporarily take control of the bus. This occurs in some systems for high-speed memory access. Some disk controllers place their data directly into memory without going through the processor. These signals are provided to insure an orderly (and peaceful!) takeover of the bus from the master.

Bus Signals

These are signals that need to be present in the system but may be generated anywhere. One of these is CLOCK*, a 2 MHz utility clock signal for general use by the system. Another is RESET* which initiates the system. The power supplies also must be present at all time.

S-100 bus signals are presented, by function, in Fig. 4-3. The rest of the story on the S-100 bus is one of timing relationships among the signals. Space does not permit a full discussion of timing considerations; several excellent references exist that include great detail on the S-100 bus standard proposal.

5
Planning the System

Planning is the most important step in the building of your computer. The worst thing you can do is to rush around and buy a lot of parts without having thought out everything first. You can spend a lot of money on items that may not do what you want or may not even work together. If you have a specific use in mind for your computer, it should be fairly easy to plan for your needs. If you want to use your computer for experimenting, or as a hobby, the decisions aren't as clear. You want to leave your options open to the greatest extent possible. Particular pieces of hardware can "lock you in" to a specific system configuration that might limit the extent to which you can expand your system later.

THE MINIMUM SYSTEM

Any computer must have a Central Processing Unit (CPU), some memory, and a way to let the user communicate with it. These elements are supported by a power supply and, in the case of a S-100 system, a backplane or motherboard for the circuit boards to plug into.

Many systems will include some EPROM, often on the CPU card, to hold routines that are constantly used. A system used for software development will also need some type of mass storage device and, eventually, a printer.

Cassettes are the least expensive mass storage system, but storing data on cassettes is slow and of moderate reliability. Disk-ettes (or disks) are more expensive, but faster and more reliable.

THE CENTRAL PROCESSING UNIT (CPU)

The CPU card is the heart of the computer and the microprocessor is the heart of the CPU card. There are S-100 CPU cards available which are based on nearly all of the currently available microprocessor chips.

We have already discussed in some detail the specifications and features of the major microprocessors. While any of the microprocessors can be used as a system base, only a few have sufficient software and hardware support to make them serious contenders. The 6502 and 6809 are both fairly well supported with software, but much of that software was written for systems with radically different hardware than is found in the usual S-100 system. A 6502 CPU card for the S-100 bus is available from California Computer Systems and a similar board for the 6809 from Ackerman Digital Systems (Fig. 5-1).

Sixteen-bit processors are represented on S-100 cards also. TMS 9900, Z8000, 68000, and 8086/8088 cards are all available— their chief drawback being, again, software. The Ithaca Intersystems Z8000 card and the Godbout 8085/8086 card have gotten around this software problem to some extent. The Z8000 card is meant to run in a system with a "host" Z-80 CPU. The Z8000 can then take temporary control of the system. The Godbout card uses both the 8-bit 8085 and the 16-bit 8086 processors on the same card.

Most S-100 systems are based on the Z-80/8085/8080 family of processors. The upward compatibility of software (e.g., software for the 8080 runs on the Z-80) has eliminated the need for major

Fig. 5-1. Ackerman 6809 CPU card (courtesy of Ackerman Digital Systems).

Fig. 5-2. Godbout CPU-Z board.

revisions in popular software, and lets users of the Z-80 and the older 8080 run the same software.

Most of the discussion in the remainder of this book assumes an S-100 and Z-80 system base. This will allow the use of the wide range of S-100 compatible hardware and the nearly universal CP/M operating system. The choice of CPU card (among Z-80 cards) will revolve around the features on each board rather than the differences between microprocessors (Fig. 5-2).

THE FRONTPANEL

Every system has some sort of frontpanel. It may be as simple as a power switch and a reset switch, or it may have many control switches and status lights.

If you plan on doing a lot of hardware development, a "full switches and lights" frontpanel has advantages and may be a good choice. If you aren't developing hardware and won't be doing your own repair work, then a "reset only" frontpanel is definitely in order. Most computer hobbyists use the "reset only" frontpanel and work out repairs as they are needed.

MEMORY

A microcomputer memory system includes both the "bulk" system RAM memory and the EPROM that holds the system monitor and support routines. The most effective EPROM in common use is the 2716. This is a 2K × 8-bit memory device that is easy to use and program. In most cases this EPROM is located on the CPU card. A memory size of 2K is convenient for the system monitor PROM. The Intel 2716 uses only one power supply (+5V). The Texas Instruments TMS 2716 requires three power supply voltages. Most CPU cards use the Intel style 2716.

The bulk or main memory usually ranges in size from 8K × 8-bits to 64K × 8-bits. With memory prices dropping so rapidly 64K systems are becoming increasingly popular. General-purpose disk-based systems generally can use all the memory they can get. Large memory systems are really useful for systems that handle a lot of text or for program development. There's a saying that computer programs expand to fill all available memory!

Systems can be set up with BASIC in EPROM. This usually requires about 8K of EPROM. With such a system, 16K of program memory (RAM) will leave you with a fair amount of room to work.

THE I/O SYSTEM

The user communicates with the computer through the Input/Output system. This communication can be achieved by the use of a serial board and a terminal, or a video board and keyboard. Screen width of 32 or 64 characters are easy for hardware development, but most larger systems, especially word processing systems, use 80-character wide screens.

Another important I/O device is the lineprinter. A fairly fast dot-matrix printer is useful for any system. Word processing systems that need high-quality print require special letter quality printers. Printers are connected to the computer through either a serial or parallel interface. Serial interfaces are easy to use and require little software overhead. The parallel interface can be much faster than the serial interface, but it requires slightly more complicated software support. A letter-quality printer often requires special software to exercise all of its features, so you should be sure that such software is available for your planned system.

Many systems have specialized I/O devices. For example, analog input (from a joystick) and output (to a speaker) both require specialized I/O devices. They are often parallel ports modified with special hardware.

MASS STORAGE

Any computer used for program development or multipurpose data handling will need some type of mass storage. Mass storage generally refers to devices that store very large quantities of data. The total storage available in a system often exceeds, by several times, the size of programmable memory.

Mass storage devices hold programs and data that are not currently needed. For example, most programs in small home systems are stored on cassette tape. When you want to use one of these programs you read it into the computer and execute it. In this case the cassette tape equipment is the mass storage system. Cassette systems are slow and many have relatively high error rates. However, the recorders, interfaces and tapes are fairly inexpensive.

Many larger systems use diskette storage systems. These are faster and more reliable than tape cassettes, but the equipment is more expensive. My system started with cassettes, moved to one diskette drive, added CP/M, added another disk drive, and then switched to double density. Each change increased the utility of my system and demonstrated one of the great advantages of building your own system—the ability to add greater capability when and if you desire it. In the beginning my system was an interesting machine to play with. It has now become a useful tool for, among other things, preparing this manuscript. A good mass storage system really makes the system easy to use.

MOTHERBOARD, POWER SUPPLY, AND ENCLOSURE

In an S-100 system the motherboard (or backplane) provides a common set of connections for all the boards. The number of slots varies from three to twenty-two, the optimum size being dependent upon the requirements of the computer.

Most S-100 systems use an unregulated but well-filtered power supply which is supplied to the individual boards through the motherboard. Each board contains its own voltage regulators.

The enclosure provides cooling air, ac power, and mechanical protection for the computer. It should also serve as a radio frequency shield for the system. It is important to have a well-grounded metal enclosure on your computer.

PUBLICATIONS

The many computer books, manuals, and other publications on the market can be of great help to you as you develop your system. There are also many excellent computer-based magazines, such as *BYTE, Creative Computing*, and *Dr. Dobb's Journal,* which can probably be found in your local libraries.

When you're looking for parts or supplies, a periodical like *Computer Shopper,* which lists products from many manufacturers can be of great value. At the end of the book, the "Suppliers" list gives names and addresses of some of the better-known suppliers.

The Central Processing Unit (CPU) and Frontpanel

The microprocessor chip that executes your programs is located on the CPU card. This Central Processing Unit can be as simple as the early MITS Altair 8080 card (Fig. 6-1) or as complex as the Teletek FDC-1 single-board computer card (Fig. 6-2). The choices that you make in selecting the CPU card will determine the character and structure of your computer system. In this chapter we will explore the functions of the CPU card.

WHAT YOU *NEED* ON A CPU CARD

There are several functions that are absolute requirements for a CPU card in a S-100 system. These requirements are, in concept, very similar for any type of computer system using almost any type of bus.

The first requirement is that the card contain the microprocessor chip itself. Each processor has its own set of requirements for power supplies, voltage levels, etc. The most common microprocessor chip for current S-100 boards is the Z-80. Many older systems use the 8080. There are CPU cards available for nearly all of the currently available microprocessors, but S-100 bus systems most frequently use the Z-80 or 8080. The specific requirements of the microprocessor chip define much of the circuitry on the CPU card.

Another important function of the CPU card is to generate a master clock signal that satisfies the requirements of both the microprocessor chip and the bus. The original (pre-standard) S-100

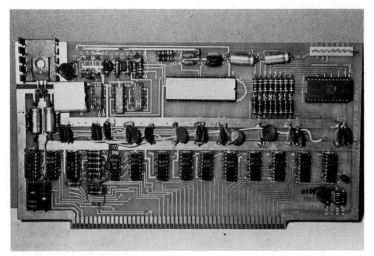

Fig. 6-1. MITS Altair 8080 CPU card.

bus computers were built using the 8080 chip; and consequently the signals on the S-100 bus reflect the signals available on the 8080 chip. This processor required a nonoverlapping two-phase clock that ran at 2 MHz. Both phases of the clock signal were on the bus, as was a 2 MHz clock signal. The Z-80 requires only a single-phase clock. When the bus standard was written, 02 was kept as the master system timing signal but the 01 definition was modified.

The new signal replacing 01 is pSTATVAL*. This signal indicates that the data on the status lines is valid. Additionally, pSTATVAL* is only valid while pSYNC, the system synchronization signal, is valid. This definition includes both the new boards which only generate pSTATVAL* when the data is valid and the old system with 01 clock signals.

A number of Z-80 CPU cards were designed between the time when the Z-80 came out and when the bus standard was written. These cards usually generated the CLK* signal at 4 MHz. This created a problem for serial I/O boards which generated their baud rate clocks by dividing the CLK* signal, assuming that it was a 2 MHz signal.

The IEEE S-100 standard now defines CLK* as a 2 MHz signal no matter what the system clock speed is. CLK* also needs to maintain no phase relationship with the master clock signal. It can, in fact, be generated by another board in the system.

The last and most complicated function of the CPU card is to handle the bus status and control signals. The CPU card must decode and generate status signals as required by the bus to allow the other cards in the system to: identify memory, I/O read and write cycles, provide synchronization with the processor and allow for slow memory or I/O devices. The boards must allow for direct memory access (DMA) cycles to allow devices to take control of the bus when necessary. All of the functions described above are necessary for a computer system to work properly.

THE "LOADED" CPU CARD

The functions we have discussed are the *minimum* that the CPU card must be able to handle. Many CPU cards now on the market include serial or parallel ports, which means you can build a system without a separate I/O card. Most of the new CPU cards include space for at least one EPROM and the circuitry necessary for the processor to automatically start execution of the program contained in it when the system is reset. The EPROM would contain a monitor program that would be used for initializing the I/O devices, performing low-level I/O functions, and, if applicable, bringing in the disk operating system.

One of the most complete CPU cards available is the Teletek FDC-1. It contains a 4 MHz, Z-80 CPU, two serial I/O ports, two parallel I/O ports, and EPROM programmer, real time clock,

Fig. 6-2. Teletek FDC-I Z-80-based CPU with ROM, RAM, disk controller, and I/O ports (courtesy of Teletek).

double/single density disk controller, and room for up to 8K of PROM or RAM.

At least one CPU card has been announced that includes eight of the new 64K dynamic RAM chips. This board, from Sierra Data Sciences, by itself forms a nearly complete system.

Few CPU cards are as complete as the two just mentioned, but most of them now have EPROM and serial I/O capability built in.

CLOCK SPEED

The older (8080) systems ran with a 2 MHz master clock. The Z-80A runs with a 4 MHz clock. There is a 5 MHz version of the 8085, and the Z-80B will run at 6 MHz. Doubling the clock speed doubles the speed at which the processor executes instructions. Increasing the system clock speed will mean faster overall execution speed (how fast programs seem to run) *only* if the rest of the system can keep up with the faster processor.

With a 4 MHz Z-80 the memory access time (the amount of time that it takes for the memory to come up with the data after you start a read cycle) needs to be about 250 ns. Running a 4 MHz system with 450 ns memory requires that a one clock-cycle-long "wait state" be entered to allow the memory to catch up with the processor. This wait state, which must occur on every memory cycle, will slow the program execution. The program will run at less than twice the rate of the same program run at 2 MHz. If I/O devices require it, you may have to add NOP (No Operation) instructions whenever you read or write to them. This will also slow the system down.

The real bottleneck in most small systems occurs during I/O transfers. For example, if you are running a data transfer program that is getting its data from a 300 baud (30 characters/second) serial port, increasing the clock speed from 2 MHz to 4 MHz may have very little effect on the amount of time that the program runs. This program is "I/O bound," i.e., the processing time is much less than the amount of time spent in I/O transfers (Fig. 6-3). The "rate-limiting step" in this program occurs in waiting for the console port to be ready—a function of the communication rate of the terminal. Text editors also tend to be I/O bound. They spend most of their time watching the console and waiting for the user to type something.

Programs are "compute bound" when the processing time is much greater than the I/O time. Routines that are compute bound will be greatly aided by an increase in processor speed because the

```
;
;
;
INPUT:    IN      STATUS    ;READ STATUS REGISTER
          RRC               ;ROTATE READY BIT TO CY
          JC      INPUT     ;JUMP IF NOT READY
          IN      DATA      ;READ THE DATA
          ANI     07FH      ;ZERO THE TOP BIT
          RET               ;DONE
```

Fig. 6-3. An I/O-bound routine.

"rate-limiting step" in this case is the instruction execution speed (Fig. 6-4). The example shown in Fig. 6-4 demonstrates a compute-bound routine; it is a little unfair since, as it does no I/O, its rate is limited by the execution speed of the processor. The moral of the story is: increasing clock speed will speed up any program that you run, but very few programs will speed up by the full amount of the increase in clock speed.

I do not want to leave the impression that speeding up the clock is of only marginal utility. A great many programs running on micros are not as one-sided as the examples just shown. A BASIC interpreter, for instance, does so much internal running around that increasing the clock speed will significantly shorten program execution times. Don't be surprised if some programs speed up to a much greater extent than others.

POWER-ON JUMP

Most microprocessor chips are designed to be reset soon after power-up. Both the 8080 and Z-80 microprocessors set their program counters to zero on reset. This means that on reset they both fetch their first instruction from address 0000H. If there is PROM at address 0000H there is no problem.

The Radio Shack TRS-80 has PROM in low memory, as do several other systems. We really don't want PROM in low memory in an 8080 or Z-80 system because we probably will want to run an operating system like CP/M which requires RAM at address zero.

In order to resolve the conflict between the processor reset address and the requirements of the operating system we have to add special circuitry to the CPU card to force program execution to begin where we want it to. One way, illustrated in Fig. 6-5, is to force the processor to execute NOP instructions. A NOP doesn't do anything except increase the program counter (PC) by one. When

```
;
;
;       LXI     H,SOURCE    ;GET THE SOURCE ADDRESS
        LXI     D,DEST      ;GET THE DESTINATION ADDR
        MVI     B,80H       ;GET THE COUNT
        MOV     A,M         ;GET BYTE
XFER:   STAX    D           ;STORE IT
        INX     H           ;NEXT ADDRESS
        INX     D           ;
        DCR     B           ;DECREMENT BYTECOUNT
        JNZ     XFER        ;JUMP IF NOT ZERO
```

Fig. 6-4. A compute-bound routine.

the PC gets to the address where we want execution to start, we turn off the NOP generation circuitry and allow the CPU to run normally. This is the type of circuit used on the Ithaca Audio Z-80 CPU card.

Another method is to force the first three bytes of the onboard PROM to respond at address 0000H just after reset. The first three bytes that are programmed into the EPROM form a jump instruction. This jump instruction causes the CPU to jump to the address where the PROM actually resides. The remapping circuitry is designed to be active only for the first instruction after a reset. This method (Fig. 6-6) is used in the SSM Z-80 CPU card.

Older CPU cards that expected the presence of a frontpanel and therefore don't have reset jump provisions onboard require the jump circuitry to be located on another card in the system. SSM makes a vector jump and prototyping card to serve just this purpose. This type of function *could* be built into the system motherboard but no one is currently marketing such a product.

Many disk controllers take control of the system on reset in order to load the disk operating system. The Tarbell single-density controller makes use of a small bipolar PROM containing very simple bootstrap routing. The board forces the processor to execute the program in the PROM which reads in one sector from the disk and transfers control to the program that was loaded into memory from that sector. This program loads another loader which loads the operating system.

The Teletek FDC-2 disk controller disables the other memory boards in the system on reset through the use of a special bus signal, PHANTOM. It then transfers the contents of its EPROM into memory, starting at 0000H. The last thing that this program does before it reads in the loader from disk is to disable the EPROM so that it no longer takes up space in memory.

All of these techniques provide special conditions for a short time after a system reset and then go away, allowing the system to run normally.

ADVANTAGES OF A FRONTPANEL

Until recently nearly all computers had a full frontpanel. This panel of lights and switches gave the operator direct control over the operation of the computer. A full frontpanel allows the operator to examine the contents of memory and in some cases the processor's registers, and to change this data if necessary. It also permits stopping and starting the program execution; in some cases a pro-

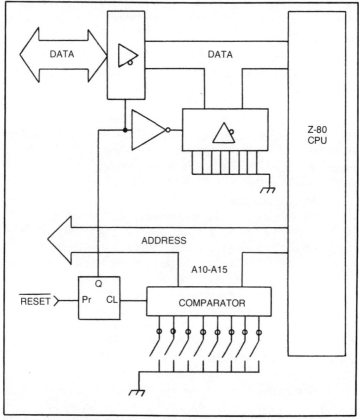

Fig. 6-5. Generation of a power-on jump by forcing NOPs into the processor.

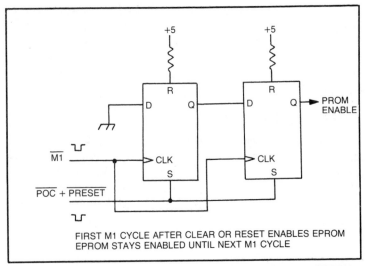

FIRST M1 CYCLE AFTER CLEAR OR RESET ENABLES EPROM
EPROM STAYS ENABLED UNTIL NEXT M1 CYCLE

Fig. 6-6. Generation of a power-on jump by relocating an onboard EPROM.

gram can be run one instruction (or clock cycle) at a time. The frontpanel of the Texas Instruments TI-960A 16-bit minicomputer is shown in Fig. 6-7.

Computers with frontpanels do not need reset jump circuitry because you can load the PC with an address and start program execution from the frontpanel. The early S-100 systems had full frontpanels. The circuitry on a frontpanel like the MITS Altair frontpanel shown in Fig. 6-8 is fairly complex, and it requires intimate contact with the CPU card in order to function properly.

In fact, the frontpanel in the early systems were really extensions of the CPU card—both were required to be operating properly for the system to run. Because the pre-standard S-100 bus was an extension of the 8080 pinout, the frontpanel was ill-equipped to handle the Z-80 CPU cards. For this reason, and because of the expense and complexity of the frontpanel, the auto-jump "turnkey" (you turn a key and it runs) systems now dominate the market.

There are some real advantages to a full frontpanel. Because you have a direct display of the address and data buses, you can easily catch problems such as shorted address lines or data lines that are stuck either high or low. You also have status lights that tell you if the system is in a wait state or a DMA cycle. The flashing lights demonstrate that the system is, in fact, running. On programs you frequently run, you get used to the light patterns and can tell immediately if the program dies. All in all, a frontpanel is nice to have when the system isn't working right but can be a pain otherwise.

While most manufacturers have moved away from the full frontpanel in favor of a frontpanel monitor in ROM, Ithaca Intersystems has moved in a different direction. Their DPS/FP frontpanel (Fig. 6-9) has, along with the standard features (examine, examine next, deposit, deposit next, reset, single step, and run/stop), a set of features designed to help in troubleshooting a failed system. It can force the processor to slow-step to make tracing program execution easier. You can set breakpoints in hardware to stop execution on a certain condition and trigger an oscilloscope from these signals. It also allows the user to force a NOP onto the data bus at any time. This in effect exercises all of the address and status lines so that you can quickly verify whether the CPU card is operating.

PROM/RAM ON THE CPU CARD

Most new CPU cards have PROM or RAM on the card itself., The system can have a monitor or a set of low-level support routines available without needing a separate PROM card. Systems that reset-jump need somewhere to jump, so most CPU cards that have one feature have the other. If RAM is available onboard it is usually in addition to or replacing some of the EPROM space on the card.

It is a real advantage to have a reliable block of memory present no matter how much main memory is available. This is the

Fig. 6-7. Frontpanel of the TI-960A computer.

Fig. 6-8. Frontpanel of the MITS Altair 8800.

place where the monitor would keep its stack, for instance, so you don't have to program a new EPROM every time you add memory and need to move the stack. If the EPROM and stack memory is placed as high in the memory space as possible it minimizes the need to bother it as you increase the total amount of memory.

The disadvantage to resident PROM is that it eats up a little bit of the available system memory. With a 64K memory board and a disk system you can bring all of the low-level I/O drivers in from the disk and live without a PROM monitor. When the disk fails, however, you are out of luck with such a system. With no PROM and a dead disk the computer won't do *anything*.

It is a tremendous advantage when trying to fix hardware problems to have the computer tell you what it thinks is wrong.

You should do one of the following:

●Live with a resident PROM monitor program.

●Have a *tested* troubleshooting monitor available to use when the system has problems.

●Be ready to spend a lot of time fixing the system when it doesn't run. You may also have to rent a logic analyzer in order to determine what went wrong.

NONSTANDARD STANDARDS

When shopping for a CPU card, check the following points:

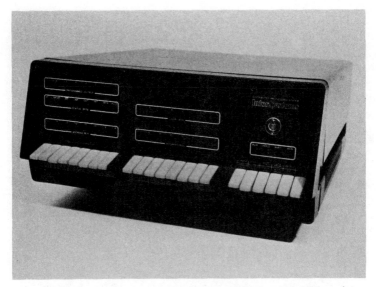

Fig. 6-9. The Ithaca Intersystems DPS/FP frontpanel (courtesy of Ithaca Intersystems, Inc.).

●Does it *really* meet the IEEE S-100 standard for signal definitions and timing? If not, where does it differ?

●Will it generate the common nonstandard signals that many cards use? (REFRESH, MREQ, pWAIT)

●Will it require forced-air cooling? Many manufacturers have a habit of loading down the regulator(s) on the CPU card to the point where they run close to their rated current. Some manufacturers will tell you that the card requires direct forced-air cooling. Some let you find out when the regulator overheats and shuts down. If the board is full of parts and there is only a single 1A regulator you will probably need cooling.

●Does it have RESET jump or does it need a frontpanel? Will it support a frontpanel?

●Is the addressing on the onboard PROM/RAM or I/O flexible? Do the I/O devices waste ports? (e.g., do five I/O registers take up eight or sixteen I/O ports?) Can you address the PROM down to the size of the device? Can you address a 2716 to any 2K block, or are you limited to a 4K block?

Memory

The memory of a computer is a vital piece of the system. All of the programs that are run, and all of the data for those programs, will at one time or another be in main memory.

In early microcomputers, four or eight thousand words (K) was a respectable amount of memory. The computer system on which the manuscript for this book was prepared has 64K of main memory. There are many 64K systems around now, and "multimegabyte" systems are not unheard of.

The growth in memory size for small computers parallels the drop in price and the increase in density of these memory devices. Today, thirty-two 16K × 1-bit dynamic chips (4116s) cost about $80.00. Only a year or so ago only eight such devices cost about $100.00. By the time this book is published the prices are certain to be even lower.

THE STATIC/DYNAMIC CHOICE

Static and dynamic are terms that you will see many times. It is important to understand the difference between these two types of memory, and to debunk some of the myths surrounding them.

Static memory differs from dynamic memory in the way that data is stored within the chip. Static memory uses a flip-flop circuit to store each bit. This requires four- to six transistors per flip-flop. The information is stored as the *state* of the flip-flop and is stable for as long as the device has power.

Dynamic memory uses a transistor-capacitor circuit with the data stored as the charge on the capacitor. The data is stable only as long as the capacitor can hold its charge. The capacitor can only hold the necessary amount of charge for about two milliseconds. This means that each cell must be "recharged" before too much charge leaks off.

Dynamic memory has advantages over static in terms of density and power. At this writing 4K static memory chips are common, as are 16K dynamic chips. New 16K static chips are just making their appearance, as are new 64K dynamic chips. This 4× difference in density is partly because the dynamic chip needs only about one-quarter as many transistors per bit as the static chip.

Dynamic memory has a power advantage over static memory of the same generation. The TI 4116 16K × 1 dynamic chip dissipates a maximum of 462 mW in operate mode and 20 mW in standby mode. The TI 40L44 (the low-power version of the 4044) 4K × 1 static chip dissipates only up to 275 mW in operate mode and 96 mW in standby mode. The Intel 2102AL 1K × 1 static chip (a generation earlier than the 4044 and 4116) dissipates 174 mW in operate and 35 mW in standby. This data is summarized in Fig. 7-1.

The disadvantages of dynamic memory are the requirements for refreshing the bit cells, and the complex and critical timing. For a static memory chip, a read cycle involves the following steps (Fig. 7-2):

●Set up the address and read/write lines and allow them to settle.

●Drop the chip select line.

●Wait through the access time.

●Read the data.

●Release the chip select, read/write and address lines.

The only real critical timing is the access time. If the processor samples the data before the access time is up it will read invalid data. Memory boards are very easy to design using static memory chips. Many boards are available, quite a few as kits. There are 64K static boards now available as well as 32K, 16K and 8K. There are

Memory Device	Size		Operating Power	STBY Power	Operating Power per K
2102 AL	1K×1	Static	174mW	35mW	174mW
40L44	4K×1	Static	275mW	96mW	68.75 mW
4116	16K×1	Static	462mW	20mW	28.87mW

Fig. 7-1. Memory power data.

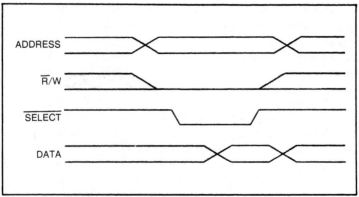

Fig. 7-2. Read cycle for a static RAM chip.

almost no 4K boards still on the market because memory is now so inexpensive that few people will accept such small increments.

The 4116 chip is now the most common dynamic memory device available for small systems. This is the device used in the TRS-80, APPLE II, Exidy Sorcerer, and most S-100 dynamic boards. A 16K device needs fourteen address bits in order to specify one bit out of 16K. This type of memory also needs +5V, +12V, −5V and ground in order to operate. Adding a chip-select line and a bidirectional data line brings the pin count up to twenty. The 4116, however, is packaged in a 16-bit DIP package by using multiplexed addressing. In this case there are only seven address lines plus a Row Address Strobe (RAS) and a Column Address Strobe (CAS). This allows packaging in a standard 16-pin package—a great advantage because it drops the cost of sockets and increases the number of parts that can be put on one board.

The price that is paid for the advantages of dynamic memory devices is higher complexity and more critical timing in the interface signals.

To read data from the 4116 system you must (Fig. 7-3):

- Set up the 7-bit row address.
- Active the Row Address Strobe (RAS*).
- Hold the row address for at least 25 ns.
- Set up the read/write line and the column address.
- Activate the Column Address Strobe (CAS*).
- Hold the column address for at least 55 ns.
- Wait through the access time.
- Read the data.
- Raise CAS* and then RAS*.

Timing is critical. The RAS* signal can stay active for only ten microseconds. A system whose RAS* is active for longer than ten microseconds risks losing a refresh cycle. If you don't catch the data when it is ready it won't hang around forever. Each memory access refreshes one column in memory so that, rather than having to refresh all 16K bits individually in two milliseconds, only the 128 columns must be refreshed in that time. Because of the speed of the signals, good power supply bypassing must be done on the board near the memory chips. This makes printed circuit (PC) board design much more demanding.

One common myth is that dynamic memory is much less reliable than static. This really isn't true. A properly designed dynamic board will work at least as well as a static memory board. The trouble has been that while almost anyone can design a static memory board that will work, you cannot get away with sloppy design on a dynamic board. A few of the early dynamic boards were so poorly designed that they gave dynamic memory a bad name.

If you wish to buy a static board there are several things to look for:

●Low power and high-speed memory chips.

●Flexible addressing. Some boards require the entire board to be addressed as one block. Many others, especially those using 4K chips, can be split into 4K blocks.

●The ability to generate wait states with fast processors. Many of the boards allow you to select up to four wait states to allow for almost any combination of memory and processor clock speed. Some boards do not have provisions for wait states. The Godbout

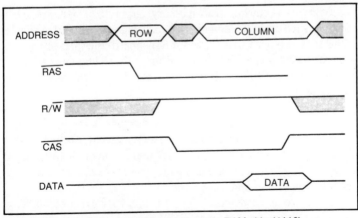

Fig. 7-3. Read cycle for a multiplexed Dynamic RAM chip (4116).

Fig. 7-4. The Godbout Econoram IIA 8K static board.

Econoram IIA (Fig. 7-4), for example, does not but it is guaranteed to run as fast as 4 MHz Z-80s and 5 MHz 8085s.

●Full buffering of data, address, and control lines.

A feature of most boards "insulates" the memory chips from the outside world by putting a TTL gate between the chip and the bus.

One of the drawbacks of static memory is the number of boards that are required to fill out a system. A 64K system would require sixteen 4K memory boards (Fig. 7-5), eight 8K boards (Fig. 7-6), four 16K boards, or two 32K boards (Fig. 7-7). In contrast, most dynamic boards hold 64K on one board (Fig. 7-8).

Systems requiring main memory larger than 64K are most practical with dynamic memory. The largest static board available at the time this was written was a 64K board; the largest (S-100) dynamic board was a 256K board. Both of these boards use "new" devices (16K static and 64K dynamic), and the prices are still quite high. The best deal on big memory is dynamic.

The other drawback of static memory is power. The system on which this was written is running on a 20A fuse in the +8V supply because of the power requirements of seven memory boards with a mixture of 2102 and 4044 memory. When I convert it to dynamic memory, only five to eight amps will be needed because the memory board will only take about one.

Here are some points to look for in a 64K dynamic board:

●The board should be able to use the Z-80 refresh facility or have the ability to do onboard refresh with non-Z-80 systems. Some boards do a real transparent refresh no matter which processor is used. This is OK, too. The point is that the memory should be refreshed when the processor doesn't need it, so that we aren't slowing down the processor with wait states during every refresh cycle.

● The board *must* be able to switch to onboard refresh automatically (independent of the CPU) to handle the following conditions:

System reset: When your finger is on the reset button the processor is stopped and can't generate refresh cycles.

Processor hold. When a device takes control of the bus for DMA, some provision must be made for refreshing because the processor is no longer driving the bus.

Long wait states. While most memory wait requests last for only one bus cycle, many I/O devices put the system into an extended wait state. Disk controllers are notorious for doing this. When the system is in a wait state the address, data, and control lines are frozen. If the wait is long enough, refresh is lost. Even if the wait is just the right length you may lose a few bits in one of the columns. All of the columns were refreshed but one (the last) waited just a little too long. Because of unavoidable differences in the bit cells, some drop out before others. The RUN/STOP switch present on many computers puts the system into a wait state. A well designed board will

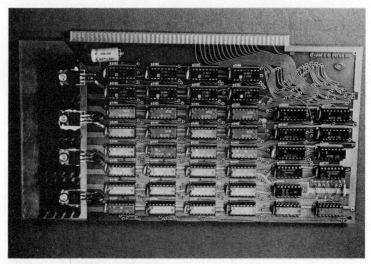

Fig. 7-5. A typical 4K static board.

Fig. 7-6. A typical 8K static board.

handle wait states of any length or from any source (I/O or memory cycle).

●The board should generate wait states only when it has to. They should *not* be generated every memory cycle or refresh cycle.

●The critical timing should *not* be handled by strings of one-shot circuits. These parts are inherently unreliable when day-to-day repeatability is critical. Many boards use digital delay lines or special refresh controllers that do all of their timing internally. It is feasible to use a monostable circuit triggered from a digital signal to generate the RAS* and CAS* pulses. The timing that determines *when* these pulses start must be done in a digital system, and the length of the pulses may be determined with a monostable device. This will minimize timing troubles. (The original Altair 4K dynamic board did *all* its critical timing with monostable circuits. The poor design helped to give dynamic memory its bad name.)

●The power supplies *must* cycle correctly. To prevent damage to the chips the −5V supply must come up first and drop last. This is often overlooked in power supply design. It is also important that the +5V and +12V supplies are shut down immediately if the −5V supply fails (blows a fuse).

If you are considering purchasing a 64K dynamic board, *buy the manual first!* If reading it leaves you with questions, *call the manufacturer and talk to the engineering department.* If they can't (or won't) answer reasonable questions, then *don't buy the board!* Most of them are OK, but there are a few bad boards on the market—so be sure to *buy the manual first.* If the manufacturer won't sell it to you, make sure that he understands that you will not buy the board unless you can see the manual first. If you still can't see one, then *don't buy the board!*

Most of the manufacturers are very helpful about giving you technical support; but some boards may not be compatible with those you already have, and since you cannot afford to buy boards that will not work in your system it is important that you have an opportunity to study the manual first. Many of the manufacturers will deduct the price of the manual from the eventual purchase price of the board.

PROM

Most computers need to have some type of program that is always available. When normal RAM memory is powered up it contains random patterns. Nonvolatile memory is not bothered by loss of power; it holds its data even after being powered down. The most common form of nonvolatile memory is Read Only Memory (ROM).

There are several types of ROM available. Mask-Programmable ROM (or just ROM) is programmed by the manufacturer during construction. Programmable ROM (PROM) is received from

Fig. 7-7. An Artek 32K static board using 40L44 4K × 1 chips.

Fig. 7-8. A typical 4116-based 64K dynamic board.

the manufacturer "blank", as all "1s" or "0s". The user can program this memory in the field.

One type of PROM uses fusible links. These links, usually made of Nichrome or Silicon, are melted during programming—thereby shorting-out or open-circuiting a transistor in the memory array. Once the chip has been programmed it cannot be erased.

Another type of PROM *is* erasable—EPROM. This type is programmed by stranding electrons on an insulated conductor. Erasure occurs when the chips are exposed to high energy ul-ultraviolet light. Interaction with the ultraviolet photons cause the charge to leak off the insulated conductor. Some types of EPROM are electrically erasable (EEPROM), and can be erased in-circuit by the computer system.

EPROM is probably the easiest type of memory for design purposes. All the common EPROMS are static and, of course, no provisions need to be made for writing data to the EPROM. (Programming an EPROM is not too difficult but it is not generally done as a routine use of the computer.)

Computers dedicated to a particular function may have a large amount of EPROM or ROM built in, and very little RAM. One example of this would be a microprocessor-based terminal. It must have at least 2K of RAM for a screen buffer (on a 24 × 80 terminal), and 2K or more of PROM to hold the terminal control program. In addition, a ROM or PROM character generator at least 1K in length is required.

For maximum flexibility, general-purpose computers should have a minimum amount of EPROM. However, a computer with BASIC in ROM will necessarily have a large quantity of memory space (8-20K) dedicated to the BASIC ROMs. If the rest of the computer memory is filled out with RAM, the result is a computer that has room for very large BASIC programs. This may be the best answer for someone who is *only* interested in BASIC.

There are many EPROM boards on the market and most of them are good. Most small computers use type 2708 or 2716 EPROM devices. When shopping for an EPROM board, look for the following points:

●The board should be able to generate wait states. Most EPROMs are 450 ns access time devices and need a wait state to run with a 4 MHz Z-80. This circuit is quite simple so there is no excuse for a board to be without it.

●The board should have some provision for de-selecting empty EPROM sockets. This allows the board to take up only as much space in memory as it needs to. There is no reason for an 8K EPROM board to take up 8K of memory space if there are only 3K worth of EPROM on it. Most boards de-select the socket with a switch that you set when the board is installed.

●The board should allow you to PHANTOM the memory "underneath" it if you need to.

●The board should be flexible enough to handle several types of EPROM. The differences between 2708, 2716, and 2732 EPROMs (1K × 8, 2K ×8, and 4K × 8-bit memories, respectively) are rather small, and one board can be made that will handle all of them. The addressing should be flexible enough to let you to place the board almost anywhere in memory. Stay away from boards using type 1702 EPROMs. These are "old technology"—small and difficult to program.

It is quite easy to design your own EPROM board. The address decoding and read/write circuitry for a simple board is shown in Fig. 7-9. Many good EPROM programmers are available. Some are designed to connect to a parallel port on the computer while others sit on the bus and use up either several I/O ports or a block of memory. If your programmer sits on an I/O port you have the advantage of not having to keep it hooked up all the time.

If you purchase a programmer that takes up memory space, be sure it can be disabled when you don't need it so that you don't have a large hole in memory. If you use a programmer that sits on the bus, you will have to open up the computer enclosure every time you want to program an EPROM (unless your programmer has an extension and a socket mounted on the outside).

Most of the on-bus programmers use a dc-to-dc converter to generate the +26V power supply needed to program an EPROM. The ones that connect through a port usually need a separate power supply for the +26V. One of the early S-100 PROM programmers used a spare S-100 bus line to feed 110Vac power to the programmer! Not a good idea!

If you work much with EPROMs you will need to be able to erase them. All of the "normal" devices (2708, 2716, TMS2716, 2732, 2764) erase with 254 nm ultraviolet light. An eraser that works fairly rapidly must have a fairly high intensity at 254 nm. This "color" UV light is extensively used for photochemical reactions and has sufficient energy to break chemical bonds. This is fairly high-energy ultraviolet and can be dangerous to eyes and unprotected skin. An EPROM eraser enclosure must be made of material that is opaque to UV light, and must have an interlock switch built in to shut off the UV light if the enclosure is opened. If you are not comfortable with the idea of the construction of ultraviolet light projects, it would be advisable to buy a commercial eraser as shown in Fig. 7-10.

HOW MUCH MEMORY IS ENOUGH?

If you plan on running a wholly cassette-based system, then 16K to 32K of main memory is sufficient. Your use of the system will be limited more by the loading and dumping time of programs on cassettes than by the total memory size. If you plan to put BASIC in EPROM, then a system with 32K of RAM would be considered quite large.

A disk-based system running CP/M 2.2 will require at least 20K in order to run at all. Many of the language compilers require at least 56K of main memory. The larger you can make main memory, the better.

If bank selection (organization of memory into banks that can be disabled) is used, up to eight 64K boards can be used by the system at once. A computer system running an operating unit like Cromemco's CROMIX will need a minimum of 128K RAM (two 64K boards for instance).

With memory prices dropping constantly, a 64K RAM system is no longer unreasonably priced, and in the near future "full" systems will become common. The newer 16-bit CPU chips have

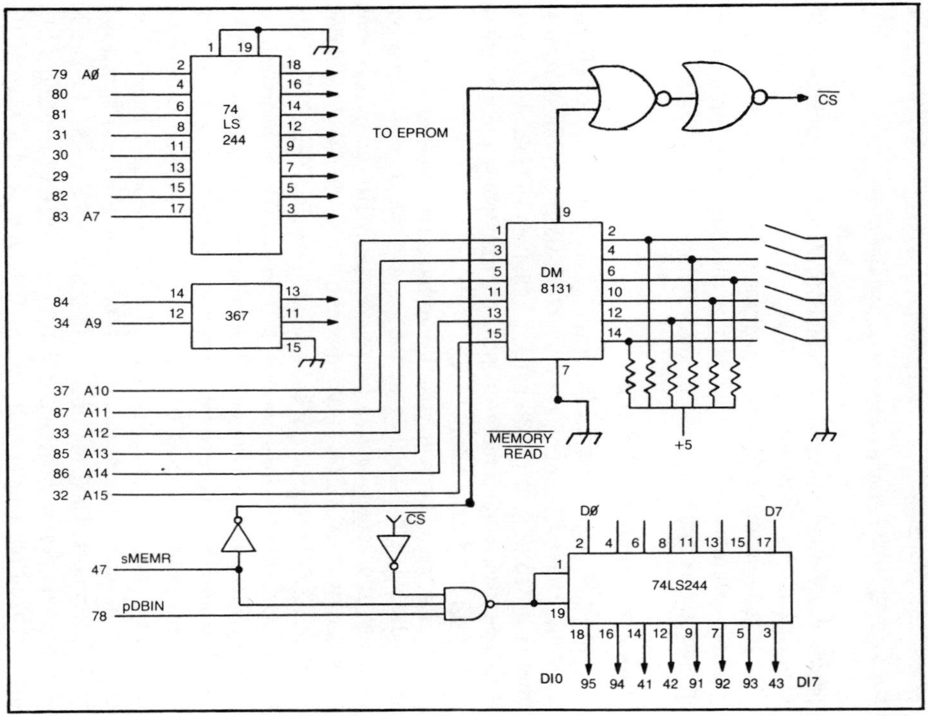

Fig. 7-9. Address decode and R/W circuitry for an EPROM.

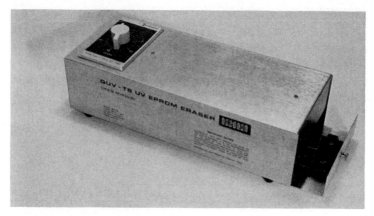

Fig. 7-10. EPROM Eraser (courtesy of Logical Devices).

provisions for addressing more than 64K of memory and the S-100 standard allows for 24-bit addressing.

It is a general "rule" that programs expand to fill all available memory! Memory is cheap (and getting cheaper all the time), so you should get as much as possible for your system.

MAGIC DISAPPEARING MEMORY

Most microprocessors (with the exception of the Z8001 and the 68000) have a 16-bit address bus. This allows for direct addressing at $2**16$ (2^{16}) or 65536 bytes of memory. There are several schemes to have more memory available than would seem possible with sixteen address bits.

It is very bad design practice to have two devices trying to drive the system bus lines at the same time. For this reason, memory addresses cannot be overlapped. However, systems equipped with a PHANTOM line allow one device to overlap another, disabling the output buffers on the data bus (Fig. 7-11). The PHANTOM line is most often used to overlap a bootstrap or monitor PROM. The Teletek FDC-II disc controller uses PHANTOM to allow the disk PROM to overlap low memory on reset, and to allow the onboard buffer to overlap a 1K space in high memory.

More than 64K of memory can be used through a bank select system. In such a system an I/O port (typically 40H) is assigned as a bank select port. The bank-enable circuitry on the memory board is wired to one or more of the port bits (Fig. 7-12). Outputting a 1 to the bit used by a bank will select it. If you send a byte of 01 (00000001B) to the bank select port, only bank 0 would be enabled.

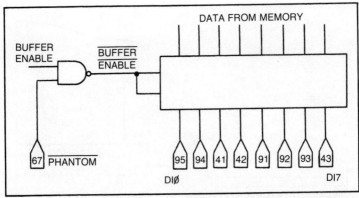

Fig. 7-11. Circuitry to allow the PHANTOM signal to disable output buffers.

Sending an 80H (10000000B) would enable only bank 7, and sending 09 (00001001B) will enable both banks 0 and 3.

Managing memory in a bank select system can be tricky. If you set up your system with two 64K memory boards, one addressed as bank 0 and the other as bank 1 and there is no PROM in the system, then executing an instruction that changes pages will send you to the other page at the address of the next instruction. There must be

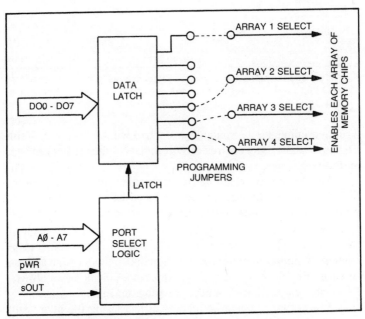

Fig. 7-12. Bank enable circuitry.

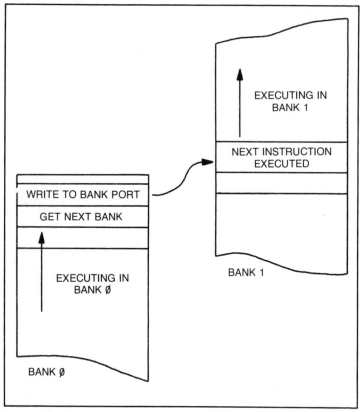

Fig. 7-13. Page swapping memory from a program running in the swapped area requires that the next instruction to be executed be at the proper address in the other page.

a routine immediately available or control will be lost (Fig. 7-13). This is possible, but requires careful control of the memory images on the two pages.

A simpler way would be to have some memory that doesn't deactivate with a change of page. Using an EPROM is one way to accomplish this. In this case the program in the EPROM supervises all page changing and the program can branch to the new page from the EPROM. This method greatly simplifies the management of the system. A similar method would give an independent page address to each 16K block, reserving the uppermost block as an always-resident area in which a supervisor program runs.

Another more versatile method of increasing the addressing range is provided in the IEEE S-100 standard. The standard has defined eight additional address lines, resulting in a 24-bit address space. A 24-bit address space translates to sixteen megabytes of main memory, or two hundred fifty-six 64K RAM cards!

The new standard also allows 16-bit data transfers if the system memory cards are equipped for it. The CPU card puts out a 16-bit request signal when it wants to transfer sixteen bits of data at a time. If the memory board answers with the 16-acknowledge signal the transfer takes place using the 16-bit word. If there is no response (from boards not equipped with the necessary hardwood) the transfer will take place as two 8-bit transfers.

Most memory cards are not equipped for 16-bit transfer, but some of the new cards will allow it. The two-byte transfer cards will catch on as the new 16-bit processors do. Their utility lies in the ability to transfer 16-bit data more efficiently in one chunk than if the same data had to be sent as two pieces.

As a postscript, the 8080 (and the pre-standard S-100 bus) had a status signal that signified when a stack operation was taking place (a PUSH, POP, CALL, RET, etc.). Evidently no one used it as such, but it could have been used as a seventeenth address line allowing separate 64K regions for the program/data area and stack memory.

Input/Output Devices

A computer must have some way of communicating with the people who use it. There must be a way to translate the data stored within the computer as voltage levels into symbols or patterns that can be understood by humans. A device that performs this translation is an input/output (I/O) device.

The major I/O device on many of the early home computers was the front panel. This device translated data and address information into light levels (ON for a one, OFF for a zero). Switches mounted on the frontpanel allowed data and instructions to be input to the computer. As you can imagine, reading lights and flipping switches was a difficult and inefficient way to communicate with the computer.

Most large computers, even if they have a frontpanel, have a system console. The console, whose name comes from the fact that it is mounted in (or directly attached to) the "box" the computer is in, is the master control terminal for the computer. The console is generally the *only* terminal needed to run the computer, and gives the operator nearly complete control over the operation of the computer system. Requests by programs for human assistance (mounting a magnetic tape on a tape drive, for instance) are printed on the console.

The console on a small computer has similar control over the operation of the system. With some special software (a monitor) it can take the place of a frontpanel, allowing the operator to examine and modify the contents of memory, and to load and run programs.

On a small system, the console is often the only terminal and all program preparation is done using it. There are two broad types of console I/O devices, a *stand-alone* console and a *system-dependent* console.

THE STAND-ALONE CONSOLE

A great many large computer systems allow access by remote users who are physically separated from the computer and often communicate with it through telephone lines. The user could be in a different building from the computer—or on a different continent. The equipment which the remote user uses obviously cannot be dependent upon the computer system for its operation. The computer terminal that he uses is standalone—with its own power supply, display, keyboard, and terminal logic that is self-contained.

The computer is basically a parallel device. This means that the data (eight bits in the case of a small microcomputer) is all available at once on separate wires (Fig. 8-1). This method of transferring data is fast and efficient but because of the need for a group of wires it is generally used only for local equipment.

In order to use a telephone line the data must be presented in a serial format. In the case of a parallel data transfer, the bits are separated in space (on different wires); in a serial data transfer the bits are separated in time (on the same wire). Most standalone computer terminals are serial terminals.

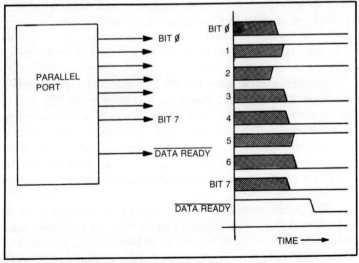

Fig. 8-1. Parallel data is available 8 bits at a time.

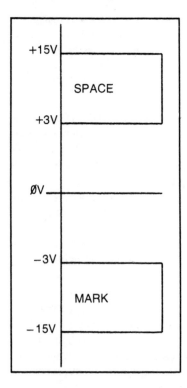

Fig. 8-2. RS-232 defines both positive and negative voltages.

In order to facilitate serial transfer over long distances several methods have been developed. Teletypes (and the original telegraphs) are current loop devices. They sense the presence or absence of current in a loop between computer and terminal. This technique is good for long distances and is relatively noise-resistant.

Another method uses the RS-232 standard communication technique. This technique makes use of voltage levels (Fig. 8-2) to discriminate between ones and zeroes. A logic *one* is represented by a voltage between −3V and −15V; and a logic *zero* by a voltage between +3V and +15V. Voltages between +3V and −3V are in the transition region and the line should never rest in this area. The logic 1 state is also known as the *mark* state while the logic 0 state is the *space* state.

The communications line rests (is idle) in the mark state. In order to coordinate data transmission the data bits are *framed* and a *start* bit, an optional parity bit, and one or two *stop* bits. The receiver is alerted to the presence of data on the line by the mark-to-space transition of the start bit.

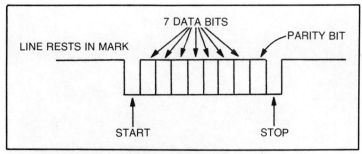

Fig. 8-3. Serial data is available one bit at a time.

The start bit serves to synchronize the receiver to the incoming data. A series of five, six, seven, or eight data bits follow the start bit. The data is transmitted with the least significant bit first. After the data bits a *parity* bit may be transmitted. This parity bit is used to check for errors in data transmission. If *even* parity is selected in the transmitter, the parity bit is set to make the total number of ones transmitted even. *Odd* parity makes the total number of one bits odd (not including start and stop bits). The serial data stream is shown in Fig. 8-3.

The remote terminal can easily be connected to a small computer through a serial I/O board. This board (Fig. 8-4) translates the parallel data on the bus into serial data and then converts the data voltages to RS-232 voltage levels. The SSM IO-4 board is such a board (Fig. 8-5) containing two serial ports and two parallel ports.

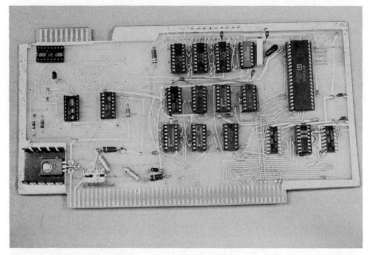

Fig. 8-4. Serial I/O boards can be quite simple.

Fig. 8-5. The SSM I/O-4 (2 serial and 2 parallel ports) I/O Board.

The California Computer Systems 2710 I/O board (Fig. 8-6) has four serial ports. Boards like these are fairly easy to design and build yourself.

There are two types of standalone terminals. The *printing terminal* (a DEC LA-36 Decwriter is shown in Fig. 8-7) usually runs at 110 or 300 baud (11 or 30 chars/sec) and provides a written log of its use. The printed output is its major advantage.

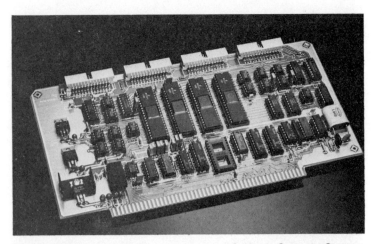

Fig. 8-6. CCS 2710 serial I/O board (courtesy of California Computer Systems, Inc.).

Fig. 8-7. The DEC LA-36 Decwriter.

The *video terminal* (a Heathkit H-19 is shown in Fig. 8-8) outputs to a television-like display. These terminals can run at up to 9600 and 19,200 baud (960 or 1920 chars/sec), and some are even faster. They have the advantage of being able to display an entire screenful of characters at once. Well-written software will allow interaction with the entire screen at one time by moving a cursor (a character that shows where the next character will be typed, see

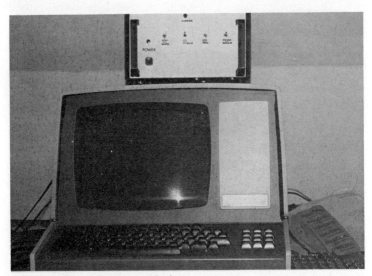

Fig. 8-8. Heath H-19 video terminal.

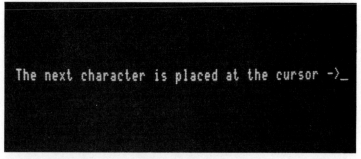

Fig. 8-9. The cursor shows where the next character will go.

Fig. 8-9) around on the screen. Most video terminals can display twenty-four lines of eighty characters per line.

The standalone terminal can be used not only on your home computer, but with a *modem* (a telephone interface device) to access large computers. The standalone terminal, being self-sufficient, can be used in troubleshooting a "sick" computer. When the system won't sign-on or prints "garbage" (random characters), the terminal can often be disconnected from the computer and tested. Many terminals have an *off-line* mode where the keyboard output is fed to its own input. If the terminal works in off-line mode the problem is in the computer. If the terminal will not work, then the computer is probably OK.

The main disadvantage of standalone console terminals is their cost. The typical terminal costs between $500 and $2000. This cost problem can be eased somewhat by purchasing a terminal board and building your own terminal. There are microprocessor-based terminal circuits, such as the one produced by John Bell Engineering (Fig. 8-10), or one by Romac Computer Equipment (Fig. 8-11). These require a video monitor, keyboard and power supply to complete the terminal.

Because of the need for serial I/O the communications speed of a standalone terminal is limited. A system-dependent console device, in contrast, runs at the full speed of the processor.

THE SYSTEM-DEPENDENT CONSOLE

System-dependent display devices became popular because of their low cost relative to a standalone terminal. A system-dependent console, as the name implies, requires the active attention of the computer system. These devices are, in general, a memory board with video generating circuitry added (Fig. 8-12).

84

Fig. 8-10. John Bell CRT Controller (courtesy of John Bell Engineering, Inc.).

Many of these boards have 16-line, 64-column displays because they fit well into memory ($64 \times 16 = 1024$ bytes = 1K) and because they do not require a high-quality video display device. A 24-line by 80-column display requires 1920 characters (nearly two K and higher frequency response from the display.

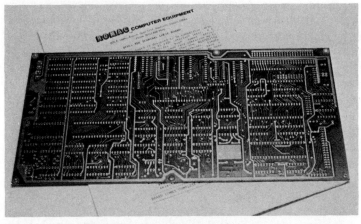

Fig. 8-11. The Romac video terminal board emulates a Heath H-19 terminal.

Fig. 8-12. Memory board with video circuitry. (Courtesy WW Component Supply.)

With most of the 16 × 64 displays you must dedicate a 1K block of memory to the display. Any character written into this block of memory will be displayed on the screen. This means that you can write characters to the display as fast as the computer can move data around in memory. This results in much higher speeds than can be obtained on a serial terminal. However, you pay for this speed in several ways.

In order to make the video act like a terminal (e.g., cursor control and scrolling display) a driver program is needed. These programs are fairly long (¼ to ½K) and must be continuously present for the display to operate.

Another penalty is the 1K hole left in memory. No programs can use this area for data or program storage without losing the display. The software for some of these displays assumed that the board would be addressed at C000H or E000H. This was pretty high up in memory for most early computers where 8-12K was a lot of memory. For a 56K or 64K CP/M system this leaves a hole in a prime memory area. These boards can all be used at alternate addresses if the software is modified to reflect the change.

If you have a system with EPROM in high memory (for instance, a monitor at F000H) and you have some unusable space behind it, the video board can be placed in this "hole" where it won't interfere with the system software. The EPROM monitor limits you to a 60K system, so putting the video board above it in memory won't be a disadvantage.

System-dependent console devices require a keyboard. Most ASCII keyboards are parallel devices, presenting an entire byte to the system at once. They can be obtained already assembled, in kit form, or can be built from scratch. Kits and assembled keyboards run from about $60 to over $200, depending upon the type of keyboard and the features it has.

To build ASCII keyboard circuits from scratch, unencoded keyboard blocks are available, as are keyboard encoder chips. A scratch-built keyboard isn't hard to make but you trade the time and effort of construction for the extra money to purchase it completely assembled. I am willing to put up with the harassment of building things in order to save money and get a custom device.

One of the greatest differences between commercial and homemade keyboards is the quality of the key switches. Some commercial keyboards use "higher technology" switches built around micro switches (high reliability mechanical switches) or Hall effect (magnetic) switches. A great many inexpensive keyboards and most unencoded boards use leaf-spring switches (Fig. 8-13). A circuit for a home-wired keyboard and the results are shown in Fig. 8-14 and 8-15.

An important feature to look for on a video board is a keyboard port. This is the parallel I/O port needed to input the data from the keyboard. Most video boards have them, but some do not. If no keyboard port is available on the board an additional I/O port is necessary. This can be on a commercial I/O board or homemade (Fig. 8-16).

Fig. 8-13. Many keyboards use a simple leaf spring contact.

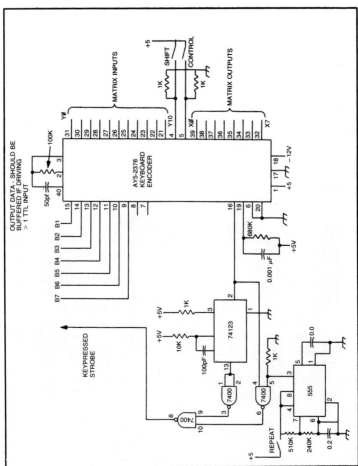

Fig. 8-14. The schematic diagram for a homemade keyboard, using an unencoded keyboard and encoder chip.

Fig. 8-15. The finished keyboard.

If you intend to buy a commercial board to get the parallel input, consider a mixed parallel/serial I/O board because you will certainly find uses for the extra I/O capability. But if you don't want (or can't afford) a mixed serial/parallel I/O board there are several very simple boards available, such as the SSM IO-2 board, which provides one parallel I/O port and a place to build more circuitry.

The video board also needs something to display *on*. Most video boards feed a standard composite video signal to a monitor. A monitor is much like a television set but without the rf and audio circuitry (Fig. 8-17). It has higher-bandwidth amplifiers in it, allow-

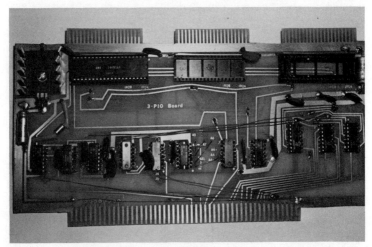

Fig. 8-16. Parallel boards can be fairly simple, using parallel I/O chips.

Fig. 8-17. A video monitor is like a TV set but without the rf circuitry.

ing a sharper display and more characters per line. The bandwidth is a measure of the high frequency response of a circuit. To produce characters the video board instructs the monitor to turn its electron beam on and off (Fig. 8-18) to produce dots. If the dot frequency exceeds the response of the display circuitry, only smears—not dots—will result.

Most monitors have 12-15 MHz bandwidth, which is easily enough for an 80-character wide display. A black and white television set has a 4-6 MHz bandwidth at best. Trying to drive a television with a 10 MHz dot signal would result in smeared, unreadable text. A color television is worse—with a bandwidth of only about 3 MHz. A color television can be used for about 40 characters across, black and white television for about 64.

In order to use a television set without making internal modifications an rf carrier must be added to the video input signal (Fig. 8-19). This modulated rf is fed to the antenna terminal of the

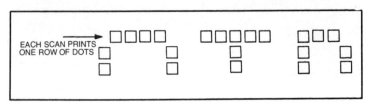

Fig. 8-18. A video terminal prints one row of dots per scan.

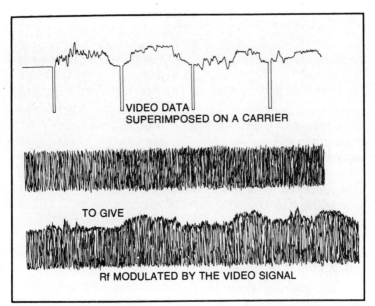

VIDEO DATA
SUPERIMPOSED ON A CARRIER

TO GIVE

Rf MODULATED BY THE VIDEO SIGNAL

Fig. 8-19. Modulated video.

television set. The device used to do this is called a video modulator (Fig. 8-20) and varies in cost from about $10 to over $40.

A video monitor is the best choice for an output device but runs in cost from about $50 to $200 (black and white). Color monitors typically cost at least $400.

Fig. 8-20. A video modulator adds an rf carrier to make the signal compatible with a TV set.

I/O SPACE AND MEMORY MAPPING

There are two common methods for defining I/O devices to the computer. Any I/O device has some type of data register where the data is read from the device or written to it. Most also have status registers used in controlling the I/O from the computer.

In the first method these registers are set up as if they were memory locations. In this system, known as memory-mapped I/O, reading and writing to an I/O device is identical to reading and writing to memory. Usually one or more 256-address pages are defined as I/O pages, and all I/O devices are located within this area. An advantage to this technique (used with the DEC LSI-11 minicomputer, and the 6800 and 6502 microprocessors) is that any instruction that references a memory location can be used to reference the I/O registers. The major disadvantage to memory-mapped I/O is that some memory space is used for the ports, limiting the total amount of available memory.

The other technique, known as port-mapped I/O, (available with the 8080, 8085 and Z-80 microprocessors) involves the definition of a set of I/O ports. These processors provide status signals that indicate whether any particular bus cycle is a memory read, memory write, I/O read, or I/O write cycle. Each memory or I/O board decodes these signals (and the address lines) to determine if it is being accessed.

A memory board will respond only when the bus address matches the range of addresses covered by that board *and* the status signals indicate a memory read or write cycle. In a similar manner, an I/O device will respond only if its port address matches the address on the bus *and* the status lines indicate and I/O operation. In this method all 64K of memory is available for program use and additional space is available for the I/O ports.

The 8080 family of microprocessors uses eight bits to specify a port address, providing 256 I/O ports. The major disadvantage to this arrangement is that only a small set of special IN and OUT instructions can be used to access these ports. These processors can also utilize memory-mapped I/O and can, in fact, mix memory-mapped and port-mapped I/O in the same system. With port-mapped I/O it is more difficult (but certainly not impossible) for a program malfunction to write into the I/O devices wreaking havoc on the system.

Most system-dependent video boards are memory-mapped, because of the large amount of memory needed for the display, and

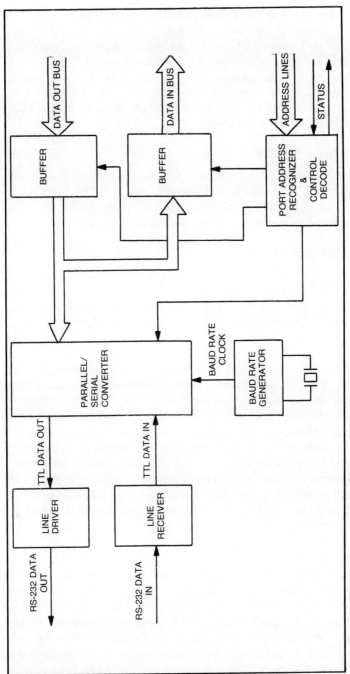

Fig. 8-21. A block diagram of a serial I/O board.

93

because of the speed advantages gained by having direct access to every character position on the screen.

A port-mapped I/O display with one data port and one status port does have something of a bottleneck, as all data must be squeezed through one port. This provides little trouble, however, because most I/O ports operate faster than the user can read. Port-mapped I/O has become the defacto standard for the 8080 family of microprocessors.

OTHER I/O DEVICES

Nearly every board in the computer, that isn't memory or the CPU itself, is an I/O board. There are really only two types of I/O devices. The first (one that we have already mentioned) is the serial board and the second is the parallel board.

Serial I/O Board

A serial I/O board is composed of several parts (Fig. 8-21). The bus interface controls the movement of data to and from the central processing unit. Any serial board requires a parallel-to-serial converter. There are two somewhat different types of parallel-to-serial converters. The first, and simplest, is the UART, the Universal Asynchronous Receiver and Transmitter. This is designed so that the number of data and stop bits are selectable, as is the parity. It also provides status information to tell the system when data is available, when the UART is ready to transmit the next character, and when an error has occurred. These devices have a standard pinout so several manufacturers' devices are interchangeable. General Instruments, for example, makes the AY-3-1013. Serial boards using a UART generally need little or no start-up programming. They have no internal registers to select operational parameters so they are ready for use immediately when the system is brought up. The only initializing they might need is to read their received data register in order to clear it.

The other popular parallel-to-serial converter is the microprocessor-compatible USART chip. These Universal Synchronous/Asynchronous Receiver/Transmitter chips are designed to be used with microprocessors. They have internal registers to allow selection of clock speed, number of bits, etc. These chips (e.g., the Intel 8251A) must be programmed before they are used. Because they are more complex than the UART chips, they can perform some functions more easily. Its register-based microprocessor-compatible architecture allows the 8251A to be

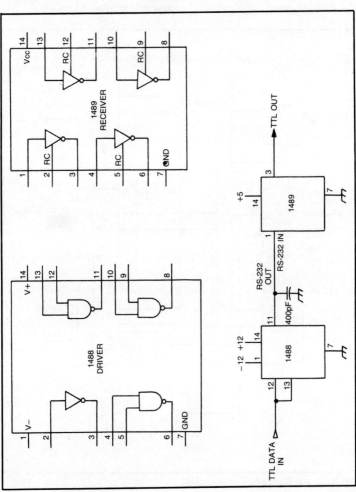

Fig. 8-22. 1488 and 1489 level-converters allow easy conversion to/from RS-232 levels.

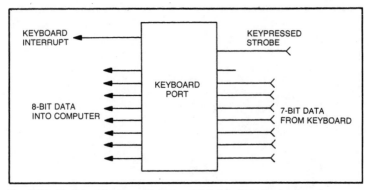

Fig. 8-23 Keyboard input port takes parallel data from the keyboard.

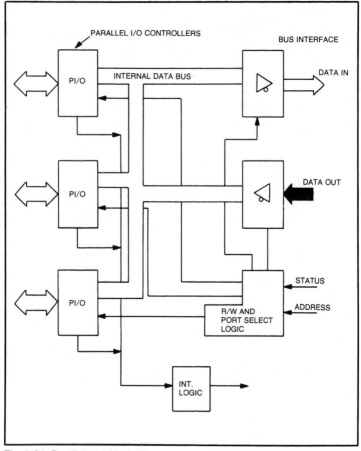

Fig. 8-24. Parallel port block diagram.

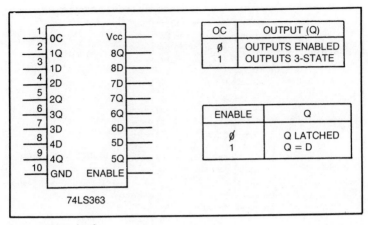

OC	OUTPUT (Q)
Ø	OUTPUTS ENABLED
1	OUTPUTS 3-STATE

ENABLE	Q
Ø	Q LATCHED
1	Q = D

74LS363

Fig. 8-25. TTL latch.

packaged in a 28-pin package, compared to the UART's 40-pin package.

All parallel-to-serial converters need some type of clock signal for a time reference. UARTs need a 16× clock (i.e., a clock whose frequency is sixteen times the baud rate). USART chips, on the other hand, can be programmed to use a 1×, 16× or 64× clock. The timebase used for the production of these clock signals is often the 2 MHz CLOCK* signal on the S-100 bus.

The last components needed on a serial board are voltage-level converters. These convert the TTL levels into, for instance, RS-232 voltage levels. There are many ways to effect this conversion, the 1488 and 1489 driver and receiver chips being easiest and most common. These chips (Fig. 8-22) take care of all of the

SELECT=1 IF $\overline{DSi}$=0 AND DS2=1

SELECT	MODE	DATA OUT
Ø	Ø	3-STATE
Ø	1	LATCH
1	Ø	LATCH IF STROBE= 0/IN IF STROBE=1
1	1	IN

Fig. 8-26. 8212 parallel port.

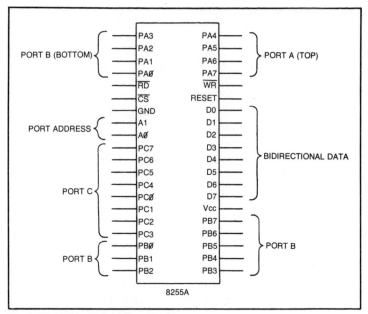

Fig. 8-27. 8255 parallel I/O controller.

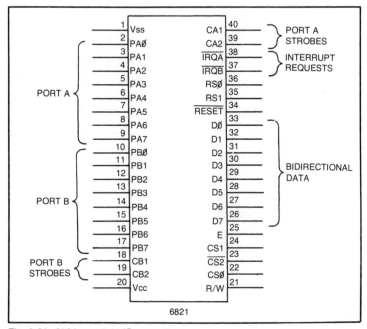

Fig. 8-28. 6821 parallel I/O controller.

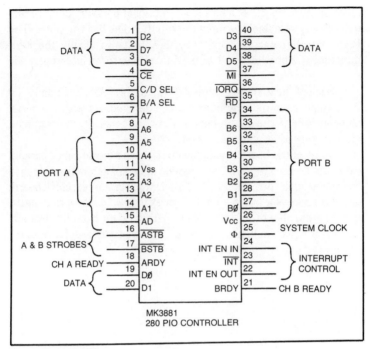

Fig. 8-29. Z-80 PIO.

voltage-level conversion needed to interface normal ICs to an RS-232 data link.

Parallel Board

Parallel boards are used where a high-speed TTL interface is needed, keyboard input ports (Fig. 8-23) are parallel input ports, while many printers run with a parallel output port. A parallel board (Fig. 8-24) has a bus interface and, instead of a parallel-to-serial converter, has a parallel controller chip. Clocks and level converters are often not necessary when parallel boards are used.

The simplest parallel I/O chip is a TTL latch, as shown in Fig. 8-25. A slightly more complex device is the 8212 8-bit I/O port (Fig. 8-26). There are more complex, microprocessor-based, parallel I/O chips. The Intel 8255, the Motorola 6821 and the Z-80 PIO chip are all somewhat different examples. The 8255 (Fig. 8-27) has two 8-bit I/O ports and a third port which can be divided into two 4-bit ports. The 6821 has (Fig. 8-28) two ports, and each bit can be individually set to be an input or output line.

The Z-80 PIO controller (Fig. 8-29) can be used as an 8-bit

99

input or output port, as an 8-bit bidirectional port, or can have bits individually selectable as input or output. It also has two ports. The PIO controller has, in hardware, the ability to supply the 8-bit interrupt vector when used with a Z-80 processor in interrupt mode 2.

Each of these more complex devices (the 8255, 6821 and Z-80 PIO) requires initializing before it can be used. As with the serial I/O controllers, the parallel controllers are generally programmed immediately after a system reset.

Many of the boards available do not bring the serial or parallel data outside the system. They instead have some function which is contained on the board itself. An EPROM programmer, clock board, or math processor board would be an example. Mass storage interface boards, also of this type, take parallel data from the bus and convert it to a form that can be recorded on a tape cassette or disk.

Mass Storage

A practical computer system needs to be able to hold a large quantity of data for long periods of time. This data may consist of programs, mailing lists, accounting data, and other information. Often this quantity is larger than the memory space available in the computer, and must be stored on some type of mass storage device.

Mass storage devices are generally slower than the computer's main memory and of much greater capacity. Unless you are building a controller using a dedicated microprocessor you would not want to keep all your programs in memory at once. With a large software-development system you would not be able to hold all of your large single programs in memory. Many Pascal compilers, for instance, require 56K bytes of system memory to run. If you had it in ROM (in addition to the operating system) all you could do would be to compile Pascal programs.

The mass storage system, in short, allows the computer to use its high speed and expensive memory for programs that are operating, while storing other programs and data on an easily accessible memory device external to the computer.

PAPER TAPE

One of the oldest mass storage methods that has been commonly used in microcomputers is paper tape with punched holes. Each row of holes corresponds to one byte of data (Fig. 9-1).

Paper tape became popular when the Teletype became a widely-used console device for small computers. Many Teletypes

Fig. 9-1. Paper tape is an obsolete way to store data.

had paper tape punch/readers built in so this became a natural means of recording programs.

Paper tape is slow. The Teletype punch/reader ran at ten characters per second (CPS). High-speed paper tape readers would run faster than this, but not a lot. Paper tape is also fragile. If the tape reader jammed during reading and ripped the tape, the program could easily be destroyed.

The main advantages of paper tape were its availability and its inexpensive nature. It has been almost completely replaced by more modern methods of storage as they have become less expensive.

MAGNETIC TAPE

Magnetic tape has been used for years in large systems for mass storage because of the large amount of data that can be stored per reel and its relatively low cost. Magnetic tape drives are also fairly fast.

Very few small systems have the stereotypical 9-track reel-to-reel tape drives which are common on large computer systems. These drives are extremely expensive—in the range of ten times the total cost of a small computer system.

Phillips Cassette

Most small systems use one of two types of magnetic tape. The more common type is the standard Phillips cassette. These cassettes and recorders are inexpensive, and the interfaces quite simple.

A number of years ago the "Kansas City Standard" tape encoding system was worked out and became popular with some computer users. This system uses a self-clocking encoding scheme that makes it relatively insensitive to variations in the playback speed. Its major drawback is its slow speed (30 characters per second). This is a result of the encoding technique, where each byte to be recorded is sent as a start bit, eight data bits, and two stop bits—much like a normal serial data channel. The difference is that in this format a 1 bit is eight cycles of a 2400 Hz sinewave, and a 0 bit is four cycles of a 1200 Hz sinewave. These frequencies are in the range that most tapes and tape recorders can best reproduce.

The most popular cassette system for S-100 computers has been the Tarbell cassette interface. This system uses a bi-phase encoding system where data and clock bits are combined into one signal. The standard interface runs at 187 characters per second—significantly faster than the "Kansas City Standard". A complete Tarbell cassette system that I occasionally use is shown in Fig. 9-2. With this system and the proper software, a single-density 8-inch diskette can be stored (as a tape backup) on one side of a C-60 cassette tape.

Both the Tarbell and "Kansas City Standard" tape recording methods use audio quality tape and inexpensive portable cassette recorders. This is because information is recorded as bursts of audio tones, much like you would record music.

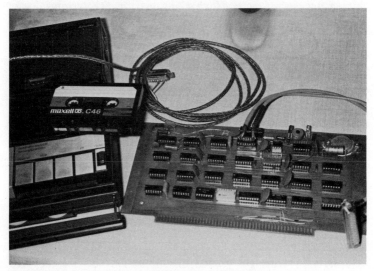

Fig. 9-2. The author's complete Tarbell cassette system.

More expensive *digital* cassettes are designed to be used with saturation recording equipment. The term *saturation* recording refers to the amount of magnetization that is placed on the tape. In saturation recording the tape is magnetized, one polarity or the other, with enough recording current to align all of the recording oxide in the same "direction".

This type of recording can be much more dense (in terms of bits per inch) than audio recording and therefore can be faster and of higher capacity. (When recording audio, you want to avoid saturation, partially because you want to get clean, nondistorted sinewaves back.) Digital cassettes are filled with tape whose oxide is optimized for saturation recording. (All diskette disk and larger tape systems use saturation recording.)

The Tarbell interface, and, for that matter, any audio cassette system, uses regular audio tape. Tarbell recommends the use of high-quality audio cassettes with its interface. One critical factor is the *drop out* rate. A drop out is a spot on the tape with little or no oxide so momentarily no signal is recorded. If you drop part of a cycle you can often drop a bit and get the whole transfer wrong. I use Maxell UD cassette tape with my Tarbell system.

Data Cassettes

The other popular tape system uses larger data cassettes designed for the storage of digital data. These are coming into increasing use as a method for backing up large disk systems. Large disks contain so much data that keeping duplicate (backup) copies is difficult. The cassettes and drives are more expensive and faster than a normal audio cassette but are about the only practical way to provide backup for large disk drives.

DISKETTES

One of the disadvantages of any tape system (paper or magnetic) is the difficulty in accessing specific portions of the data. If you want to load a program that is in the middle of the tape you have to read your way through the tape until you find the program. If you have a large data base on tape and need to access one record in the middle, it is necessary to read along in the data file until you locate the record that you want. If you want to update that record you would probably have to make a new copy of the tape file with the new record in it.

Disk systems get around this limitation because they are random access devices rather than sequential. If you want to access

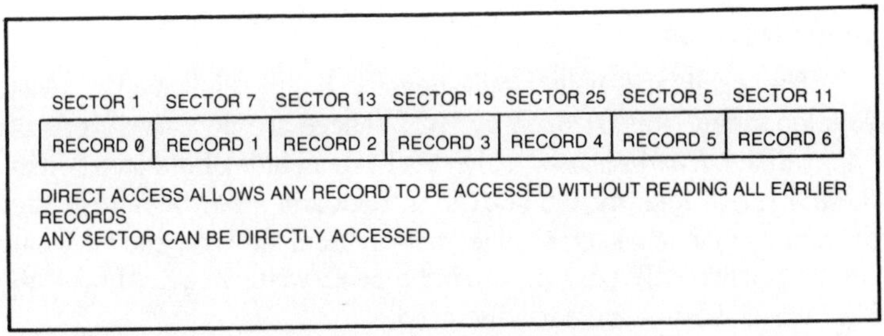

SECTOR 1	SECTOR 7	SECTOR 13	SECTOR 19	SECTOR 25	SECTOR 5	SECTOR 11
RECORD 0	RECORD 1	RECORD 2	RECORD 3	RECORD 4	RECORD 5	RECORD 6

DIRECT ACCESS ALLOWS ANY RECORD TO BE ACCESSED WITHOUT READING ALL EARLIER RECORDS
ANY SECTOR CAN BE DIRECTLY ACCESSED

Fig. 9-3. Direct Access disk files can be read in any order.

a program that is stored out in the middle of the disk, you can go directly to the start of the program file without having to read other data. If a file is structured properly you should be able to access only the record you want and update it without rewriting the entire file (Fig. 9-3).

Most small computers that have disk systems use *diskettes*. These are flat mylar disks coated with high-quality magnetic recording oxide. They are placed in a plastic or heavy paper jacket with holes for access by the read/write head and the mechanism that centers and turns the disks (Fig. 9-4). The disks are partitioned into *tracks* which are concentric bands of data 26 *sectors* in length. The sector is generally the smallest amount of data that can be read or written at one time.

5¼-inch Diskettes

The 5¼-inch diskette is popular on many small systems. Originally designed as a cassette tape replacement, these diskettes hold up to 256K bytes per side depending upon the number of tracks, sectors and the recording density. One of the difficulties with 5¼" diskettes is the lack of an industry-wide standard for the number of tracks and sectors. Some 5¼-inch diskettes have 77 tracks and some have 48. This makes software interchange among diskette users much more difficult. The 5¼-inch diskette drives are compact and easy to build into a computer enclosure.

The drives require several dc voltages. The main drive motor (spins the diskette) runs on dc and can be shut off entirely when the drive is not in use. While this has the advantage of reducing noise, wear, and power consumption, it has the distinct disadvantage of requiring a long time (up to one second) to start the motor and bring the disk up to speed before the data can be read or written. This delay can become considerable if each disk access is preceded by a one-second delay.

105

8-inch Diskettes

The original 8-inch single-density floppy disk system was developed and standardized by IBM. There are now two types of floppy disks. *Hard-sectored* diskettes have an index hole punched in the platter to identify the start of a track and a sector hole at the beginning of each sector. The disk system always knows what sector is currently passing over the read/write head. Almost all 5¼-inch diskettes are hard-sectored.

The second type is the *soft-sectored* diskette. This type has only the index hole. There are no sector holes, so the disk system has to rely on sector information data recorded on the diskette itself.

The IBM standard is soft-sectored. With soft sectoring you give up a little storage area to sector header information. IBM standard soft-sectored single-density 8-inch diskettes have 77 tracks and 26 sectors per track, while an equivalent hard-sectored disk might have 77 tracks and 32 sectors.

An advantage of soft-sectored diskettes is the ability to reformat them for different sector sizes. You can run with the IBM standard 128-byte sectors; or you can reformat for 256-, 512- or 1024-byte sectors. The system runs faster by getting more data per sector read and thereby doing fewer sector reads.

Most of the system's disk access time is taken up waiting for the desired sector to come past the read/write head. Reading the

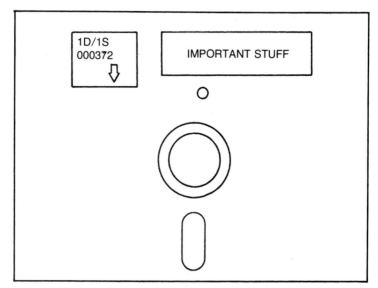

Fig. 9-4. Diskettes are an efficient and inexpensive way to store data.

data generally doesn't take as much time as waiting for the disk to get into position. If you can reduce the number of sectors read you will speed up the whole process.

I had a single-density disk controller with onboard ROM containing the necessary service routines. The ROM programming contained time delay routines to allow the head motion on the drive to cease after movement. (The heads, like any mechanical system, oscillate for a while after they are moved.) The ROMs were programmed assuming a 4 MHz system; but my system ran at 2 MHz, meaning that the delay routines would run twice as long as necessary. Since these delays were in the millisecond range, it didn't appear that the slower execution speed would make any real difference.

However, I had an opportunity to run the system with both 4 MHz and 2 MHz ROMs. A test program was developed to write successively larger files until the disk was full. With the 2 MHz ROMs (in a 2 MHz system) the program took 13 minutes to complete. With the 4 MHz ROMs in the same system it took 23 minutes to complete the same test on the same data. I finally determined that the extra delay time allowed the disk to rotate far enough that the desired sector had already passed the head—and the system had to wait for another complete revolution of the disk before it could complete the operation. This is an extreme example of the delays that can be associated with disk accesses.

CP/M 2.2 systems can be "trimmed up" to match the speed of the computer. Standard CP/M diskettes use a sector skew of six. This means that, instead of writing on sectors 1, 2, and 3 in succession, it writes on sectors 1, 7, and 13. This is done because most computers aren't fast enough to access successive sectors.

To explain: After sector 1 is written the system does some housekeeping. By the time it is ready to write the next sector, sector 2 has passed the head and the system must wait through another complete revolution of it. With a skew of six, after sector 1 is written the computer is fast enough to be ready to work again before sector 7 comes by. It is, of course, much faster to wait through only six sectors than it is to wait through twenty-five.

Decreasing the skew factor will speed up disk accesses if your computer is fast enough to keep up. When "trimming up" the system, each time you decrease the skew factor the system should speed up. When decreasing the skew slows down the operation you've gone too far. If you do modify the sector skewing, *please* leave at least one drive as single density with a skew factor of six so that you remain compatible with standard single-density CP/M volumes. Single-sided, single-density disks generally hold about 256K bytes; a double-sided, double-density diskette will hold about one megabyte.

HARD DISK

Floppy diskettes are the lower end of the disk family. For years large computers have used hard disks for mass storage. A hard disk is an aluminum platter coated on each side with magnetic recording oxide. It spins much faster than the floppy disk, and commonly holds at least one megabyte. Hard disk design falls into two categories. Characteristics of each are described below.

Removable Media

The first category contains the designs that use removable media. In these designs the medium, i.e., disk (protected by a plastic housing) can be removed from the drive and replaced—much like a floppy diskette.

These disks are fast and provide several megabytes of storage. The major drawback of a drive of this type is the requirement that the disk be kept extremely clean. The heads on this type of disk do not touch the surface but ride on a microscopic cushion of air. A hair, a fingerprint or a particle of cigarette smoke on the disk surface would stick up far enough for the head to hit it. The disk would not stop or even slow down (its rotating mass is too high) but the dirt particles could bounce the head away from the platter. If the head then touches the disk surface as it rebounds, it will chip off a piece of oxide and bounce off again. It will repeatedly strike the disk surface, chewing off the oxide, scraping, and possibly destroying the head as well as data on the affected track. If the damaged disk is inserted into an uncrashed drive, in an effort to recover the remaining data, it will be likely to crash that drive also. The new head will run into particles of oxide on the disk that were thrown around when the original damage occurred. The high-pitched squeal that you hear when the head crashes means that your disk and heads have just "bought the farm".

Nonremovable Media

The second category of hard disk includes designs with non-removable platters. The most popular of these is the Winchester-technology disk. Winchester disks tend to have higher density and lower cost than a removable-platter disk of the same diameter.

The heads on a Winchester drive are extremely lightweight. They are designed to touch the disk surface when the drive is turned on or off. Most designs use a special landing area for this, rather than on the data area. The head slides along the surface as the platter starts up. As the rotational speed of the disk increases, the air cushion builds up and the heads take off.

These disks are factory sealed to keep the surface clean. Winchester disks are available in 5¼-, 8-, 10-, and 14-inch diameters with total storage from 5 to 152 megabytes.

The term Winchester disk apparently was coined from the first drive of this type—the IBM Model 30. The Model 30 was, of course, the Famous Winchester repeating rifle.

DISK ALLOCATION PROCEDURES

Any disk operating system must make the best use of available space on the disk. It should also be reasonably efficient and fast. These requirements are often at odds with each other—an efficient and fast system (in terms of processing speed) may be quite inefficient in its use of disk space.

Each operating system resolves this problem in its own way. One method, used in Digital Equipment Corporation's RT-11 operating system for the LST-11, allocates disk space sequentially. As files are erased, space opens up on the disk. If a new file can be recorded in one of these spaces or at the end, well and good. If the entire file will not fit in the open space, then none of it is used. All files must be recorded in one piece, not spread all over the disk. Eventually you will get the disk full enough so that no more data can be recorded. There may be enough empty space to hold the file, but if it is not continuous it cannot be used. At this point the disk must be *squeezed*: the files are compacted to move the unused space to the end of the diskette.

The advantage of sequential allocation is that the operating system always knows where it has to read or write next, and it doesn't have to spend a lot of time moving around to find pieces of the file scattered all over the diskette. The disadvantage is that if a problem develops during the squeeze operation, the data on the disk becomes worthless.

CP/M, on the other hand, uses a different approach. Since the CP/M operating system runs on 8-bit processors (with the exception of CP/M-86) the amount of 16-bit arithmetic needed to be minimized. Digital Research (CP/M software developer) divides the disk into 1K blocks starting at Track 2, Sector 1. These blocks (assuming a standard single-density disk) are composed of eight sectors of 128 bytes each. Since each disk has less than 256 blocks, the block numbers can be one byte long. When a file is written to disk, the system uses the lowest block numbers available. Therefore, as files are deleted the holes that open up, are filled when new files are created. This eliminates the squeeze and its problems, but at the cost of some speed.

As a file is written the system finds open blocks from a bit map that it has built up in memory. As each open block is filled, the bit representing it is set. The file is closed by updating its directory entry to record the blocks that the file occupies. If a file isn't closed the system will act as if it were never recorded because the blocks that it used weren't recorded in the directory entry. With this system, only a disk problem in writing the directory would be likely to destroy all of the data on disk.

In each of the above cases, the operating system was well matched to the computer system on which it was to run. CP/M could have allocated blocks 256 bytes at a time, like RT-11; but that would have meant taking 16 bits per block number, and doubling the size of the directory entries and the bit map in core. RT-11 could have made easier use of disk space by allocating files into open spaces on disk like CP/M; but it would have eliminated the speed advantage of not having to skip all over the disk to record a file.

Power Supply,
Motherboard, and Enclosure

Some of the most neglected components in discussions of the design of small computer systems are the motherboard (backplane), power supply and enclosure. There are relatively simple parts but they can have a great effect on the overall performance of the computer system.

The computer must have stable power supplies, a noise-free bus, and a well-ventilated and mechanically secure enclosure. The enclosure and power supply both serve to isolate the computer from the outside world (and the world from the computer).

THE MOTHERBOARD

The motherboard, or backplane, provides a common set of connections for all the boards in the system. While not true of all bus systems, the S-100 bus is position-independent. It makes no difference which slot (connector) any board is placed in. Neither memory nor I/O addresses are dependent upon the slot; nor is the interrupt structure.

Backplane cards are generally of very heavy-duty construction, often ⅛-inch or thicker fiberglass/epoxy. They are available with three, six, twelve, fifteen, eighteen or twenty-two slots. A three-slot motherboard is only useful for a system built around a single board computer (CPU, I/O, disk controller, and EPROM on the same card) and a 64K memory board. This still leaves only one slot for expansion. If you are building your own computer you *don't* want a three-slot motherboard.

A six-slot system is a reasonable size for a system with more extensive I/O needs. The extra slots provide sufficient room to expand the system. Six-slot systems are a good choice for single-purpose system (word processing, for example). The hobbyist or computer experimenter really needs one of the larger motherboards. The twelve-through twenty-slot motherboards provide enough room for memory and I/O expansion.

A limitation that applies to any motherboard involves the use of wirewrapped boards. A wirewrapped board will take up *two* places on the motherboard because the wirewrap pins stick out far enough to prevent installation of another board in the slot behind the wirewrap card.

Unless small size is a major concern, the hobbyist interested in building boards should consider a backplane with at least twelve slots.

TERMINATION

Because of the length of the traces on the motherboard, ringing and reflection of signals can be a problem. If severe enough, these effects can cause data problems during bus cycles. In order to control these effects the bus should be *terminated*. Termination for TTL systems generally means holding the bus lines at about 2.5V when they are not being driven. This allows the TTL gate to source and sink current as intended, and minimizes the impedance of the line.

A simple way to provide this termination is with a resistive voltage divider; but this has the disadvantages of requiring a lot of power and generating a lot of heat. Such a passive terminator will typically use between 0.5 and 1 amp from the +8 V power supply.

A better method—active termination—has been developed to minimize the current requirements. The Godbout Active Termination circuit uses an operational amplifier to generate 2.6V, which is supplied to the bus through a series of 270-ohm resistors. Normally the circuit will need to supply only a small amount of current to the bus because the number of lines pulling current from the terminator will about equal the number of lines supplying current. This circuit is used on the Godbout motherboards and their active terminator card. With this card (Fig. 10-1), you can add termination to a motherboard that doesn't have it built in. The major disadvantage is the loss of one bus slot.

Another common termination method involves providing the 2.5V by putting a resistive voltage divider on the ground connection of a common three-terminal +5V regulator. Some motherboards have been designed with a ground plane surrounding each line. This cuts down on noise and crosstalk but still doesn't terminate the bus.

Many manufacturers recommend placing the CPU card as far as possible from the termination circuitry. The other boards should be placed in relation to their frequency of use. The memory boards should be close to the CPU with high speed I/O devices next.

It is quite possible to wirewrap a backplane but several factors argue against it: The power supplies can be required to carry a lot of current so separate (non-wirewrapped) wiring would have to be supplied. More important, a wirewrapped backplane is likely to be noisier and more prone to crosstalk than one constructed on a printed circuit card.

CONNECTOR SPACING

The major factor that affects connector spacing has already been mentioned—that of using two bus slots for every wirewrapped board. The only place where you can plug in a wirewrapped board and not lose a slot is in the last position. In this position the pins can stick out over the termination resistors.

For an experimenter planning on wirewrapping circuit boards, an 18-slot or larger motherboard is recommended. To make best use of such a motherboard, install only about 12 sockets. Starting at the end away from the termination resistors, install sockets in the first six positions. Skip the seventh and all remaining odd-numbered positions, installing sockets in the remaining even-numbered positions (Fig. 10-2). This results in seven slots with nothing immediately behind them—good places for wirewrapped cards.

Many of the larger motherboards have their "front" socket (the one farthest from the termination circuitry) offset slightly, with more space between it and the next socket. This was originally done

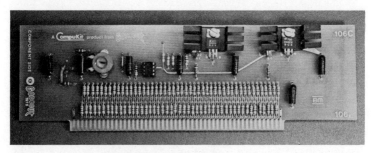

Fig. 10-1. The Godbout active terminator card.

to facilitate inclusion on an Imsai chassis. The Imsai frontpanel plugged into the first slot on the motherboard. The wider spacing was to allow the frontpanel to bolt onto the front of the enclosure and still provide enough clearance for a board to be plugged in.

SYSTEM POWER SUPPLIES

There are two types of power supplies that your computer can use. One is an unregulated but filtered supply for use with boards that carry their own local regulators. The other is a filtered and regulated supply that can be fed to circuits directly without further regulation.

The main system power supplies in an S-100 system are filtered but unregulated. The backplane carries +8V, +16V, and −16V unregulated power supplies. These are commonly very heavily filtered and of high current capacity. Power supplies for disk drives are normally voltage-regulated because the drives do not provide on-board regulation.

All S-100 boards have their own regulation circuitry mounted on them. This is what allows the use of unregulated power supplies in the system. The regulators used on these boards are generally of the three-terminal, monolithic, fixed-voltage type, requiring only one or two capacitors. They have the advantage of being tolerant of many problems (shorts, overheating, etc.). If a regulator mounted on a board fails it can damage only that board—the rest of the system is protected. In contrast, if a central regulated power supply fails, the entire system could be damaged.

On-board regulation has some disadvantages, however. In a central regulated supply, the heat generated by the regulation process is localized and easily handled. When the voltage regulators are on the boards, the heat is distributed around the system and more work must be done to keep the system cool.

GROUNDING AND FUSING

It is imperative that your computer system be well grounded. The frame of the computer should be firmly grounded to the ac power-line ground, both for safety and rf noise suppression. Grounds within the power supply itself should be frequent and heavy. Ground connections to the motherboard should be made with #18 or larger wire.

The ac power input should be fused immediately after it enters the computer enclosure. Everything inside should be protected by this fuse on the primary power line. The fuse should be a delayed

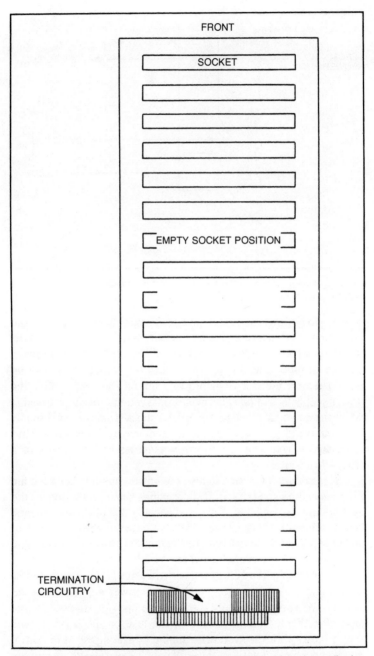

FRONT

SOCKET

EMPTY SOCKET POSITION

TERMINATION
CIRCUITRY

Fig. 10-2. An 18-slot motherboard can be populated with 12 sockets, allowing easy expansion with wirewrapped boards.

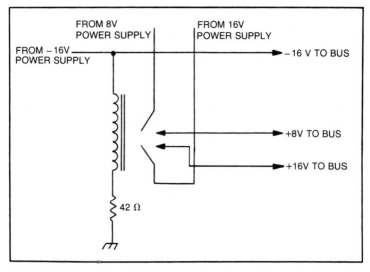

Fig. 10-3. A relay on the −16V line can protect dynamic memories in case the −16V supply is lost.

action (slow-blow) fuse rated at 1 to 3 amps, depending upon the equipment. A standard-action fuse usually can't be used because the inrush of current needed to charge the filter capacitors is normally enough to blow a standard fuse. The filter capacitors should be equipped with bleeder resistors to drain off the charge after the power supply is shut off. This makes the system a lot safer to handle when the power is off. You won't get a shock from the +8V supply but you could get quite a shock (and maybe blow up a filter capacitor) if you drop a screwdriver across the terminals of a charged capacitor.

It is common practice to fuse the power supplies between the filter capacitors and the bus. This provides some protection for the system and the supplies. This is especially useful if experimental boards are tested because these tend to have a higher incidence of power supply problems. Protective fusing can be a problem in some circumstances, however, for dynamic RAM boards.

For example, the 16K dynamic RAM chips (416s) require +5V, +12V, and −5V power supplies. These power supplies *must* be sequenced. The +5V supply should come up *before* the others and drop *after* them. Difficulty arises if the fuse on the +16V power supply blows while the system is running. Operating the 4116 chip on +12V and +5V, but without the −5V supply can cause them serious damage. To remedy this, the +8V and +16V supplies should be shut

116

down immediately if the −16V supply drops out. This is not difficult to accomplish, but it does require additional circuitry. A simple relay across the −16V supply to ground will cut off the +8V and +16V supplies when the −16V supply is lost (Fig. 10-3).

A quicker way to cut off the positive power supplies would be to use a version of the crowbar circuit. This circuit (Fig. 10-4) uses an overvoltage protector and an adjustable voltage divider. The divider is set to a voltage near ground when the supply is active. If the −16V supply shuts down, the overvoltage circuit comes up to nearly the surviving voltage, firing the protector and blowing the fuse.

BUILD FOR EXPANSION

The system power supplies should be designed to provide more current than the initial system will need. This extra capacity allows you to expand the system without running out of power.

A 15-slot (or larger) motherboard in an experimenter's system should have a 20A to 25A capacity on the +8V supply. The +16V and −16V supplies should be able to provide two to three amps each. The power supply should be integrated with the enclosure design to efficiently carry away heat.

The ± 16V supplies usually have much greater capacity than the system uses, especially before much expansion takes place. This results in these voltages being present on the bus at ± 20V or

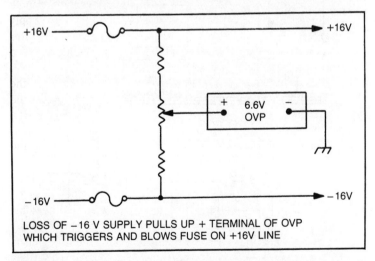

LOSS OF −16 V SUPPLY PULLS UP + TERMINAL OF OVP WHICH TRIGGERS AND BLOWS FUSE ON +16V LINE

Fig. 10-4. A crowbar/divider circuit can also provide protection for dynamic memory.

117

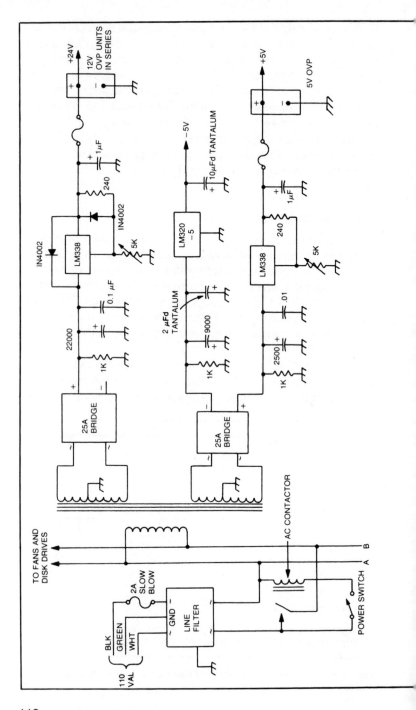

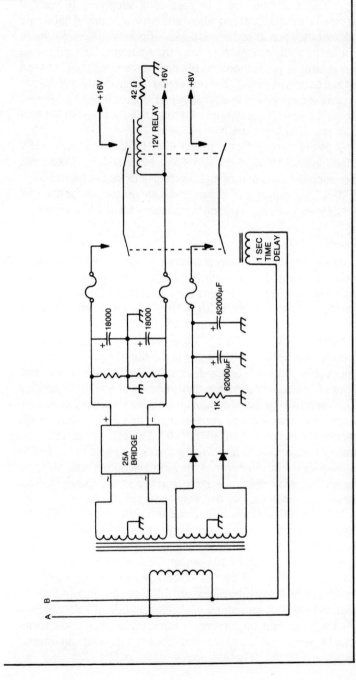

Fig. 10-5. This power supply provides +8V at 20A, (±) 16V regulated at 5A, +24V regulated at 5A and −5V regulated at 1A.

higher. These supplies must be capable of supplying 16 volts at their rated current (2.5A) but when only several hundred milliamps are drawn they run at higher voltages. Higher voltages put more strain on the voltage regulators since the amount of heat generated in a regulator is proportional to the difference in voltage between input and output terminals. Some systems use dropping resistors to bring this voltage down, which really just creates heat in a different place (in the power supply rather than on the boards)—but the heat can be removed more easily.

A power supply that provides the +8V, +16V, and −16V needed for an S-100 system; and +5V, +24V and −5V regulated power supplies for a pair of eight-inch disk drives is illustrated in Fig. 10-5. This supply provides overvoltage protection for the +5V and +24V supplies and sequencing circuitry for the bus voltages.

COOLING

Any electrical or electronic device produces heat because of losses within the device itself. In a computer system, the logic components can get warm, but their contribution to the total heat generated by the system is fairly small. The voltage regulators generate the most heat in the system.

Some computers (the APPLE II, for instance) use a central switching regulator to supply power to the system. These regulators can be quite efficient and, as a result, generate only a small amount of heat. They generate their output voltage by integrating (with a capacitor) pulses of a higher unregulated voltage. One of the reasons why these supplies are efficient is that they quickly switch the transistors from "full on" to "full off". This takes relatively little power in comparison to a transistor operating in its linear region (i.e., partway on). However, switching regulators can be quite complex and may require a large number of components. This increases the cost and can decrease their reliability.

Most S-100 systems use three-terminal series regulators. These regulators contain a very large transistor that is used, in effect, as a variable resistor. Any voltage higher than the regulated output voltage is converted into heat. The resistance of the pass transistor is controlled by the other circuitry in the regulator. Internal self protection circuitry provides current limiting on the output and thermal protection of the regulator's circuitry. These regulators will limit their current output rather than allow themselves to be damaged, and will shut themselves off if the internal circuitry overheats. These features and the fact that only two

Fig. 10-6. The TO-3 power transistor package.

external components are necessary make these regulators very popular.

Three-terminal series regulators are available in both the TO-3 power transistor package (Fig. 10-6) and the TO-220 tab package (Fig. 10-7). The TO-3 package has better thermal characteristics, but the TO-220 is in more common use. In either case, if the regulators are going to run at any large fraction of their rated power, heat sinks are necessary. These heat sinks greatly increase the surface area available to dissipate heat.

Fig. 10-7. The TO-220 power transistor package.

Fig. 10-8. A fan that is used to cool the computer.

Some computers that run at fairly low temperatures are ventilated by natural convection currents. Only a small amount of airflow is necessary to keep the components at a reasonable temperature.

Systems that produce a lot of heat should have active air circulation (S-100 computers are usually of this type). The most common way to provide this is with a small electric fan (Fig. 10-8).

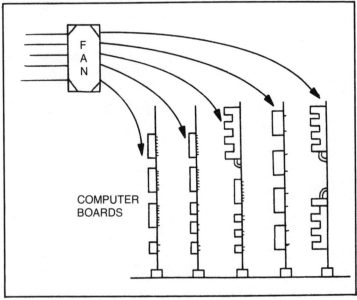

Fig. 10-9. Blowing air over the tops of the boards helps cool them.

While blowing air over the top of the boards (Fig. 10-9) is usually satisfactory, blowing air through the boards is far superior (Fig. 10-10). Screens and filters should be placed over the fans to protect fingers and keep out dirt.

RFI AND TVI PREVENTION

Computers create radio-frequency interference (rfi) and television interference (TVI). This interference is usually high-frequency noise that can disrupt local radio and television reception. Computers radiate a wide range of radio frequencies, some extending into the low 50 MHz range used by the lower VHF television channels. A computer with a 2 MHz clock can generate interference in the 50 MHz range because of the speed at which the signals change state. A 2 MHz clock signal has rise times for the level transitions in the nanosecond range or less. This high-speed transition causes the high-frequency interference. In order to have sharp edges on a pulse, the signal must be composed of a great many high-frequency components (Fig. 10-11), and it is these that cause the interference. This is a basic "fact of life" in digital electronics.

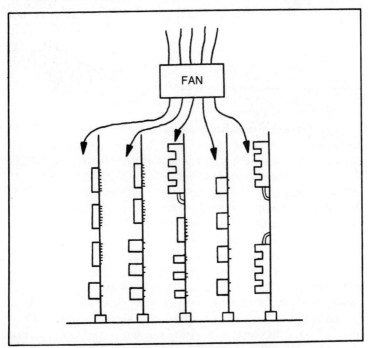

Fig. 10-10. Blowing air through the boards cools more efficiently.

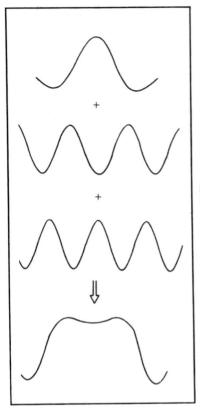

Fig. 10-11. A pulse is made of many high frequency components.

The Federal Communications Commission (FCC) takes a dim view of television interference caused by computers and other electronic devices. They have set up rules to ensure that home computers do not cause undue television interference. The APPLE II computer, designed and built before these FCC regulations were in force, is housed in a plastic case and is notorious for causing TVI. Atari home computers were designed to comply with the regulations and, as a result, have a substantial metal case under the plastic outer one. The Ataris do not cause TVI.

The most important step in controlling radio-frequency interference is to provide your computer with a good ground. The enclosure should be a metal box with as few holes as possible. The cooling fan holes should be covered with metal screen securely grounded to the case. The ac power cable should have an rf filter installed after the fuse, just inside the enclosure. Other cables should be shielded to prevent them from acting as antennas.

When your computer is completed you should test it for television interference by running it in the same room as a television. Check especially for interference on TV channels on the low-frequency end (channels 3 and 5, for example). There should be little problem with the higher-frequency channels (8 and above) and no problem at all in the UHF band (channels 14-80),

RACK AND TABLE-MOUNT ENCLOSURES

Most home computers are built in tabletop enclosures. These are built to sit on (and look good on) a table or desk top. Most of the commercial S-100 computers are available in tabletop enclosures. Many homebuilt computers are also built in this type of enclosure because of its practicality (Fig. 10-12).

Commercial equipment is also commonly available for mounting in the industry-standard 19-inch relay rack (Fig. 10-13). This is practical because equipment can be bolted directly to the rack, and makes the system modular. Power supplies, disk drives, and the computer can each mount separately in the rack. 120Vac power can be distributed easily to each component in the rack. The disadvantage of the standard rack system is that rack mounts weren't made to be pretty.

A middle ground does exist, however. There are tabletop enclosures available with standard rack frames installed. They let

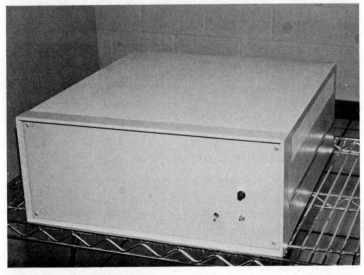

Fig. 10-12. A tabletop enclosure.

Fig. 10-13. A rack-mount enclosure.

you use rack-mounted equipment in a nice looking enclosure small enough to fit on a table (Fig. 10-14). Desks are also available with rack-mount frames installed (Fig. 10-15).

It makes little difference *how* the system is enclosed, but for physical protection, good cooling and rfi prevention, it is important that the system *is* enclosed. Your enclosure should provide easy

Fig. 10-14. A table/rack-mount enclosure.

Fig. 10-15. A desk-mount system enclosure.

access to all components for servicing and testing. The enclosure is what people see when they look at your computer. A nice-looking enclosure seems to be much more impressive than piles of boards and a tangle of wires!

Software

The most sophisticated and technically advanced computer ever designed would be completely useless without the software to run it.

Software used by a computer system can be organized in pyramid fashion (Fig. 11-1). At the bottom are the low-level device-driver routines and other simple but vital software (for example, to communicate with the console terminal).

The next level up is generally some type of operating system. This system is (or should be) designed to allow the user to forget all of the nitty-gritty details of system operation (how to allocate space on diskettes to store files etc.). Above that level are language processors. These compilers and interpreters allow the user to develop programs. Again, these programs should allow the user to forget about details and concentrate on the concepts involved in writing the program at hand. At the top of the pyramid are the applications programs. These should hide almost all the details of the hardware from the user.

The illustration given in Fig. 11-2 demonstrates how much time and effort a program can save for the user of the machine. Imagine that you are running a program and it asks you "Do you wish to save the data? You answer "Yes." If the program was written in Pascal it probably has to execute a Pascal "rewrite" instruction in order to create the file in which the data will be saved. This instruction has, however, been translated by the Pascal compiler into a "create file" code for the operating system. The operating system must enter the new file into its directory, and in order to get to the directory it must first reset one of the floppy disk drives to track 0. The operating system calls a "home selected drive" routine which sends the disk controller a "reset drive" command. The user doesn't even need to know that there *is* a "reset drive" command for the disk controller. He just answered "Yes" to a simple question and the system did the rest.

SYSTEM MONITOR

A *system monitor* program performs the same functions that would be handled by a hardware frontpanel. A simple monitor program has the facility to deposit data into memory and start executing at any address.

Minimum Requirements

The system monitor contains the routines needed to initialize the system, and to read and write to the console. If these routines are well-written they will be fast, efficient, and accessible to other programs. There is no reason for an application program to include separate console I/O routines when they are already available in the monitor. Since the monitor is in EPROM these routines are always available and at a constant location in memory. This logic can and should be extended to printer and modem service routines, binary/hexidecimal conversion routines, disk drivers, real-time clock support, and, in general, anything that needs to be in memory at all times.

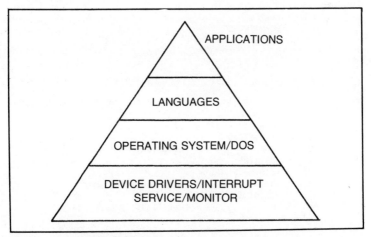

Fig. 11-1. The software pyramid.

Application Level:

    Do you wish to save the data? (Y/N):

Pascal source:

```
  repeat
        write(' Do you wish to save the data? (Y/N):');
        readln(YesNo);
  until YesNo in ['Y','N','y','n'];

  if YesNo in ['Y','y']
        then
          begin
                rewrite(DataFile,Filename);
                .
                .
                .
```

Assembler produced by compiler:

```
PSTNG:  MVI     C,PrintString
        LXI     D,Message
        CALL    BDOS
        CPI     'Y'
        JZ      MAKEFILE
        CPI     'y'
        JZ      MAKEFILE
        CPI     'N'
        JZ      L4000
        CPI     'n'
        JZ      L4000
        JMP     PSTNG
Message:        DB      ' Do you wish to save the data? (Y/N):$'

MAKEFILE:
        MVI     D,FCB1
        MVI     C,MAKECODE
        CALL    BDOS
        .
        .
        .
```

The operating system calls, among others, the "Home drive" Routine:

```
HOME:   PUSH    PSW
        MVI     A,HOMECMD
        OUT     DSKCTL          ;Send command to controller
WAIT:   IN      DSTATUS
        ORI     STATMASK
        JRNZ    WAIT            ;Check for home done
        IN      DSTATUS
        ANA     A               ;set flags
        RET
```

Fig. 11-2. A hypothetical program example.

130

A well written monitor will usually begin with a *jump table* as illustrated in Fig. 11-3. Once the jump table is in place it doesn't matter at what address a particular service routine starts, as long as the jump table points to it. Succeeding generations of the monitor may include major software changes that alter the position of the service routine, but the jump table remains in the same position. If the jump table is located at address F000H and the second element in the table is jump to the console input routine, a program calling location F0003H will end up reading from the console. As long as the same jump table structure is maintained the actual address that the jump points to is irrelevant. As long as the jump to the console input routine remains at address F0003H, it makes no difference what address the jump points to. Any routine that must be available all of the time should be in the monitor.

ZMON 62

ZMON 62 is the current version of the monitor program used in my computer system. It provides for all of the basic frontpanel functions, some extended frontpanel functions, and includes low-level support routines for the I/O devices.

This monitor (see Appendix B) is constructed with a jump table at the beginning of the program. The command *parser* is of very

```
Start of monitor jump table

JMP      INIT     ;Cold Start monitor
JMP      CONIN    ;Console in
JMP      CONOUT   ;Console out
JMP      CONSTAT  ;Console status
JMP      PNT      ;Printer out
JMP      PNTSTAT  ;Printer status
JMP      HOME     ;Seek disk to TK 00
JMP      SELECT   ;Select disk drive
JMP      TRACK    ;Set the track
JMP      SECTOR   ;Set the sector
JMP      READ     ;Read disk
JMP      WRITE    ;Write disk
JMP      SETDMA   ;Set transfer address
JMP      ERROR    ;Monitor error handler
```

Fig. 11-3. A monitor jumptable allows easy access to the routines in it.

simple design. I experimented with a more complicated and less "brute force" method, but the system of multiple comparisons (an IF-THEN-ELSE structure) was decided upon for several reasons: The multiple-compare method is simple to implement, simple to expand, and is much shorter than other methods tried. Because this is a simple command parser (and spends most of its time waiting for input from the user) the less time-efficient but more space-efficient compare form was used.

The monitor allows the user to switch into a frontpanel mode where only numbers need to be entered. No explicit "examine" command needs to be used—you simply type an address and that location is examined. Hitting the space bar causes the contents of the next memory location to be displayed. Typing a hexidecimal number after a location is examined causes that number to be deposited in the current location. The location is re-examined and the contents printed out. The next location is then examined. One limitation in the monitor is the requirement to type a full field of numbers (i.e., you have to type all four digits of an address or both digits of data).

The "M" command allows a section of memory to be displayed in hexidecimal. The "B" command causes the monitor to boot the operating system.

Some of the low-level support routines that were included allow reading and writing to the console, a status check on the console, printer initialization and print character routines, and real-time clock support. The listing shown in Appendix B is heavily commented and should be easily deciphered.

OPERATING SYSTEM

The operating system (OS) or disk operating system (DOS) is the program that handles the creation and maintenance of disk files. It has the job of creating new disk files when necessary, allowing these files to be updated or deleted, and keeping track of what files are available and where they are.

While the operating system will typically also handle the console, its major function involves keeping track of files on disk. This program relieves the operator of much of the work associated with keeping files in a disk-operated system. The operating system figures out how much disk space to allocate for a file, and what tracks and sectors to put it on. Several operating systems have become popular for use on small systems. These will be discussed in the following sections.

132

CP/M Built in commands:

SAVE	Save an area of memory to disk
ERA	Erase a file
REN	Rename a file
DIR	List the disk directory
TYPE	List a file to the console
USER	Set user area number
B:	Make drive B the default drive (works for drives A through O)

Fig. 11-4. The CP/M built-in commands.

CP/M 1.4 AND 2.2

The CP/M operating system, a product of Digital Research, is the most popular 8080/Z-80 disk operating system available. The 1.4 version was designed to handle single-density 8-inch diskettes while the 2.2 version can handle nearly any disk system from one single-density 5¼-inch diskette up to fifteen 8-megabyte devices.

The CP/M operating systems are constructed in three parts. The first, and the lowest in memory, is the Console Command Processor (CCP). This module will take care of interaction with the user console, and it defines and processes the built-in commands (Fig. 11-4). The CCP reads the command line that the user types. This module can be replaced by an application program if necessary but doing so requires that the operating system be re-read when the application is finished.

The next section of CP/M is the BDOS, or Basic Disk Operating System. This module is the one that manages the disk system. It has a number of commands available through a call to an entry point that allows a program to create, read, write, erase, and rename files, among other things.

The final CP/M module is the BIOS or Basic I/O System. This is a user-customized area where I/O handling is done. The specific hardware-dependent routine for controlling the disk drives, printer, and console are contained in the BIOS. Some of these may be implemented as jumps to your monitor. The advantage of this organization is that only the BIOS needs to be changed from one implementation to another.

The remaining memory area, with one small exception, makes up the Transient Program Area, or TPA. The TPA begins at address 0100H in a standard system. The exception mentioned above is the area between addresses 0000 and 00FFH. This area is used for vectors into CP/M, the restart addresses, and some default buffer areas. A memory map of a typical CP/M system is shown in Fig. 11-5.

The TPA is used for transient programs. If you type a word such as "BASIC" the CCP first checks to see if the word is one of the built-in commands. If it is, the CCP causes the BDOS to execute the command. If it is not, the disk is searched for a file named "BASIC COM." If a file by that name is located it is loaded into memory beginning at 0100H, the beginning of the TPA. Execution also begins at 0100H. The "COM" extension means that the file is a

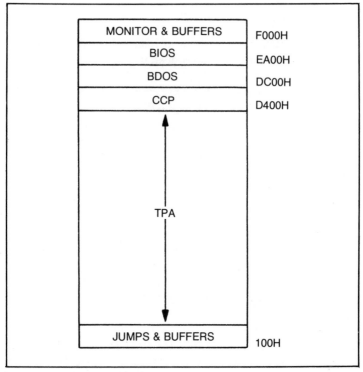

Fig. 11-5. A CP/M memory map.

memory image, (i.e., an assembled and loaded program designed to run starting at 0100H).

CP/M is, simply, a large program (8-12K depending upon the version) that simplifies file handling by the computer. It also allows users with widely different equipment to exchange programs.

INDUSTRY SUPPORT

CP/M, like the S-100 bus, is heavily supported by independent manufacturers. In fact, the vast majority of programs available to run under CP/M were written by someone other than Digital Research.

There are also several large CP/M Users' Groups around the country. One of these has more than fifty 8-inch single-density diskette volumes available. Several of the languages have developed their own users groups which are also quite active.

OTHER SYSTEMS

CP/M-86 is available for the 8086 family of 16-bit microprocessors. This is normal CP/M recoded for the 8086 processor and has all the features of "normal" CP/M. CP/M is a somewhat limited system, however given the power of a 16-bit computer. Many of the newer 16-bit processors run under more complex operating systems. A large number of the available operating systems for the Z8000 and 68000 series of microprocessors are based on the UNIX system developed by Bell Laboratories.

There are some alternate operating systems available for Z-80 systems also. These fall into two distinct groups. The first group consists of the CP/M extensions. Some are CP/M recoded for the Z-80; and some, like Cromemco's CDOS, are extensions to CP/M. Cromemco adds some additional operating system calls to CP/M 1.4.

The other type of operating systems consists of those which are "different from CP/M" systems. Cromemco Cromix is an example, as is the OASIS system from Phase 1 systems. These systems may sacrifice CP/M compatability in order to gain features such as advanced file security. These two systems are also designed to be multi-user systems. MP/M is Digital Research's multi-user system. It is, for the most part, compatible with CP/M systems.

When CP/M 2.2 was released some additional advanced features were added. In their newer versions CP/M and CDOS have diverged to the point where they are now incompatible in many respects.

PROGRAMMING LANGUAGES

Once the hardware for your computer is assembled you are only half done. You presumably want the computer so that you can *do* something with it. While there are many good commercial programs available to do all sorts of useful things you will want to have the capability to write your own programs. There are many different languages available in which to write your programs; some of them are more suitable than others for a particular task.

Machine Language

Your computer has a set of built-in instructions that it understands. These are represented by one or more bytes. If an 8080 microprocessor reads memory to receive its next instruction and it reads a byte of C3H (a bit pattern of 11000011) it knows that this is a jump instruction, and that it must read the destination address from the next two consecutive memory locations. The set of *opcodes* (operation codes) built into the microprocessor chip are the *only* instructions that it can execute.

You can program the computer by entering the bytes corresponding to the instructions in memory. This method (slow, cumbersome, difficult, and prone to error) is called *machine language* programming.

Assembler

The "original" programming language (if there is one) is Assembly language. All computer manufacturers have developed lists of short words (*mnemonics*) that represent each instruction. For example, the jump instruction mentioned previously is represented by the mnemonic JMP.

A program can be written to translate these mnemonics into the proper machine codes. This program is an Assembler. Some typical Assembler code is illustrated in Fig. 11-6. Assembler provides the fastest and most efficient programs. It is difficult to write in Assembler because you have to keep track of what is going on in each register of the machine.

Assemblers can be quite complex. One powerful type of assembler is the Macro Assembler. A *macro* is, simply, a group of instructions that you will want to use in more than one place where a

136

```
;
; OSTR   String Printer
;        ENTER with HL pointing to the string to print
;        EXIT when a byte of 00 is found
;
OSTR:   MOV     A,M      ;GET BYTE
        ANA     A        ;SET FLAGS
        RZ               ;RET IF ZERO
        CALL    CONOUT   ;CONSOLE OUTPUT ROUTINE
        INX     H        ;GET TO NEXT BYTE
        JR      OSTR     ;JUMP(RELATIVE) TO PROCESS NEXT CHAR
;
```

Fig. 11-6. An example of an Assembler program.

subroutine will not work. You just put together the group of instructions and give it a name. When you need to use it in your program you simply use the macro name rather than rewriting the whole set of instructions.

If you write a program which needs to write to several different I/O ports you can develop a WRITE Macro, as shown in Fig. 11-7. It would be invoked in the program by using its name as shown in Fig. 11-8. When the Macro Assembler finds the instruction "WRITE" it determines that it is not a legal machine instruction so it checks to see if a macro called "WRITE" has been defined. If "WRITE" is found, the code in the macro is inserted where the write statement has been located. The resultant code is shown in Fig. 11-9. Two of the most common Macro Assemblers are MAC, written by Digital Research, and Macro-80 by Microsoft.

```
;;
;;       WRITE - MACRO TO WRITE TO A PORT
;;
WRITE   MACRO   PORT,MASK
;; PORT IS STATUS PORT # WITH DATA AT PORT + 1
;; MASK IS STATUS READY MASK
        LOCAL   READY
READY:  IN      PORT     ;READ STATUS
        ANI     MASK     ;ISOLATE READY BIT
        JRNZ    READY    ;LOOP IF NOT READY
        MOV     A,C      ;GET BYTE FROM C
        OUT     PORT+1   ;WRITE BYTE
        ENDM             ;;END OF MACRO
```

Fig. 11-7. A Write Macro.

```
GRAPH:   EQU     10H     ;DEFINE BASE PORT #
GMASK:   EQU     01H     ;DEFINE MASK
         .
         .
         .
         LXI     H,SCREEN        ;GET ADDRESS OF DATA BUFFER
         MOV     C,M             ;GET BYTE
         WRITE   GRAPH,GMASK     ;WRITE BYTE TO INTERFACE
         .
         .
         .
```

Fig. 11-8. Invocation of the Write Macro.

BASIC

In order to simplify programming higher-level languages are used. These free the programmer from worrying about which register is which, etc. The most common higher-level language for small computers is BASIC.

BASIC was designed to be easy to write and debug. It is generally available as either an interpreter or a compiler. An *interpreter* reads each line of BASIC code, figures out what it needs to do, and then does it. The interpreter itself is executing the program. A *compiler* reads the program and translates it into machine language. When the program is run the compiler no longer takes part.

Where an interpreter is another program following the instructions of the BASIC program, the compiler "writes" an assembler program from the instructions in the BASIC program. One of the

```
Macro is expanded to:

GRAPH:   EQU     10H     ;DEFINE BASE PORT #
GMASK:   EQU     01H     ;DEFINE MASK
         .
         .
         .
         LXI     H,SCREEN        ;GET ADDRESS OF DATA BUFFER
         MOV     C,M             ;GET BYTE
??5:     IN      10H     ;READ STATUS
         ANI     01      ;ISOLATE READY BIT
         JRNZ    ??5     ;LOOP IF NOT READY
         MOV     A,C     ;GET BYTE FROM C
         OUT     11H     ;WRITE BYTE
         .
         .
         .
```

Fig. 11-9. Expansion of the Write Macro into the code.

advantages of the interpreter is that the programs are easier to debug because the program is always there and generally has some built-in editing facilities. A compiled program must be re-edited and recompiled every time a change is made; the compiler makes up for this in faster execution speed. In an interpreter each line must be re-interpreted each time you come upon it. This results in much of the code being re-interpreted many times (code within a loop is an example). The compiler, having created a self-sufficient program, is not active when the program runs. As a result a compiled program runs much faster than the same interpreted program.

BASIC is easy to learn but its limitations make it difficult to write correct, structured programs. Many BASIC programs are a jungle of meaningless variable names (e.g., A1 or B$) and a rat's nest of GOTO and GOSUB statements. All variables exist everywhere in the program (they are global). If you use the variable R3 both in a subroutine and in the main program for different purposes, each call to the subroutine will alter the value of R3 in the main program. An example of a BASIC program is shown in Fig. 11-10.

Pascal

The Pascal language was developed by Niklaus Wirth in Switzerland and has great utility both as a production language and as a language to teach programming. Pascal features a rigid, strongly typed structure which is designed to force the programmer to write in a clear, readable and correct way.

If Pascal has one overridding rule, it is that everything must be defined before it is used. All variables must be declared before they are used, *and* all procedures must be defined before they are invoked. This requires a "backwards" structure for Pascal pro-

```
0005    REM THIS PROGRAM FINDS THE BIGGEST NUMBER IN ARRAY A
0007    REM  AND PUTS IT IN B. ITS INDEX GOES IN N
0010    DIM A(50)
        .
        .
        .
        .
0280    N=0
0290    B=-32758
0300    FOR I=1 TO 50
0310    IF A(I)>B THEN B=A(I):N=I
0320    NEXT I
```

Fig. 11-10. BASIC example.

```
const
        NumberOfElements        = 50;
        InitialValue = -MAXINT;             (often 32738 )
type
        sca     = ARRAY[1..50] of INTEGER;
var
        Scales  : sca;

        Index,
        BiggestNumber,
        IndexOfBiggestNumber    : INTEGER;
begin
  BiggestNumber := InitialValue;
  for Index := 1 to NumberOfElements do
        begin
           if Scales[Index] > BiggestNumber
                then
                   begin
                        BiggestNumber := Scales[Index];
                        IndexOfBiggestNumber := Index;
                   end;
        end;
end;
```

Fig. 11-11. Pascal example.

grams. Most BASIC and FORTRAN programs are written (and must be) with the main program first, followed by the subroutines that it calls. A Pascal program, in contrast, must be written with the global variable declarations first, then each procedure (subroutine), and finally the main program. This structure greatly simplifies the compiler structure also.

The major flaw in Pascal is probably the I/O handling. There is little or no formatting of printed lines in standard Pascal. Most Pascal packages have extensions for I/O and console-handling functions.

Pascal packages generally come in two forms: the compiler and the p-code compiler/interpreter. The first form, used in Intersystem's Pascal/Z and MT Micro System's Pascal MT, translates Pascal code into Assembler for later assembly. This has the advantage of fast execution and easy linkability to assembler routines.

The other form, used by Sorcim's Pascal/M, is the p-code compiler/interpreter. This method translates Pascal to an intermediate "p-code". This forms the instruction set of a "Pascal machine". The p-code instructions are then interpreted by the Pascal system when the program is run. Western Digital's Pascal

Microengine is a multi-chip microprocessor that executes p-code directly, for fast execution. Figure 11-11 shows an example of Pascal code.

C Language

The C language is a successor of the B language. C and the legendary UNIX operating system are both products of the equally legendary Bell Labs. C is a structured language along the same lines as Pascal. The system is wildly different from Pascal but the same structural concepts are at work in both. C allows the programmer more access to the computer hardware than does Pascal. This makes C an ideal tool for the development of systems software.

The UNIX system mentioned above demonstrates the utility of C for this type of programming. According to *The C Programming Language* by Kernighan and Ritchie:

> " . . . the UNIX operating system, which is written almost entirely in C. Of 13000 lines of system code, only about 800 lines at the very lowest level are written in assembler. In addition, essentially all of the UNIX applications software is written in C."

C allows all of the logical operations that you need to do when handling hardware interface programming. Its syntax allows powerful functions to be created with a minimum of code. If Pascal is a bit verbose, C is terse. C is not as strongly typed as Pascal. The data types in Pascal are practically inviolate, whereas C allows the programmer some flexibility. With this flexibility comes, however, the ability to write cryptic, obscure code that is not nearly as readable as Pascal.

All of the common C systems for CP/M are compilers, with only one exception. Tiny-C (by Tiny-C Associates) is a limited and slow interpreted subset of C. Tiny-C and its manual excel at teaching structured programming in general and some aspects of C in particular.

Small-C is a public domain C compiler executing a subset of UNIX C. The outstanding feature of Small-C is that complete source code (in C) is available in listing form in the May 1980 issue of Dr. Dobb's Journal and on disk from The Code Works.

Another outstanding C compiler is BD Software C, written by Leor Zolman and distributed by Lifeboat Associates. Written by a lover of C, it is enthusiastically supported by the author and a BDSC Users' Group.

Tiny-C Associates also market the Tiny-C TWO compiler, which supports the same syntax as the interpreter. The Tiny-C syntax is a variant of standard C. Standard C programs will *not* run, unchanged, under Tiny-C and vice versa.

Both Supersoft and Whitesmiths market C compilers. The Whitesmiths compiler is a big-bucks big-memory full C compiler. Potential users should be warned, however, that some of the C standard functions have different names in the Whitesmiths implementation. A sample of C code is found in Fig. 11-12.

Other Languages

There are many other programming languages around. Many of these are available under CP/M. FORTRAN, the oldest of higher-level languages, is available from several sources, as is COBOL. I see no reason to use either language unless you already have a large library of programs written in one of them.

Digital Research distributes PL/I-80—a subset of IBM's monstrous PL/I language. This seems to be an excellent product including compiler, assembler, linker, and library support.

Algol, the predecessor of PL/I, Pascal, and C, is available from CP/M Users Group. This is a product of the Naval Postgraduate School, as was BASIC-E (an old BASIC compiler) and NPS COBOL.

Several FORTH systems and dialects are available. FORTH seems to be a mixture of assembler, higher level language and religion. Its proponents love it; its opponents hate it; and most people say "What good is it?"

```
{
        int     bisnumber,bisindex,index,array[50];

        bisnumber = -23754;
        index = 1;
        while (index <=50){
                if( array[index] > bisnumber )
                {
                        bisnumber = array[index];
                        bisindex = index;
                        ++index
                }
        }
}
```

Fig. 11-12. C example.

```
FINDBIG: PROCEDURE;

    DECLARE ARRAY(50) FIXED,
            MAXIMUM FIXED,
            INDEX   FIXED;

    MAXIMUM = -32762;
    DO I = 1 TO 50;
        IF ARRAY(I) > MAXIMUM
            THEN
                DO;
                    MAXIMUM = ARRAY(I);
                    INDEX   = I;
                END;
    END;
```

Fig. 11-13. PL/I example.

Another "what good is it" language is LISP. Its strength seems to lie in a built-in tree structure. It is heavily used by practitioners in the field of artificial intelligence, but they seem to be the only ones who understand it.

APL (A Programming Language) is another interesting, if somewhat strange language. APL's strength—the use of special characters to stand for complete functions not available in most languages—is also its weakness. Most terminals do not have the APL character set built in, and many do not have it available as an option. With APL you can manipulate matrices in one stroke, compressing to one line a function that would take many lines in another language. APL also suffers in readability because of the strange character set. Some examples of these languages are found in Figure 11-13.

YOUR SOFTWARE INVESTMENT

It would be a mistake to believe that your computer is complete just because the hardware is assembled and working. If you are planning a disk-based system it is likely that you will want to run CP/M or a related operating system.

The initial purchase for a CP/M system should be CP/M 2.2 from Digital Research. The package includes the following:

ED : A line editor designed for use with a printing terminal.

ASM: An 8080 assembler.

PIP: The general purpose "data movement" program
to allow copying, etc.

DDT: The assembly language debugger.

There are several more "systems" programs included with the package for maintenance of the system, allowing you to generate new system disks, etc.

If you have a video terminal you will want to consider a screen editor. This allows you to use the CRT terminal as a window into the file you are working on. One of these, Wordmaster, is available from Micro Pro and is the "little brother" of their word processing program Word Star. Another, Vedit, was designed to use the special function keys available on many terminals. This is from CompuView Products. There are a number of other editors on the market, some from user's groups, which are worth investigating.

If a BASIC system is what you want, there are two ways to go. The "standard" CP/M BASIC is Microsoft's. Microsoft distributes this system as a compiler or an interpreter. Most people would start with the interpreter and later purchase the compiler. While this runs into a lot of expense (at least $600) you do get two major advantages. The first is that you have a matched set. You can develop a program using the superior diagnostic and editing facilities of the interpreter and, when the program is working correctly, compile it to make use of the speed of a compiled program. The other advantage is that the compiler package includes the Macro-80 Macro Assembler, Link-80 linker, and the library manager.

If you do not want the Microsoft system there are several alternatives. The CBASIC-2 compiler is popular and moderately priced. Tarbell BASIC is an interpreter that is available both from Tarbell and (in an older version) from the CP/M User's group. In addition, source code is available from both sources.

Most computer people will want a Macro Assembler if they intend to do much assembly language programming. The two most widely used Macro Assemblers are MAC from Digital Research and Macro-80 from Microsoft. These approach the problem of the Z-80 instructions in two different ways.

MAC uses the original Intel (8080) mnemonics with "look-alike" extensions for the Z-80 instructions. Macro-80 uses Zilog mnemonics which differ greatly from the Intel set.

Both assemblers have their strong points. Macro-80 produces relocatable code. This means that all code is assembled starting at address 0. The data produced by the assembler includes information

144

that allows a linking program (Link-80 in this case) to determine which instructions must be modified to allow the program to run at a different address. Figure 11-14 demonstrates this process. The use of relocatable code allows a group of pre-assembled libraries to be developed and linked into an application program if needed.

MAC does not produce relocatable code. (A version of MAC distributed with PL/I-80 does, however.) It will produce a symbol file. This file is made up of an entry for each label used in the program and its address. This allows the Digital Research Symbolic debugger SID or its Z-80 version, ZSID, to insert the proper alphanumeric label into an instruction instead of just the address, making the tracing of program execution much easier. This process is illustrated in Fig. 11-15. I would recommend the purchase of SID or ZSID with MAC.

For higher-level languages there are several possibilities. If you really want FORTRAN, the Microsoft FORTRAN compiler is available. It includes Macro-80, the linker, and the librarian programs. Another FORTRAN compiler that has received favorable reviews is the one by SuperSoft. I don't, however, see any reason to bother with FORTRAN when the newer languages—Pascal, C, or PL/I are available.

If you are interested in C, buy a copy of Small-C from The Code Works. For $15.00 including source code you can't beat it. For more serious C programming the BD Software C compiler is outstanding. It is a subset of UNIX C, but a complete enough subset to allow major systems work to be done.

For Pascal enthusiasts, several options exist. Pascal M from Sorcim is a p-code compiler/interpreter, and as such is slower than a full compiler. It has many of the advantages of an interpreter at a substantial cost savings over the full compilers. Pascal/Z and Pascal MT are both full compilers. They offer high execution speed compared to an interpreter but at a considerable increase in cost. Both Pascal/Z by Ithaca Intersystems and Pascal MT by MT Microsystems are fairly complete packages. Pascal/Z includes compiler, assembler, linker, library, and symbolic debugger.

The Digital Research PL/I-80 package is also quite a complete programming package including relocating assembler, linker, etc. I do not have sufficient data to compare PL/I-80 and, for example, Pascal/Z as programming systems. It does seem that either would be suitable for major programming jobs.

Some software naturally "teams up" well together. The Microsoft BASIC compiler and interpreter were designed to be used

145

Relocation: All routines assembled at address 0000
         Addresses resolved when linkage occurs

address	data	code		
0000	211500	A::	LXI	H,MSG
0003	CD0000G		CALL	PNTST
0006	211B00		LXI	H,BUFF
0009	0620		MVI	B,20H
000B	7E	A1:	MOV	A,M
000C	CD0000G		CALL	CONOUT
000F	23		INX	H
0010	05		DCR	B
0011	C8		RZ	
0012	C30B00		JMP	A1
0015	48454C502024	MSG:	DB	'HELP $'
001B		BUFF:	DS	100H
011B				

and:

address	data	code		
0000	EB	PNTST::	XCHG	
0001	0E09		MVI	C,STRPNT
0003	CD0500		CALL	BDOS
0006	C9		RET	

Becomes, after relocation and linkage:

address	data	code		
0100	211501	A::	LXI	H,MSG
0103	CD0005		CALL	PNTST
0106	211B01		LXI	H,BUFF
0109	0620		MVI	B,20H
010B	7E	A1:	MOV	A,M
010C	CD06F0		CALL	CONOUT
010F	23		INX	H
0110	05		DCR	B
0111	C8		RZ	
0112	C30B01		JMP	A1
0115	48454C502024	MSG:	DB	'HELP $'
011B		BUFF:	DS	100H
021B				

and:

address	data	code		
0500	EB	PNTST::	XCHG	
0501	0E09		MVI	C,STRPNT
0503	CD0500		CALL	BDOS
0506	C9		RET	

Fig. 11-14. Example of relocation and linking.

146

together. Digital Research's MAC and SID were also designed to work with each other. BDS-C also works well with these two as it can produce a symbol table that is SID/ZSID-compatible.

The software in a system gives it "feel"—the way that it interacts with the user. A BASIC in ROM system (using the cas-

```
Symbolic debugger uses data in a symbol file to assign
        symbols to addresses that it encounters.

If in disassembling it finds:

            •
            •
            •
        LXI     H,0157
        MOV     A,M
        CALL    0527
        DCR     H
        JMP     0339
            •
            •
            •
```

And the symbol file holds:

ADJUST: 0237	BREAK: 0110	BOOT: 0520
C100: 0389	C200: DFC0	C300: A100
DELTAT: 0424	ERROR: F016	FINAL: CD00
KILL: 104B	LOOP: 0339	LOOP1: 0502
NOTCHAR:0224	OCTAL: 0CB2	R3: 0504
STATUS: 0157	VERSION:0527	WIDTH: 0047
YEAR: BC02		

The Debugger will display:

```
            •
            •
            •
        LXI     H,STATUS
        MOV     A,M
        CALL    VERSION
        DCR     H
        JMP     LOOP
            •
            •
            •
```

Fig. 11-15. Example of the use of a symbolic debugger.

147

sette version of Tarbell BASIC, for instance) will interact diffe-rently with the user than will a CP/M system running Pascal. A disk-based, flexible system is the ultimate goal because it makes writing and using programs so much easier.

One of the most important sources for programs are users' groups. The CP/M User's Group has over seventy volumes of public-domain software available. Each volume is one (full) 8-inch single-sided, single-density CP/M diskette and currently costs $8.00 including postage.

SIG/M from New Jersey has over twenty volumes of software available. There is also a group for BDS-C, as well as one for users of Pascal/Z—both providing users' support for the respective lan-guages. Some of the best software available to run under CP/M is obtainable practically free from these users' groups. The groups are sources also for software patches, device drivers, languages, editors, assemblers, disassemblers, and a host of games and other software.

Hardcopy

After developing programs on a computer that is equipped with only a CRT, the advantages of being able to produce hardcopy (printed data) become obvious. It is difficult to develop and debug a program using only a CRT output device. Many times in developing software you need to see the big picture. A CRT display can usually show you only a 24-line window into the program. You can't easily flip between pages and can't leave yourself marginal notes. The solution to this problem is of course some type of printer. The type that you need will depend on the type of work that you intend to do with the system.

The major decision you have to make is "Do I need a letter-quality printer?" If your major purpose is to produce programs listings for software development, then the answer is no. If, however, you plan on using the system for word processing (typing letters, preparing articles, etc.) then you probably do want a letter-quality printer.

Not long ago the design of the printer determined the quality of the type. Now, as printing technology is refined, the print quality of all types of printers is improving.

DOT MATRIX PRINTERS

Dot matrix impact printers make characters by printing dots in an array, much like a CRT display device. Common matrix sizes are 5 dots × 7 dots, 7 × 7, or 7 × 9. All of them work on the principle that the eye will blend adjacent dots into a continuous line. The

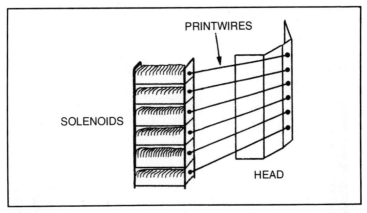

Fig. 12-1. A dot matrix printhead. The solenoid throws the printwires against the paper.

denser the matrix, the better this blending will work. Dot matrix printers print one vertical column at a time—in contrast to CRT displays which print one horizontal row at a time.

The dot matrix printhead (Fig. 12-1) consists of a set of solenoids, a set of print wires, and a guide block. A platen backs up the paper. As each column is printed the solenoids that correspond to the dots that are to be printed are switched on momentarily. When a solenoid is turned on the magnetic field it produces throws the associated printwire out of its rest position. The wire, guided by the guide blocks, hits the ribbon and forces it against the paper. When this combination hits, and is stopped by, the platen the dye on the ribbon is transferred to the paper and the dot is printed. The printwire then rebounds back to the rest position in the solenoid.

Dot matrix printers tend to be fast. Speeds of 40-60 lines per minute are common for inexpensive (under $1000) printers. These printers have a good, but not letter-quality, type face. They are especially useful for producing program listings because of their speed.

One printer of this type is the Integral Data Systems ID-440 (Fig. 12-2). A similar, but faster and more expensive printer is the Texas Instruments TI-820. This printer (Fig. 12-3) will print bidirectionally (both forward and backward) with logic seeking. *Logic seeking* means that the print head moves only as far as it has to, so that if a long column of numbers is being printed the head doesn't move all the way back to the left margin for each line (Fig. 12-4).

The print quality of a dot matrix printer can be improved in several ways. The first is to reprint the line several times, with each

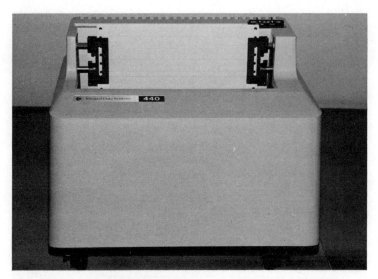

Fig. 12-2. The IDS-440 printer.

pass offset slightly from the others. This method, used in the Sanders Media 12/7 printer, can provide excellent print quality which rivals that of an office typewriter. This procedure (Fig. 12-5) fills in the gaps left between previous dots. Another way to improve the print quality is used in the IDS-460 printer. The printhead in this case contains offset wires (Fig. 12-6). This technique serves

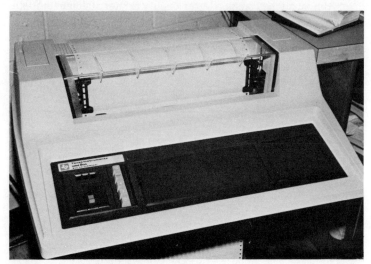

Fig. 12-3. The TI-820 printer.

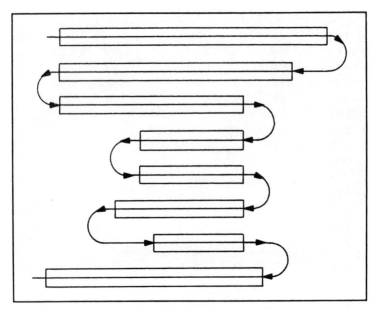

Fig. 12-4. Logic-seeking printing moves the head only as far as necessary.

the same purpose without the need for multiple reprinting of the same line.

GOLFBALL, DAISYWHEEL, AND THIMBLE PRINTERS

Almost all the common letter-quality printers fall into the category of impact printers working like conventional typewriters.

Golfball

The golfball-style printer is, more commonly, an office typewriter—the IBM Selectric. This type of printer is often built

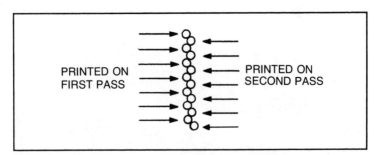

PRINTED ON FIRST PASS   PRINTED ON SECOND PASS

Fig. 12-5. Offset dots can be used to increase the quality of the printed characters.

152

with the same mechanics as the office typewriter but with a new bottom plate and a set of computer-driven solenoids. These solenoids act on a set of activator bails which cause the typeball to move to the selected character, print, and move the paper.

The typeball is a hollow plastic ball with the typeface characters raised from its surface (Fig. 12-7). These characters are arranged in several bands around the ball. In order to select a character the ball tilts and rotates to center the character over the print area (Fig. 12-8). The head then impacts the ribbon and paper, and the character is printed.

One advantage of this type of printer is the capability to change the typeball. The typeface can be changed in a matter of 30 seconds or so. The printer makes very high quality listings but is typically quite slow (15 CPS). The use of the Selectric mechanism means that service is available at many places that service office typewriters.

Daisywheel

The daisywheel printer also gets its name from its type element (Fig. 12-9). The wheel is shaped like a flower or starburst, with the typeface at the outside of the wheel.

The character to be printed is selected by rotation of the wheel. Since the index or rest position of the wheel can be sensed

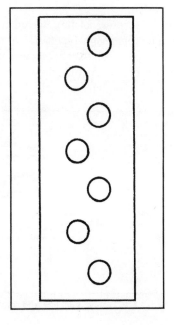

Fig. 12-6. Offset wires can be used to improve print quality.

Fig. 12-7. A typeball in an IBM typewriter-type printer.

by the printer, the electronics within it can easily determine how far to turn the wheel to print any character. When the wheel has stopped with the character in position a solenoid-fired hammer impacts against the back of the wheel and prints the character (Fig. 12-10).

Printers of this design can be quite fast (45CPS) and have interchangeable typefaces but tend to be expensive ($2000-$3000). A typical printer of this type is the Diablo 630 (Fig. 12-11). This printer is also available with a tractor-feed attachment to allow the use of continuous forms.

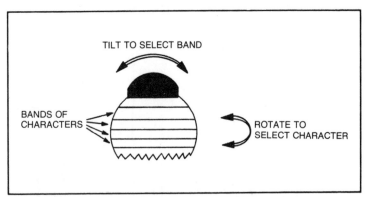

Fig. 12-8. The typeball tilts and rotates to select the right character.

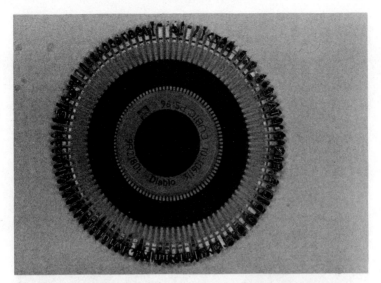

Fig. 12-9. A daisywheel type-element that spins to select the character.

Thimble

Thimble printers are very similar in design to the daisywheel but the typefaces are along the outside edges of a thimble-shaped element (Fig. 12-12). These printers, manufactured by NEC, have nearly the same features as the daisywheel units.

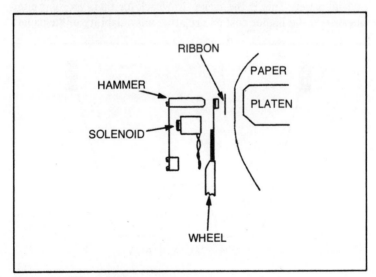

Fig. 12-10. The daisywheel mechanism.

Fig. 12-11. Diablo-630 daisywheel printer.

ELECTROSENSITIVE AND THERMAL PRINTERS

These printers are all based on different principles. One feature which they do have in common, however, is their need for special paper. This is the major drawback for this type of printer because of the higher cost and relative unavailability of the paper.

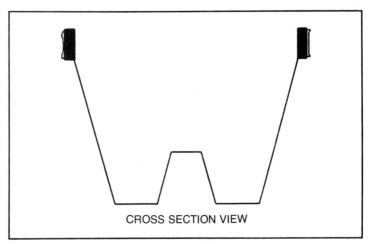

CROSS SECTION VIEW

Fig. 12-12. Thimble-type element cross-section.

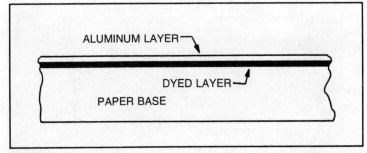

Fig. 12-13. Cross-section of electrosensitive paper.

Electrosensitive Printers

These printers are quiet and quite fast. They use paper (Fig. 12-13) that is composed of a paper base, black (or dark) coating and a thin layer of aluminum covering the dark coating. This means that the printed sheet is silver with black letters. It does photocopy well, but it would be a major inconvenience to have to copy each sheet. The sheets do not fade.

Printing on this paper is accomplished by using a spark to move aside (or eject) the aluminum layer and let the black show through. If the print elements are arranged across the width of the paper an entire line can be printed very rapidly (Fig. 12-14). The only moving parts on a printer of this type are the platen and the paper. Electrosensitive printers can also be built with a moving head, much as a dot matrix impact printer.

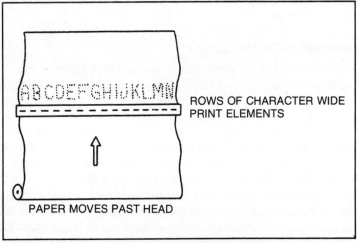

Fig. 12-14. Print elements across the paper allow a line to be printed at once.

Fig. 12-15. The Texas Instruments Silent 700 terminal uses a thermal printhead.

Thermal Printers

The thermal printer (e.g., the Texas Instruments Silent 700 terminal) has a printhead which is a matrix of special resistors (Fig. 12-15). When current is passed through a resistor it gets hot; the paper used with this type of printer is heat sensitive. Normally a light buff color, it darkens rapidly when heated. Printing with a thermal printer is quiet and can be quite fast; the paper does tend to darken with age.

PRINTERS AND PRINT QUALITY

High-quality (or letter-quality) printers have always tended to be impact printers: the golfball, daisywheel, and thimble versions described above are the types mainly used in small systems. Larger computer systems are able to use higher technology printers. An example is the ink-jet printer, which sprays droplets of ink at the paper. The reason that you don't end up with black blotches instead of letters is that the droplets are electrically charged and steered to the right place by electrostatic fields (Fig. 12-16).

As mentioned above, the print quality of the dot matrix printer has been increasing significantly. As the quality of multi-pass and staggered-wire technology improves there will be less demand for the typewriter-style printers. One reason for this is the typeface interchangeability problem. It is difficult to use a typewriter-style printer if it is necessary for you to change type elements often.

If, for example, you needed Greek letters in equations in the middle of a document and the normal printwheel did not include them you would have two alternatives: Stop every time you needed a Greek letter and change the type elements; or print the entire page, skipping the special characters, move the paper back to the top, and overprint the Greek letters after changing the type elements.

With a high-quality dot matrix printer the typefaces are all electronic (stored in a character-generator ROM). Any additional characters could be defined either in RAM or an additional ROM. When you needed a special character you would just use the alternate pattern. Multi-pass dot matrix impact printers also have the advantage of a fast single-pass mode. In this way only one printer is needed to produce both listings and letter-quality output.

PRINTER INTERFACING

Most printers are set up for either serial RS-232 or 8-bit parallel interface. The RS-232 serial printers can be used directly with any source of RS-232 serial data. These printers can often be connected directly to a modem and used as a remote printer.

The major reason for the popularity of serial printers is the simplicity of the interconnection. Parallel interconnection is an advantage for high speed printers because the byte-at-a-time format can be much faster than a serial format.

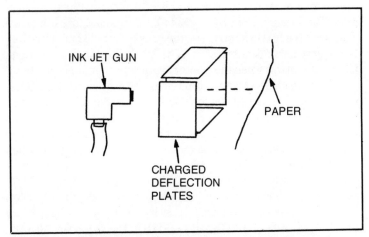

Fig. 12-16. An inkjet printer sprays ink at the paper.

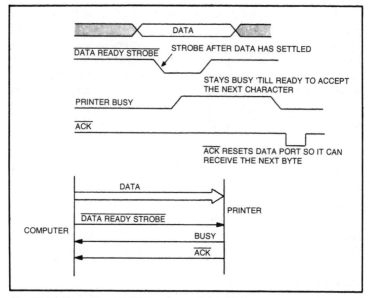

Fig. 12-17. Typical parallel timing for a printer interface.

Using either type of interface, the printer is still much slower than the computer system which runs it. This requires some form of communication from the printer to the computer so that the printer can signal its readiness to accept another character. This handshaking has to be handled differently for a serial interface than for a parallel interface.

With a serial interface several handshaking methods are common. The Integral Data Systems-440, for example, uses the Data Terminal Ready (DTR) signal on the standard RS-232 interface (pin 20) to coordinate data transfers. The DTR signal is dropped to its false state (mark) when the printer can accept no more characters.

The Heath H-14 serial printer has two handshake methods. One, similar to that used on the IDS-440, uses the RS-232 Request to Send (RTS) signal. When RTS is false the printer can accept no more data. The other method used in the H-14 requires that the printer send data along a serial channel back to the computer. When the line-buffer memory in the printer is full it sends as ASCII Control-S character ($\wedge$S,XOFF,DC3, or 13H). When the system sees a $\wedge$S it should stop sending characters. It should, however, continue to monitor the printer's serial input port, waiting for an ASCII Control-Q ($\wedge$Q,XON,DC1 or 11H). The $\wedge$Q means that the computer can continue to send data.

160

Handshaking with a parallel interface is different, but similar in concept. The parallel interface on the IDS-440 has three control lines (Fig. 12-17). One, the STROBE* line, is used to signal to the printer that there is valid data on the data input lines. This signal takes the place of the start bit, data, stop bit sequence used in a serial transmission. When the STROBE* signal is received the printer activates the second of the control lines, the BUSY line. This signals that the printer is busy processing the input character and cannot accept another character. When the printer has completed processing the character and is ready for another, the BUSY line becomes inactive and the ACKNOWLEDGE* line pulses. This pulse can serve as the strobe signal to reset the computer's parallel interface if desired.

Both the IDS-440 and the H-14 are line printers. This means that both "save up" characters in a print-buffer memory until they have a full line or see the ASCII CR character (carriage return). The H-14 can buffer up to 256 characters, as can the IDS-440. The Integral Data Systems printer can also have an expanded (2K) buffer if it is purchased with the graphics option. These printers can remain in the "not ready" state for a long period of time when the buffer fills up. Both are designed to manage the buffers for maximum throughput.

With disk-based computer systems, several programs are available to allow the system to be printing while you are doing something else. These programs take advantage of the fact that most of the time that you spend using an editor is spent with the computer idle, waiting for input. This idle time is used to send data to the printer.

Special Hardware

Any computer system can be enhanced by adding on special equipment to perform new tasks—or to perform old ones more efficiently. Some of this special equipment (to produce pictures or sound, for instance) will be treated in a later chapter. For now we will concentrate on relatively simple things that can produce a large increase in efficiency with only a small increase in complexity.

INTERRUPTS AND INTERRUPT HARDWARE

Most small computers are single-user systems, with only one person using the computer at any given time. When a system must service more than one person at a time or run more than one program at a time, the computer cannot afford to sit around and wait for a user to type something on a terminal.

In order to make the best use of the computer's time a change can be made in the way the system handles I/O devices. In many simple systems the console (or other I/O device) is polled. This means that, while waiting for you to type something, the computer reads the status register of the console input port. If the flag in the status register indicates that no character is ready, the computer rereads the status port and rechecks the flag, looping continuously until a character-ready indication occurs. At that point the port data register is read and the computer can process the data. An example routine and a flow chart are shown in Figs. 13-1 and 13-2. This is a simple and straightforward way to handle the console but it is inefficient if several ports or several programs are involved.

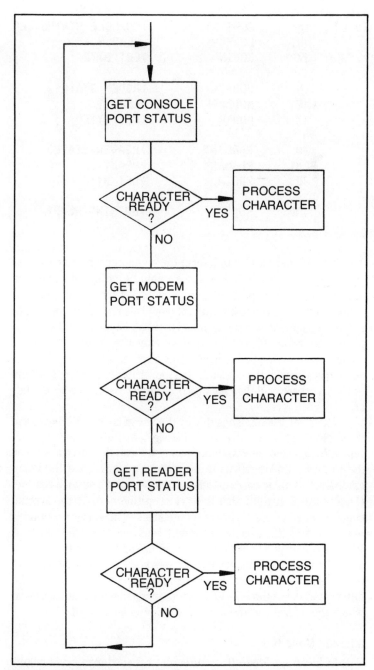

Fig. 13-1. Flow chart for polling routine.

```
POLL:    IN       CONSTAT        ;CONSOLE STATUS REG
         ANI      CONMASK        ;READY?
         JZ       CONIN          ;GET BYTE
;
         IN       MODSTAT        ;MODEM STATUS
         ANI      MODMASK        ;READY?
         JZ       MODIN          ;GET BYTE
;
         IN       RDRSTAT        ;READER STATUS
         ANI      RDRMASK        ;READY?
         JZ       RDRIN          ;GET BYTE
;
         JMP      POLL           ;NOTHING READY
```

Fig. 13-2. Polling routine.

If there were a way to inform the computer when a character has been typed (using hardware) it could be off doing something useful like printing a program listing instead of screaming around in a loop waiting for you to hit a key. It would also be nice to be able to tell the computer something important has happened (like the ac power has gone off) while it is busy executing a program. Most computers are equipped to handle interrupts in some form. What is needed is a way for the computer to stop whatever it is doing, attend to the interrupt, and then pick up the original process where it left off.

The Z-80 accomplishes this by the use of special hardware and three interrupt modes that are software selectible. When an interrupt is recognized several things happen. First, the current value of the Program Counter (PC) is saved on the stack. Next the PC is loaded with a value corresponding to the start of a service routine. Usually the first thing that a service routine does is to save the contents of all of the registers on the stack. The service routine is executed and the register contents restored from the stack. A RETURN instruction is executed, loading the PC from the stack. If all of the programming was correct this stack value is the value of the program counter that was saved at the time of the interrupt. The differences in the three Z-80 interrupt modes involve the manner in which the address of the service routine is addressed.

Interrupt Mode 0

In Interrupt Mode 0, an interrupt-acknowledge cycle begins when the processor recognizes an interrupt. During this cycle the

164

Mnemonic	Hex. code	Address
RST 0	C 7	0000 H
RST 1	C F	0008 H
RST 2	D 7	0010 H
RST 3	D F	0018 H
RST 4	E 7	0020 H
RST 5	E F	0028 H
RST 6	F 7	0030 H
RST 7	F F	0038 H

Fig. 13-3. Restart instructions and addresses (8080/Z-80).

interrupting device will place an instruction on the data bus which will be executed immediately by the CPU. Most commonly used is one of the RESTART instructions that serve as single-byte CALL instructions. There are eight restart instructions, RST 0 through RST 7. Each works in a similar manner. When a restart instruction is executed the current contents of the PC are pushed onto the stack and execution begins at an address that is dependent upon the restart instruction that was used. The actual address that the restart instruction points to is eight times the restart number. Figure 13-3 illustrates this, listing the restart instructions and their corresponding addresses. JUMPS to the actual service routines would usually be placed at the locations pointed at by the restart instructions.

Interrupt Mode 1

Interrupt Mode 1 fixes an address for use by the interrupt. When an interrupt is recognized with the processor in Mode 1 an automatic jump is made to location 0038H. This is a straightforward, minimum-overhead method for a single-interrupt system.

Interrupt Mode 2

Interrupt Mode 2 makes use of the Z-80 interrupt register. In this mode, upon recognition of an interrupt the processor allows the interrupting device to place an eight-bit vector on the Data In bus. This vector (the least significant bit must be a 0) forms the lower half of an address. The contents of the interrupt register form the high-order byte of the address. The address so assembled is within an interrupt-service-routine address table. The processor assembles the address as discussed above and fetches the byte at that address and also the next byte. The bytes form the actual address of the interrupt service routine (low-order byte first) and therefore are loaded into the program counter (Fig. 13-4).

The assembled vector points to an address which contains the address of the interrupt-service routine. This is clearly a powerful way to handle interrupts as each device can carry its own vector and, through manipulation of the I register and the contents of the service routine address table, point to many different service routines. Peripheral chips made specifically for the Z-80 have circuitry to deliver this vector byte automatically.

Maskable Interrupts

All of this discussion involves the response of the Z-80 to the Maskable Interrupt input (INT). The name implies that this interrupt input can be masked or disabled. The processor disables its maskable interrupt upon reset and it stays disabled until an Enable Interrupt (EI) instruction is executed. This allows the system to run through its initialization program without danger of being interrupted by devices that aren't programmed yet.

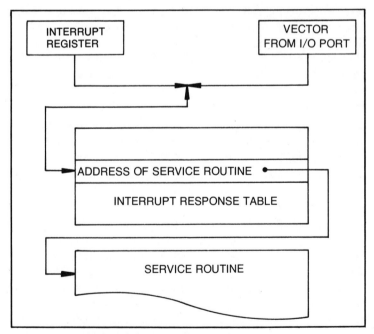

Fig. 13-4. Z-80 IM2 makes up a pointer to a table during the interrupt response; the table contains addresses for service routines.

When an interrupt occurs the processor either ignores it if interrupts are disabled, or services it if interrupts are enabled. When an interrupt is recognized, further interrupts are automatically disabled. This prevents the interrupting device from interrupting its own service routine if the request signal is held active until the port is serviced.

This also permits the system to do some things that should not be interrupted. If another interrupt occurred in the middle of a time-critical or data-critical routine it could cause unpredictable results or loss of data.

As an example, some I/O devices (card readers, cassette recorders, and some disk controllers) supply data at a constant rate. The computer must be available to handle this data when it becomes available or it will be lost. An interrupt that occurred in the middle of such a transfer would cause some of the data to be lost. For this reason a Disable Interrupt (DI) instruction is provided.

Nonmaskable Interrupts

Some occurrences are so important that the system must be made aware of them no matter what it is doing. A computer controlling industrial equipment *must* know when ac power to the computer is lost. A power supply can give the system enough warning to allow it to perform a "crash" routine before the power supplies drift out of regulation. For this use the Z-80 provides a Nonmaskable Interrupt (NMI). When the NMI input is activated the processor jumps to location 0066H.

Interrupt Hardware

In any mode the interrupt system, if it is to be used, needs a special consideration in hardware. A port that is to run with interrupts must, of course, be able to generate the interrupt signal. In Interrupt Mode 1, this is enough but the jump location of 0038H is inconvenient when running CP/M as this corresponds to the Restart 7 Jump location which is used by the debugger, DDT. You cannot use this for an interrupt service routine and still use DDT. Mode 1, with its single-interrupt capability, is not too useful in such a system anyway, as you generally need more than one interrupt.

In a CP/M system, RST 0 and RST 7 instructions are not too useful because the system uses the RST 7 location for DDT and the RST 0 location as the warm start entry to the operating system. This leaves six usable restart locations.

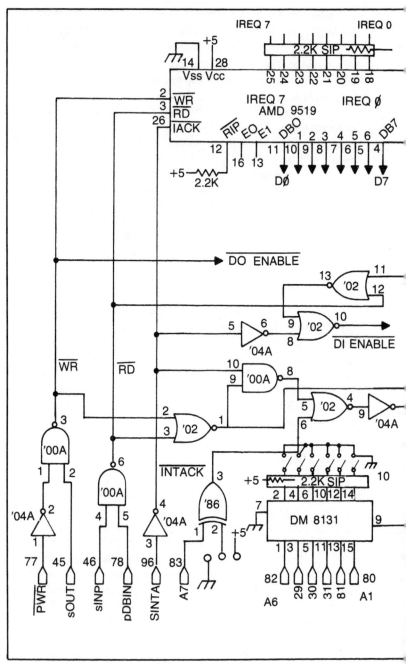

Fig. 13-5. S-100 interface for the 9519 interrupt controller.

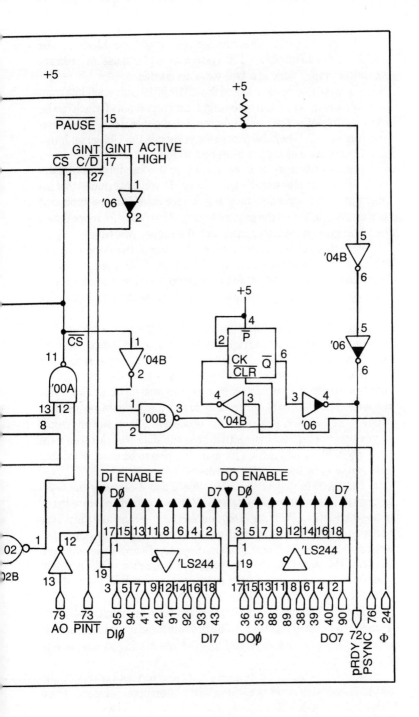

169

The most flexible interrupt system would use Mode 2. The easiest way to do this in a S-100 system would be to use an interrupt controller chip. There are two ways to do this.

The first would make use of the AMD 9519 Universal Interrupt Controller chip. This chip takes eight interrupt inputs (which can be arranged in several priority schemes) and generates a processor-interrupt signal. When the processor responds the Universal Interrupt Controller can supply from one to four bytes.

The priority system is an advantage if some interrupting devices are more important than others. If you determine that an interrupt from the console meaning "I have data" is more important than an interrupt from the printer saying "I am ready for more data", then you give the console interrupt the higher priority.

With this system, if two interrupts occur at the same time the higher-priority interrupt gets serviced first. Also, the system can be set up so that if you are in an interrupt-service routine only an interrupt of higher priority than the one that is being serviced can be accepted.

The 9519 allows for a programmable response table. The response to a Mode 2 interrupt is the one-byte vector, as was discussed above. For Mode 2 interrupts only single-byte responses are programmed. Single-byte responses would also be used to supply a Mode 0 interrupt with a restart instruction. The other response lengths (two, three, and four bytes) would be used in Mode 0. Remember, in Mode 0 the processor allows the interrupting device to place an instruction onto the data bus. A three-byte response table would allow a Jump instruction to be used, providing a direct jump to the service routine.

The hitch is that of the 8080, 8085, and Z-80, only the 8085 generates interrupt response signals for the second and third bytes of the instruction. With the 8080 and Z-80 the second and third byte accesses look just like normal memory read cycles. It is for this reason that the Godbout System Support Board generates the PHANTOM signal during the response sequence. This problem does not occur with single-byte responses, either RST instructions in Mode 0 or vectors in Mode 2.

The 9519 allows the use of more than one interrupt controller. Two 9519s chained together would provide for sixteen interrupts. It is fairly simple to design, with Fig. 13-5 illustrating an interface to the S-100 bus.

Intel (and others) made a very simple interrupt controller, the 8214. This device accepts eight priority interrupts, compares them to a processor-determined current status level, and, if the interrupt has high enough priority, generates a processor interrupt. When the interrupt is acknowledged the chip provides a three-bit priority level. The original data on this chip saw this as an ideal way to generate RST instructions by using the circuit shown in Fig. 13-6.

This 8214 chip can be used (with a slight modification) to provide the Z-80 Mode 2 vector as shown in Fig. 13-7. This method does require the response vector table to reside on a sixteen-byte boundary but this is hardly a problem in most systems.

The Intel 8259 is a "smarter" controller than the 8214 but suffers some from this factor. The 8259 will put out a CALL instruction as an interrupt response. The calling location is fully programmable but it *always* generates a CALL. This effectively eliminates its use in Mode 2. It is only usable in Z-80 Mode 0 or with an 8080 or 8085.

REAL TIME CLOCKS AND RTC HARDWARE

One device that every computer should have (but few do) is a real-time clock. This device—not to be confused with the system clock—tells real (or wall) time.

You might wonder why this would be useful. Imagine yourself in the middle of developing a program. You have piles of printout stacked around the computer. How will you tell for sure which printout is the current one when you resume work the next day? At

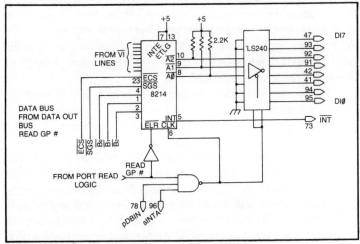

Fig. 13-6. Generating RST instructions with the 8214.

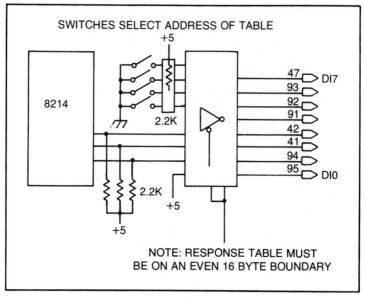

SWITCHES SELECT ADDRESS OF TABLE

NOTE: RESPONSE TABLE MUST
BE ON AN EVEN 16 BYTE BOUNDARY

Fig. 13-7. Generating Mode-2 vectors with the 8214.

best, you must read through it to find the changes. If you could print
the time, day, and date on a header at the top of each page you could
easily find the newest version of your program. It would be nice if
CP/M allowed you to date each file in the directory when it is
created or updated, but it doesn't—yet.

The real-time clock is a good place to use interrupts because
the time must be updated for each "tick" of the clock. There is no
good way to update the clock every second except with an interrupt.
Without one, each program would have to try to keep track of the
time by itself. This would require every application program to
check the clock at regular intervals.

An efficient way to handle clock data is to keep it in memory.
All any program needs to know is the address of the data and its
format. As far as application programs are concerned, the data
magically appears at the predefined spot.

There are several ways to produce a real-time clock. The
simplest is to generate a pulse every second using simple circuitry.
The circuit shown in Fig. 13-8 uses a National Semiconductor
MM5369 timebase chip, a 3.58 MHz colorburst crystal and a simple
TTL divide-by-60 circuit to provide 1 Hz pulses. These pulses can
be used to generate an interrupt. The interrupt service routine (Fig.
13-9) does all the work of updating the time. This circuit requires

172

that you set the correct time whenever the computer is fired up or reset. Software must be provided which prompts for and converts the time and date to BCD.

A more complex way would be to use the timebase circuit discussed above with counters to provide hours, minutes, and seconds in hardware (Fig. 13-10). These would need to be set on reset or power-up, and would reduce the software complexity somewhat at the expense of a large increase in hardware complexity. It would still be most practical to handle the date in software, updating it when the 24-hour point was reached. (Fig. 13-11)

One of the advanced counter/timer chips could be used (the AMD 9513 for example) to reduce hardware complexity, but this still wouldn't get you away from setting the clock every time the system is reset. There is, however, a way around this problem.

The development of the digital watch brought low-power (CMOS) clock circuits that could operate for quite a while on battery power alone. One of these devices has been modified and repackaged into a DIP package. This is the OKI MSM 5832 Microprocessor Real-Time Clock. It keeps track of year, month, date, day of week, hours, minutes, and seconds.

Normally operating from +5V, the 5832 will maintain timekeeping with supply voltages as low as 2.2V. At low voltages it draws very little power (90 microwatts at 3V), so it can operate for a long time. Most designs using this chip power it from the +5V TTL supply with a battery to supply backup power when the system power is shut off.

The MSM 5832 is read and programmed via a 4-bit address bus, a 4-bit bidirectional data bus, and several control lines. It can be used in many ways. The data sheet that describes this device illustrates its use with an 8255 peripheral controller chip. Figure

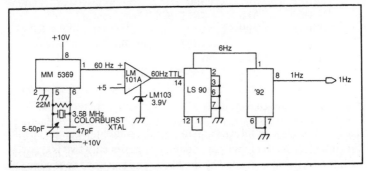

Fig. 13-8. A 1Hz pulse generator.

```
;
;          RTC SERVICE ROUTINE
;                    ASSUMES ALL REGISTERS ARE ALREADY SAVED
;                    BEFORE WE GET HERE
;
CLKINT: LDA     SECONDS ;GET SECONDS BYTE
        INR     A       ;ADD 1
        DAA             ;DECIMAL ADJUST
        STA     SECONDS ;SAVE IT
        CPI     60      ;IS IT > 60?
        RNZ             ;NO DON'T WORRY
        XRA     A       ;GET A ZERO
        STA     SECONDS ;SAVE IT
        LDA     MINUTES ;GET MINUTES BYTE
        INR     A       ;ADD 1
        DAA             ;ADJUST
        STA     MINUTES ;SAVE IT
        CPI     60      ;IS IT > 60?
        RNZ             ;NO
        XRA     A       ;YES-GET A ZERO
        STA     MINUTES ;SAVE IT
        LDA     HOURS   ;GET HOURS BYTE
        INR     A       ;ADD 1
        DAA             ;
        STA     HOURS   ;SAVE IT
        CPI     24      ;IS IT > 24 ?
        RNZ             ;NO
        XRA     A       ;GET A ZERO
        STA     HOURS   ;
        LHLD    DAY     ;GET DAY INTO HL
        INX     H       ;ADD 1
        SHLD    DAY     ;SAVE IT
        MOV     A,H     ;GET 100'S
        CPI     1       ;100?
        RNZ             ;NO
        MOV     A,L     ;GET REST
        CPI     6DH     ;
        RNZ             ;NOT > 16DH DAYS
        LXI     H,0     ;
        SHLD    DAY     ;HAPPY NEW YEAR
        RET             ;
```

Fig. 13-9. RTC service routine.

13-12 illustrates an interface using 8212 parallel port chips. While this interface has a higher part-count it requires only two I/O ports, rather than the four needed by the 8255. The software needed to set and read this interface is shown in Figs. 13-13 and 13-14. The

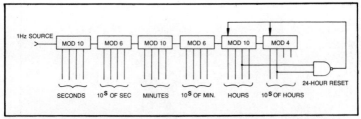

Fig. 13-10. Counters to generate hours, minutes, and seconds in hardware.

interrupt (one per second) is generated by leaving the clock chip selected to read with an address of OFH.

The CP/M Users Group has several programs and patches for existing programs which make use of the date and time when listings are printed. Pascal/M from Sorcim has time/day/date support built in, using a "Wall Time" function.

ADVANCED MATH PROCESSORS

One thing that the average 8-bit processor is not very good at is, surprisingly enough, mathematics. All microprocessors have built-in ADD and SUBTRACT instructions. Many have these instructions for both 8- and 16-bit data. Very few 8-bit microprocessors have DIVIDE or MULTIPLY instructions. These functions are found on most of the 16-bit processors, but even processors that have built-in MULTIPLY instructions handle only integer functions.

Multiplication and division in an 8-bit processor, and floating-point functions in any microprocessor, must be supplied from out-

```
;
;       FLIP DAY
;               DAY IS STORED AS 16 BIT BINARY NUMBER
;               STARTING AT 0 AND NOT ACCOUNTING FOR LEAP YEAR
;
FLIP:   LHLD    DAY     ;GET THE DAY
        INX     H       ;ADD 1
        SHLD    DAY     ;SAVE IT
        MOV     A,H     ;GET 100'S DIGIT
        CPI     1       ;100?
        RNZ             ;NOT 100H DAYS YET
        MOV     A,L     ;GET THE REST
        CPI     6DH     ;
        RNZ             ;NOT YET
        LXI     H,0     ;
        SHLD    DAY     ;MADE ANY RESOLUTIONS?
        RET             ;
```

Fig. 13-11. 24-hour day flip-in software.

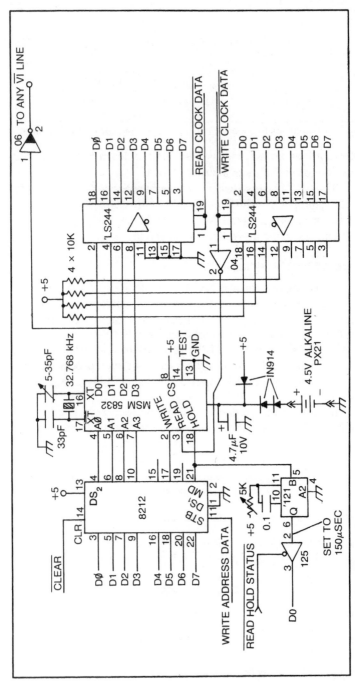

Fig. 13-12. 8212 interface to OKI clock chip.

```
;
;       SET TIME FOR OKI CLOCK CHIP
;               ASSUMES BCD TIME,DATE IN MEMORY BUFFER
;               BEFORE WE GET HERE
;
SETIT:  LXI     H,TIME          ;SET UP FOR TIME/DATE TABLE
        MVI     A,10000000B     ;SET TO HOLD
        OUT     CLKCTL          ;WRITE TO CLOCK CONTROL PORT
        PUSH    PSW             ;SAVE
SET1:   IN      CLKCTL          ;READ CTL PORT
        RRC                     ;GET HOLD BIT IN CY
        JC      SET1            ;NOT READY
        POP     PSW             ;
        MVI     A,0             ;WRITE TO S1
        OUT     CLKDAT          ;
        MVI     A,10000001B     ;WRITE TO S10
        OUT     CLKCTL          ;CLEARS S10
        OUT     CLKDAT          ;
        MVI     A,10000010B     ;
        OUT     CLKCTL          ;
        CALL    SMALL           ;
        MVI     A,10000011B     ;SET TO M10
        OUT     CLKCTL          ;
        CALL    BIG             ;
        MVI     A,10000100B     ;SET TO H1
        OUT     CLKCTL          ;
        CALL    SMALL           ;
        MVI     A,10000101B     ;SET TO H10
        OUT     CLKCTL          ;
        CALL    BIG             ;
        MVI     A,10000111B     ;SET TO D1
        OUT     CLKCTL          ;
        CALL    SMALL           ;
        MVI     A,10001000B     ;SET TO D10
        OUT     CLKCTL          ;
        CALL    BIG             ;
        MVI     A,10001001B     ;SET TO M1
        OUT     CLKCTL          ;
        CALL    SMALL           ;
        MVI     A,10001010B     ;SET TO M10
        OUT     CLKCTL          ;
        CALL    BIG             ;
        MVI     A,10001011B     ;SET TO Y1
        OUT     CLKCTL          ;
        CALL    SMALL           ;
        MVI     A,10001100B     ;SET TO Y10
        OUT     CLKCTL          ;
        CALL    BIG             ;
        MVI     A,10000110B     ;SET TO DAY OF WEEK
        OUT     CLKCTL          ;
        CALL    SMALL           ;
        RET
;
SMALL:  MOV     A,M             ;GET DATA BYTE
        ANI     0FH             ;MASK UPPER NYBBLE
        OUT     CLKDAT          ;WRITE IT
        RET                     ;
;
BIG:    MOV     A,M             ;GET MIN BYTE
```

```
        ANI     0F0H                ;MASK BOTTOM NYBBLE
        RAR                         ;ROTATE
        RAR                         ;  TO
        RAR                         ;   BOTTOM
        RAR                         ;    NYBBLE
        OUT     CLKDAT              ;WRITE IT
        INX     H                   ;BUMP POINTER
        RET                         ;
;
;       CLOCK BUFFER AREA
;
TIME:   DS      6                   ;MIN,HOUR,DAY,MON,YEAR,WEEK
```

Fig. 13-13. Set-time software for OKI clock chip.

side the microprocessor. The most common way to supply these functions is in software. The major drawback here is, of course, speed. It takes a long time to do the calculations necessary in a multiplication routine.

Integer functions involve the use of a fairly small range of numbers. An eight-bit integer can only hold numbers in the range of $+127$ to -128. A sixteen-bit integer can handle numbers between $+32,767$ and $-32,768$. Thirty-two bit integers (four bytes) can cover a range from $+2,147,483,647$ to $-2,147,483,648$. Even this range may be insufficient for some scientific calculations.

Floating-point functions make use of a modified form of scientific notation. Normal scientific notation expresses any number as a number in the range of -9.9999 to $+9.9999$ multiplied by a power of ten. (The number of places to the right of the decimal point is dependent upon the precision required, or available, in the measurement.) Figure 13-15 illustrates some numbers and their scientific notation (four places). A modification of this representation commonly used with computer programs makes the mantissa (the fractional part) between ±0.9999; the digit to the left of the decimal point is equal to 0. Just as the decimal point denotes the boundary between positive and negative powers of ten, a binary point denotes the place where the powers of two change sign (Fig. 13-16).

A 32-bit floating-point number involves a fractional mantissa and a power of two as a multiplier. One way to handle 32-bit floating-point numbers is shown in Fig. 13-17. The six-bit exponent allows powers to the range of ±64. This produces a range of decimal numbers of about $10^{\pm19}$ whereas the 32-bit integer has a range of about $10^{\pm9}$. This is still not stupendous in terms of some scientific calculations but is much better than the straight integer. While the floating-point number has a greater range than the integer it has less

```
;
;        READ TIME SOFTWARE FOR OKI CHIP
;
READ:   LXI     H,TIME          ;POINT AT TIME BUFFER
        MVI     A,10000000B     ;SET TO HOLD MODE
        OUT     CLKCTL          ;
R1:     IN      CLKCTL          ;READ STATUS
        RRC                     ;GET RDY BIT
        JC      R1              ;NOT READY
        MVI     A,11000000B     ;SET UP FOR SECONDS
        OUT     CLKCTL          ;
        CALL    LOW             ;
        MVI     A,11000001B     ;SET FOR S10
        OUT     CLKCTL          ;
        CALL    HIGH            ;
        MVI     A,11000010B     ;SET FOR M1
        OUT     CLKCTL          ;
        CALL    LOW             ;
        MVI     A,11000011B     ;SET FOR M10
        OUT     CLKCTL          ;
        CALL    HIGH            ;
        MVI     A,11000100B     ;SET FOR H1
        OUT     CLKCTL          ;
        CALL    LOW             ;
        MVI     A,11000101B     ;SET FOR H10
        OUT     CLKCTL          ;
        CALL    HIGH            ;
        MVI     A,11000111B     ;SET FOR D1
        OUT     CLKCTL          ;
        CALL    LOW             ;
        MVI     A,11001000B     ;SET FOR D10
        OUT     CLKCTL          ;
        CALL    HIGH            ;
        MVI     A,11001001B     ;SET FOR M1
        OUT     CLKCTL          ;
        CALL    LOW             ;
        MVI     A,11001010B     ;SET FOR M10
        OUT     CLKCTL          ;
        CALL    HIGH            ;
        MVI     A,11001011B     ;SET FOR Y1
        OUT     CLKCTL          ;
        CALL    LOW             ;
        MVI     A,11001100B     ;SET FOR Y10
        OUT     CLKCTL          ;
        CALL    HIGH            ;
```

179

```
        MVI     A,11000110B     ;SET FOR WEEK
        OUT     CLKCTL          ;
        CALL    LOW             ;
        RET                     ;
;
LOW:    IN      CLKDAT          ;READ THE DATA
        MOV     M,A             ;SAVE IT
        RET                     ;
;
HIGH:   IN      CLKDAT          ;READ THE DATA
        RAL                     ;ROTATE
        RAL                     ; IT
        RAL                     ;  LEFT
        RAL                     ;   4X
        ORA     M               ;OR IT WITH MEMORY
        MOV     M,A             ;SAVE IT
        INX     H               ;BUMP POINTER
        RET                     ;
;
;       TIME BUFFER
;
TIME:   DS      7               ;SEC,MIN,HOUR,DAY,
                                MON,YR,WEEK
```

Fig. 13-14. Read-time software for OKI clock chip.

precision. Integers must be used where maximum precision is a necessity.

The floating-point software necessary to handle numbers in this format is relatively involved, requiring that the mantissa be

Number	Representation in Scientific Notation
1.000	1.000×10
73.24	7.324×10^1
10,000.04	1.000×10^4
0.0004271	4.271×10^{-4}
602,300,000,000,000,000,000,000.0	6.023×10^{23}

Fig. 13-15. Examples of scientific notation.

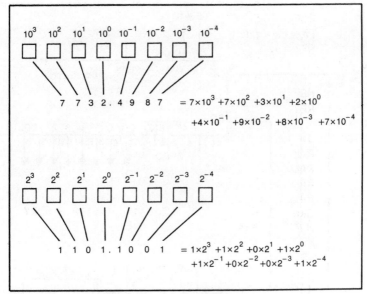

Fig. 13-16. A binary point is like a decimal point.

normalized and the exponent adjusted after every calculation. The multiplication of two floating-point numbers in software takes up quite a lot of time.

The AMD 9511 Arithmetic Processing Unit and the 9512 Floating-Point Processor are two devices designed to help solve this problem. The 9511 (second-sourced by Intel as the 8321) is a general-purpose mathematics-support device. It will perform add, subtract, multiply and divide operations on 16- and 32-bit integers, and on 32-bit floating-point numbers. (The 32-bit floating-point format shown in Fig. 13-17 is the one used in the 9511.) Using its

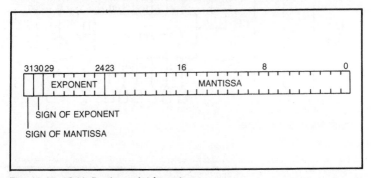

Fig. 13-17. 32-bit floating point format.

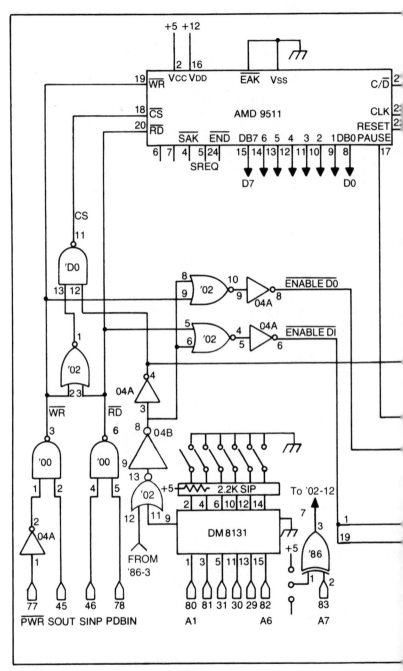

Fig. 13-18. S-100 interface for the 9511 math chip.

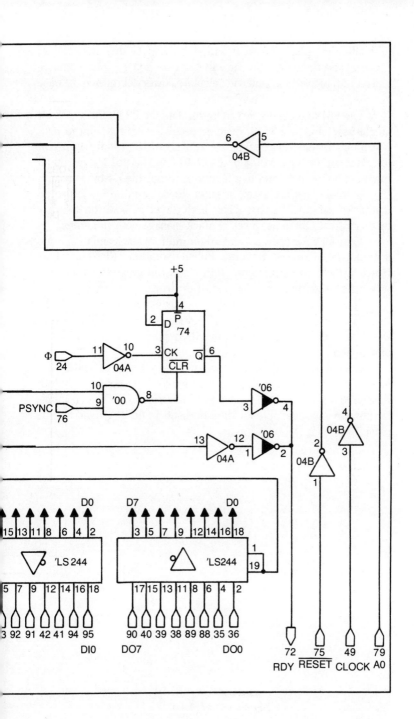

183

32-bit floating point format it will also compute the sine, cosine, tangent, and their inverses; it will compute square root, common and natural logarithms, and will calculate powers of ten and the base e.

The 9512 (second-sourced by Intel as the 8232) uses a 32-bit single-precision or a 64-bit double-precision floating-point format. The 32-bit format has a decimal range of about $10^{\pm38}$ while the 64-bit format has a decimal range of about $10^{\pm308}$! The 9512 gives up all fixed-point (integer) and trig functions to get the 64-bit format.

Both devices are stack-oriented processors optimized to do mathematical calculations. They both have, in addition to their mathematical functions, a set of stack management functions.

They load the operands onto their internal stack and then issue a command, like the Reverse Polish Notation (RPN) used by Hewlett-Packard calculators. Both chips can generate interrupts when their functions are finished, if desired.

These devices are relatively easy to design with (Fig. 13-18), their major drawback being price. They run well over $100 apiece at the time this is being written but their power and versatility is unmatched.

Inclusion of 9511 routines in a language to replace the software function calls will speed up programs by a large factor. Both Pascal/M and Pascal/MT+ have 9511 libraries available, and similar libraries are available for the Microsoft FORTRAN and BASIC compilers.

Graphics

Most computer display devices are text oriented, displaying only letters and numbers. However, the advent of small computers has made built-in graphics equipment increasingly common.

A computer game, for example, can be much more enjoyable if you have a graphic display to look at. Some data can only be useful handled with a picture. A line drawing presents data in a much more useful manner than a list of line endpoints or points. That is why blueprints are drawn rather than just listed as headings and distances from a common point (Fig. 14-1).

There are two major ways to draw pictures under computer control. The first is to draw lines directly. This method (vector graphics) works with devices that can draw continuous lines. The other important graphics method is raster graphics. In this case, a CRT display is used, and dots in the raster are turned on and off to produce a picture.

VECTOR (LINE DRAWING) GRAPHICS

The most basic vector-display device is an oscilloscope with x and y inputs. A voltage on the x input moves the spot along the x-axis and the y input has a similar function on the y-axis. The real trick with vector graphics is to convert the digital data into voltages.

Simple D/A Displays

The simplest way to generate the voltages necessary to drive a vector display is through the use of a digital-to-analog (DAC) con-

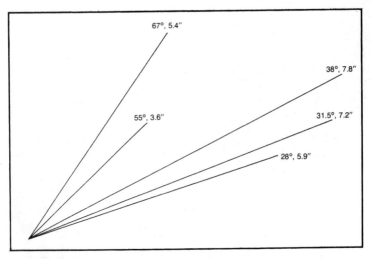

Fig. 14-1. Describing a figure by headings and distances makes it hard to visualize.

verter. These devices take a digital word and convert it to an analog voltage. More discussion of these converters will be found in the next chapter.

It would seem that all you need do to draw a line is to write the starting point to the converter and then write the endpoint. While this *will* draw a line you won't be able to see it. The beam would be driven so quickly between the two points that the line would not be visible. What is needed is some way to slow down the drawing of the line. A graphic interface designed by Steve Ciarcia and published in the November, 1976 issue of *BYTE Magazine* does this by the use of a vector generator consisting of a monostable multivibrator circuit that delivers a 100-microsecond "draw" pulse, some analog switches, and an operational amplifier circuit of the type shown in Fig. 14-2. Another way to provide the sweep would be to use an op-amp integrator circuit as shown in Fig. 14-3.

Any simple analog vector-graphics display needs to be "tuned" so that it draws proper lines, and this tuning will have to be repeated periodically. Most simple displays ignore some important details. In a normal oscilloscope-type display, the brightness of the plotted line is a function of how fast the beam moves. The faster that a line is drawn, the lighter the line will be. A display that takes the same amount of time to draw every vector and does not compensate for line brightness will have short lines which are much brighter than

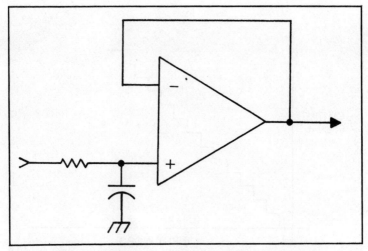

Fig. 14-2. The sweep generator circuit used in Ciarcia's BYTE article.

the long lines. This can be quite disconcerting in a complex displayed figure.

Complex Systems

Vector systems can be built which produce the vector motion in digital circuitry rather than analog. If you found the difference be-

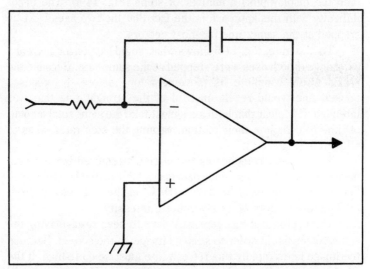

Fig. 14-3. An op-amp integrator can also be used as a sweep generator.

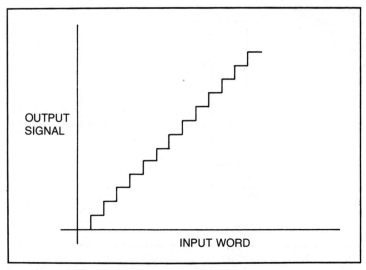

Fig. 14-4. A DAC counts through a number of steps.

tween the starting and ending coordinates in each axis you would know the number of digital-to-analog converter (DAC) steps that would be needed to draw the vector. Sending the initial coordinates to the x and y DACs would position the beam at the starting point. If you "counted up" to the final coordinates the DACs would produce (and the display plot) a number of steps (Fig. 14-4). The major difficulty with this approach is the fact that the two axes can't be stepped at the same time for most vectors.

To illustrate, Fig. 14-5 shows what would happen for an 8x and 3y change if both axes were stepped at the same rate. Because the y-axis would complete its movement long before the x-axis a hooked line would result, instead of the straight line that was intended. It is clear that both axes must take the same total amount of time to complete their motion, varying the step rates so as to allow this (Fig. 14-6).

This greatly complicates the circuitry required but can produce very nice displays. Since data is available on the length of each vector, it can be used to drive a DAC on the z (intensity) axis, keeping the vectors of nearly uniform intensity.

The vector systems generally have to keep re-displaying the same vector list in order to keep an image on the screen. Because the image fades rapidly this refresh rate must be quite high. If the whole screen isn't refreshed at a rate well over 30 Hz the flicker will be visible. The drawing speed of such a system is generally a

188

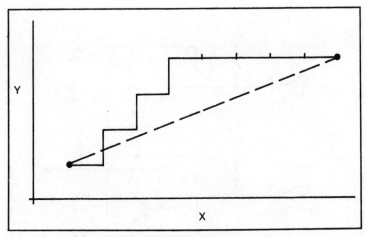

Fig. 14-5. A vector generator can't count uniformly on both axes because you won't always get straight lines. (An 8x, 3y measurement is shown.)

trade-off between flicker-free operation and speed of the DACs and display electronics.

One way to eliminate the refresh problem is to use a storage display. This type of display has a special electrode behind the screen that can be charged to maintain the image on the screen. The disadvantages to this type of display are a decrease in writing speed (because of the design of the tube) and a bloom effect which causes stored lines to be fatter than the original beam.

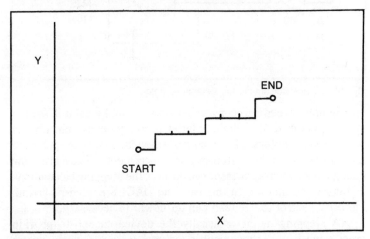

Fig. 14-6. Varying the rate between two axes allows you to draw "straight" lines. (An 8x, 3y measurement is shown.)

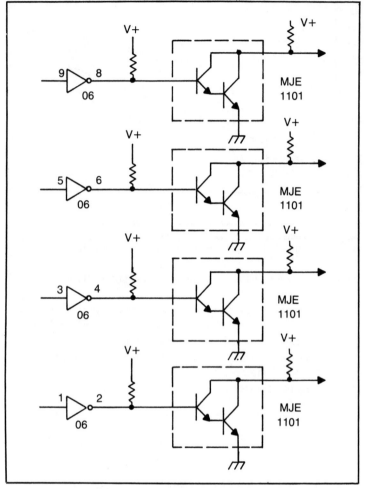

Fig. 14-7. Transistor drivers for a stepping motor.

Simple sweep and conversion circuits can be used if writing speed is not critical. A digital plotter is an x-y device, usually run with stepping motors. These motors, when their coils are pulsed in the correct order, will step in small increments. They are slow enough that a microprocessor can do all of the stepping calculations and drive the motors. In this case, no DACs are needed, and no intensity control (other than pen up/down) is necessary.

A stepping motor is usually the device chosen to provide precise mechanical movement in a digital system. A fairly simple circuit (Fig. 14-7) can be used to convert from the logic signals to the high power levels that are needed by the stepping motor. The sequence that is used to energize the coils to make the motor step is shown in Fig. 14-8, and it is easy to see how a microprocessor could generate it. In fact, to obtain maximum speed from a stepping motor it must be accelerated and decelerated—a clear use for the programming power of a dedicated microprocessor.

RASTER DEVICES

A raster-scan-output device, be it character-oriented video terminal or graphics interface, will use a television-like display. The terms "raster device" or "raster graphics" come from the name for the scan pattern used to draw on the screen of a television. The electron beam starts in the upper lefthand corner of the screen and sweeps horizontally to the right (Fig. 14-9A). The beam then rapidly returns to the left side of the screen, somewhat below the starting point (Fig. 14-9B). In this manner the whole screen is covered (Fig. 14-9C). When the beam reaches the bottom it quickly moves back to the top lefthand corner of the screen, where the whole display process repeats (Fig. 14-9D). The horizontal and vertical retrace occur with the beam turned off so no line is drawn during retrace. Standard video rates would have a horizontal sweep frequency of 15720Hz, and a vertical rate of 30Hz or 60Hz, depending upon whether interlace is used. Interlace "interweaves" two raster fields making a denser display. A "real" raster, obtained by turning up the brightness on a video monitor is shown in Fig. 14-10.

It is clear that with this system lines cannot be drawn with the freedom exercised in a vector system. All drawing on the screen is

		WINDING			
		1	2	3	4
STEP	1	1	0	1	0
	2	1	0	0	0
	3	1	0	0	1
	4	0	0	0	1
	5	0	1	0	1
	6	0	1	0	0
	7	0	1	1	0
	8	0	0	1	0
	1	1	0	1	0
	⋮		⋮		

Fig. 14-8. Stepping motors must be sequenced through a particular pattern.

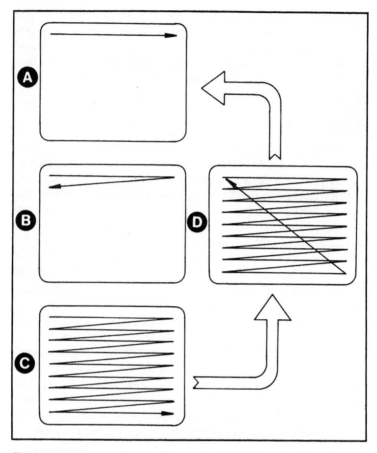

Fig. 14-9. A video raster starts at the upper left-hand corner (A) and sweeps horizontally. It then returns to the left side, one line down. (B). The beam sweeps over the screen in this manner until it gets to the bottom righthand corner (C). It then begins the vertical retrace (D) ending up at the upper lefthand corner. Normally, both the horizontal and vertical retrace sweeps are done with the beam blanked so no line is drawn.

done by turning the beam on or off at the proper time. A video monitor draws its letters (Fig. 14-11) by turning on and off dots on the screen.

If a video-interface board is built to display dots (rather than characters) then it is called a raster-scan-graphics device. The screen would be mapped into, for instance, a 256 × 256 dot array. Drawing is accomplished by turning on and off the dots in this array. 256 × 256 graphics requires 65336 dots, or 8K bytes or memory. In contrast, a video terminal 80 columns wide by 24 lines deep would require only about 2K of screen memory.

It is evident that this method requires a fair amount of memory. This has been, in fact, the major limitation to raster-graphics devices in the past. Now, however, as memory prices drop drastically, raster graphics is becoming the preferred method of video graphics. The electronics to control a fairly sophisticated vector display can cost well over $200.00, *not including* the microprocessor and memory needed to run it. In comparison, with 16K bytes of memory now available at around $20.00, the entire raster-graphics device can be built for the same amount of money.

The difficulty with raster graphics involves the software. In order to draw a line using a vector device only the endpoints need to be specified, whereas in a raster device each dot in the line must be turned on explicitly. This requires the graphics software to calculate which dots must be turned on, and then turn them on.

Raster-graphics devices allow the area of the drawing to be shaded. If a box is drawn it is relatively simple to turn on all of the dots within the box. With a vector display, area filling is very difficult. The best that can generally be done is a very fine crosshatch pattern. Raster patterns can also generate a gray scale. Most vector systems must use their intensity control capability to provide equal line intensities for various length vectors.

Fig. 14-10. A real raster showing the horizontal traces.

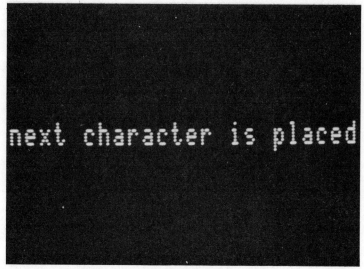

Fig. 14-11. A raster device displays its characters as dots.

A "single-plane" raster system that is 256 × 256 pixels requires 8K bytes of display memory and provides one bit of intensity data (Fig. 14-12). This single bit yields two possible intensities: full on (bright) and full off (dark).

If an additional 8K of memory is added and the pixel density maintained at 256 × 256, the result is a "two-plane" system. This system has two bits of intensity data per pixel, providing four intensity levels. This adds two intermediate intensity values. Now each pixel can be either full on, full off, one-third of the maximum intensity, or two-thirds of the intensity of the full-on state. The result is two intermediate shades of gray. Adding another 8K memory plane would provide three intensity bits per pixel and a total of eight available shades of gray, including black (full off) and white (full on).

COLOR GRAPHICS

All of the devices discussed so far are monochrome units (black and white). Vector displays are almost universally monochrome systems. There are color vector displays available but they are astronomical in cost and they will not be discussed here. If you could afford one, you wouldn't be thinking about building a microcomputer!

The vast majority of color graphics are, then, of the raster scan variety. Raster-scan color displays come in two styles. The first (and most common) takes composite video signals. These signals are a combination of horizontal and vertical sync pulses, video data, and color-burst signal.

Composite video is what a television set produces after the rf carrier is stripped off the received signal. Composite video requires that the horizontal and vertical sweep frequencies be identical to standard broadcast video rates. If the frequencies are much different from the standard then incorrect colors (or no colors) will be displayed.

Displays which require higher bandwidths (higher frequencies, higher density) generally use an "RGB" monitor. This type of monitor has separate inputs for directly driving the Red, Green and Blue (RGB) electron guns as well as a separate sync input. This separation facilitates the use of nonstandard frequencies and produces better results. RGB monitors are, however, more expensive than composite video (color television) monitors.

There are several ways to generate the color image. One is similar to a monochrome display; the others use new integrated graphics controller chips. The most popular (and the oldest) is the Motorola 6847 Video Display Generator. The Texas Instruments TMS 9918A Video Display Processor is newer and more capable. The most advanced graphics chip is the NEC μPD 7220/GDC Graphics Display Controller.

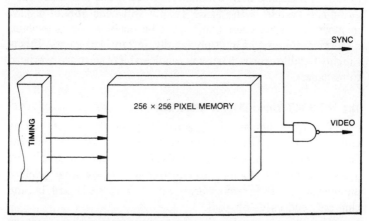

Fig. 14-12. A single-plane monochrome system has one intensity bit per pixel, so only two states (on and off) are possible.

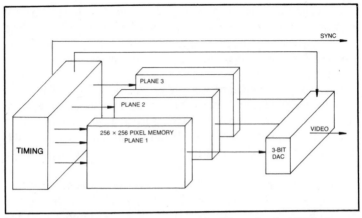

Fig. 14-13. Three planes of memory connected through a fast DAC give you eight brightness levels.

Combination of Monochrome Systems

The three-plane monochrome graphics system weights the three intensity bits differently, using a digital-to-analog converter (Fig. 14-13). If the DAC is removed each plane can be made to drive one color input of an RGB monitor. One plane would be green dots, one red, and one blue (Fig. 14-14). This is the simplest change that can be made to obtain color graphics. If more than two intensity levels are wanted for the color planes, more memory must be added. The only difficulty with this is that a single-plane RGB system will require 24K of memory for 256 × 256 resolution but a two-plane system of the same density will need 48K of display memory. Each 8K color plane must be doubled. As is evident, memory requirements multiply rapidly, in 24K increments. This is a highly flexible approach but will require a lot of software overhead to manage.

The MC 6847 Video Display Generator

The first common video graphics chip was the MC 6847. This chip, in a 40-pin DIP package, was designed for use with the 6800-series microprocessor. The 6847 is designed with thirteen address and eight data lines to interface with an external graphics memory array. The memory array can be up to 8K in size, but the chip only addresses 6K of it.

The chip has twelve display modes. One of these uses an internal character generator allowing 32 characters across by 16 lines down. An alphanumeric mode of the same density is available to use an external character generator. Two "semigraphics" modes are available, one using a four-element block (Fig. 14-15A) with 64 × 38 elements per screen, and the other (Fig. 14-15B) a six-element block with 64 × 48 elements per screen.

There are eight "full graphics" modes available with the 6847. These fall into two basic groups: The first maps one byte of display memory into four *pixels* (Fig. 14-16A) and is available in several densities. The other group maps one byte of display memory into eight pixels (Fig. 14-16B), and is also available in several densities. The colors of each pixel are dependent upon the data byte read from memory, while the mode in use is selected through a set of input pins.

The 6847 generates composite video (black and white) and some extra signals that are designed to be fed into an MC1371 rf-modulator chip to produce a color display. Updating the video-graphics memory is meant to be done directly when the 6847 is in a vertical retrace cycle to avoid breaking up the video image (Fig. 14-17).

The TMS 9918A Video Display Processor

The TMS 9918A Video Display Processor (VDP) was designed to do nearly everything necessary, by itself, to manage a graphics display. It was intended for use in home computers and arcade games, and it will display graphics on a home-color television.

The 9918A looks like an I/O port to the processor; this greatly simplifies the interface hardware. The VDP also manages the graphics-display memory (VRAM). It was designed to be tied di-

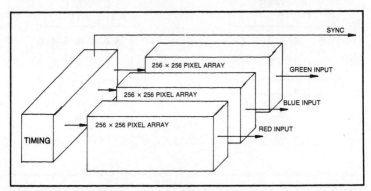

Fig. 14-14. A three plane system can also drive the red, green, and blue inputs to a color monitor, yielding eight colors.

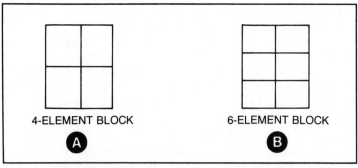

Fig. 14-15. The MC6847 color graphics chip, in its lowest resolution modes, can use 4-element (**A**) or 6-element (**B**) pads.

rectly to 4K or 16K dynamic RAM chips. All display memory activity is managed through the 9918A. When the processor wants to change the display memory it writes the address and data to be changed to the VDP and it, in turn, writes it to the display memory. This total control of the VRAM allows the video display processor to manage refresh, display, and read/write activity to eliminate screen tearing during microprocessor access.

There are four distinct display modes:

Text mode allows display of 24 lines of 40 characters. There is no built-in character generator, but up to 256 different character shapes can be defined, and any of the 96 character positions can use any of the characters so defined. Only two colors are available (but

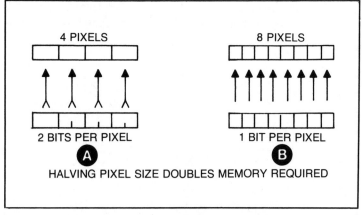

Fig. 14-16. The higher resolution modes of the 6847 can have two bits per pixel (four pixels per byte) and four possible colors (**A**), or a one bit per pixel (eight pixels per byte) resolution yielding two possible colors (**B**) per pixel.

any two of the sixteen possible colors); one defining the color of the characters, and one defining the background color.

Multicolor mode provides a 64 by 48 display of color blocks. All sixteen colors are available.

Graphics I Mode provides a display of 256 × 192 pixels, using any of the sixteen available colors. Graphics 1 allows the definition of 256 different patterns, any of which can be used in any of the 768 pattern positions on the screen. Each pattern may be any two colors of the sixteen.

Graphics II Mode also allows a 256 × 192 display but provides for 768 different patterns—one for each display position. Each line of the eight-by-eight pattern may use two of the sixteen colors.

The multicolor and graphics modes also allow for 32 sprites. A *sprite* is a movable, independent graphic image. In these modes the display can be thought of as a stack of 35 sheets or planes. The external video plane (the chip allows for input from another video source) is at the back, with the lowest priority. In order for an image on the external video plane to show through in any spot, all of the other 34 planes must be transparent ("transparent" is one of the sixteen colors) at that spot. Next is the backdrop plane, used for the background color and to provide a border. The next plane is the

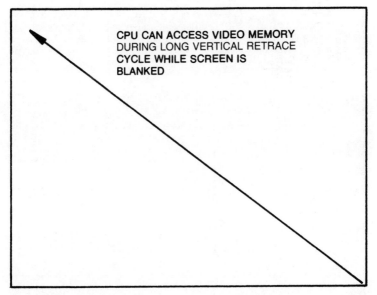

CPU CAN ACCESS VIDEO MEMORY DURING LONG VERTICAL RETRACE CYCLE WHILE SCREEN IS BLANKED

Fig. 14-17. The 6847s screen memory should be updated during retrace cycles so as not to disturb the screen.

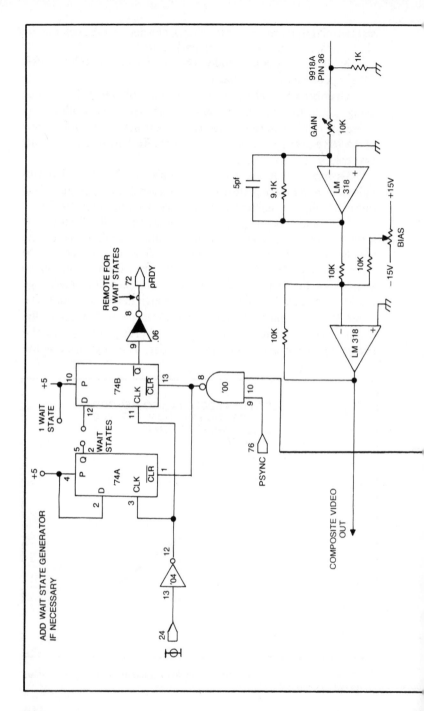

ADD WAIT STATE GENERATOR
IF NECESSARY

1 WAIT STATE

WAIT STATES

REMOTE FOR 0 WAIT STATES

pRDY

74B

74A

'00

'04

PSYNC

9918A PIN 36

GAIN

LM 318

BIAS

LM 318

COMPOSITE VIDEO OUT

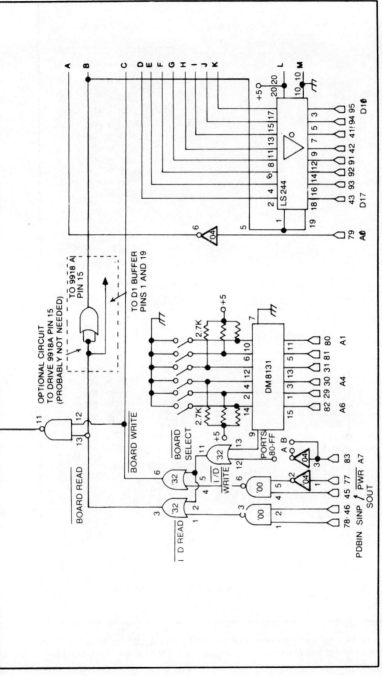

Fig. 14-18. The bus interface controller and video output for an S-100 color graphics board based on the Texas Instruments TMS-9918A.

201

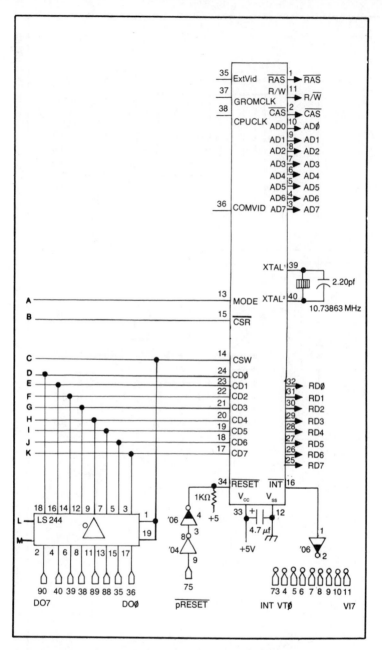

Fig. 14-18. The bus interface controller and video output for an S-100 color graphics board based on the Texas Instruments TMS-9918A. (Continued from page 201.)

pattern plane (or multicolor plane). The image defined on the multicolor or graphics modes is displayed on this plane. The text-mode image is also displayed on this plane, but in this case it is the outermost active plane. The remaining 32 planes are sprite planes. They are transparent except for the sprite on the plane. The sprites are normally patterns of 8 × 8 pixels but can be expanded to 16 × 16 or 32 × 32. Each sprite has its own entry in the "sprite attribute table". Each sprite specifies the name (one of the 32 possible sprites), the color, and the x-y coordinates of the sprite. The sprite can be moved to any pixel position by specifying its x-y coordinates.

In contrast to a "normal" graphics system, where much (or all) of the screen must be rewritten in order to change the position of an object, the sprite can be moved by changing only two bytes in the attribute table! Also, there are no address complications in determining the sprite position because it is specified directly as x and y coordinates.

Further, sprites have a priority arrangement, with the outermost sprite having the highest priority. When two sprites overlap, the one with higher priority is displayed, and the overlapping portions of the lower-priority sprite are blanked. If, however, the higher-priority sprite has areas which are defined as transparent the other sprite will show through! A flag is set in the status register when two sprites overlap. Only four sprites can be active simultaneously on a horizontal line. If this rule is violated the four highest-priority sprites on the line are displayed. This is apparently a result of running out of hardware within the VDP chip itself.

The TMS-9918A VDP is quite easy for a designer to use. A complete S-100 bus interface for a TMS-9918A VDP is shown in Figs. 14-18 and 14-19. The parts list is given in Fig. 14-20. The 9918A generates standard composite-video signals which can be fed directly into a video monitor or through an rf modulator to the antenna input of a color television set. The VDP has an onboard crystal oscillator needing an external 10.73868 MHz crystal and a tuning capacitor. This chip is probably the best available for small computers to be used with a home-color television.

The NEC uPD 7220/GDC Graphics Display Controller

The NEC uPD 7220/GDC (second-sourced by Intel) is the most powerful graphics-controller chip on the market. Like the TMS 9918A, it is intended to manage the video-display memory, with all microprocessor access to the display RAM done through the GDC. Unlike the 9918A, however, the GDC does not generate

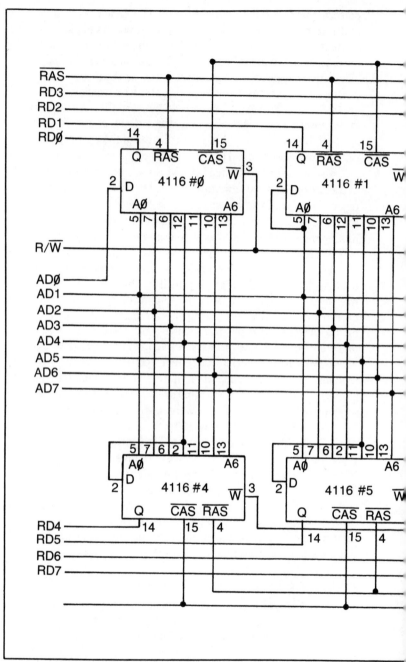

Fig. 14-19. The memory array for the TMS-9918A graphics board.

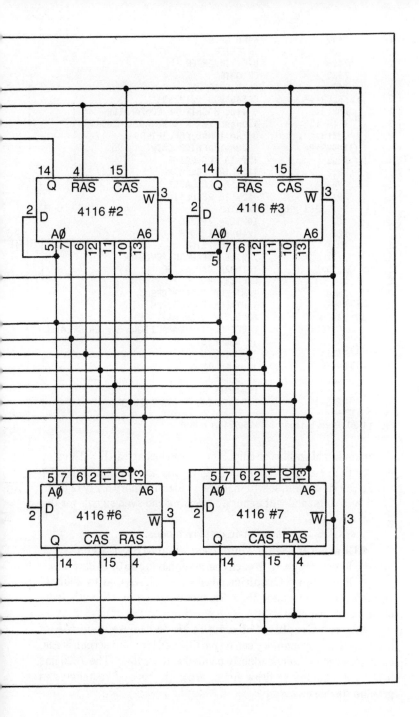

205

1	7400	NAND GATE
1	7404	INVERTER
1	7406	O.C. INVERTER
1	7432	OR GATE
1	7474	FLIP FLOP
2	74LS244	OCTAL BUS DRIVERS
1	DM8131	6-WIDE MAGNITUDE COMPARATOR
8	4116-15	150nsec 16K X 1 DYNAMIC MEMORY
2	LM318	OPERATIONAL AMPLIFIERS
1	TMS9918A	COLOR GRAPHICS CHIP
1	7805	+5V 1A REGULATOR
1	7812	+12V 1A REGULATOR
1	7905	-5V 1A REGULATOR
1	7912	-12V 1A REGULATOR
1	10.73863 MHz	CRYSTAL
2	10K	10 TURN TRIMPOTS
2	10K	1/4W RESISTORS
1	1K	1/4W RESISTOR
1	2.7K	7-WIDE SIP PACK RESISTOR
1	2-20pF	TRIMMER CAPACITOR
2	5pF	CAPACITORS
2	2mFd	TANTALUM CAPACITORS
2	10mFd	TANTALUM CAPACITORS
12	.1mFd	MONOLITHIC CAPACITORS
3	40-100mFd	ELECTROLYTIC CAPACITORS 30V OR GREATER
5	14pin	IC SOCKETS
9	16pin	IC SOCKETS
2	20pin	IC SOCKETS
1	40pin	IC SOCKET
1	----	HEATSINK
1	8802-1	PROTOTYPING BOARD (VECTOR)

Fig. 14-20. Parts list for the TMS-9918A board.

the video signal within the chip. Since it can manage a 1K × 1K color display the resultant video-dot frequencies are too high to handle within the chip itself. It will manage a video-memory array of up to 256K × 16 bits, and will generate blanking and sync signals for the display.

The GDC has three basic display modes:

●**Characters-Only Mode** can use up to 8K of 16-bit words for character storage, with each character having up to 13 data bits.

●**Bit-mapped Graphics Mode** can address up to 256K of 16-bit words, allowing a 2K × 2K monochrome or 1K × 1K four-plane color display.

●**Mixed Graphics/Character Mode** can use up to 64K of memory. Display memory can be partitioned into four screen areas; each area can be independently panned and scrolled. The 7220 has hardware included to draw lines, arcs, circles and rectangles in graphic memory.

206

A greater number of integrated circuits is needed to make an interface to the GDC than to the TMS 9918A, but this is because of the extreme power of the 7220. External circuitry must be added to generate the video signal because of the high frequencies involved. The minimum system requires sixteen 4164 64K × 1 dynamic memory chips! Only the rapidly decreasing cost of memory allows

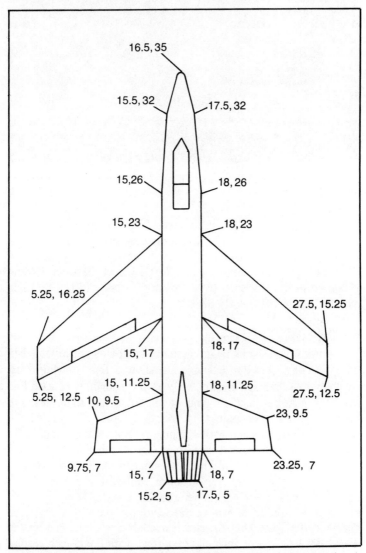

Fig. 14-21. An inefficient way to digitize a drawing is to assign endpoints by hand.

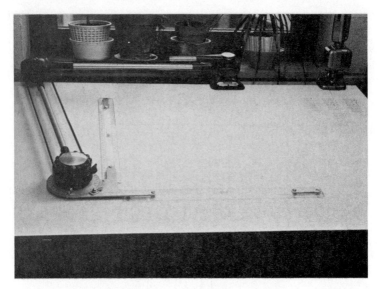

Fig. 14-22. A drafting machine can be fitted with encoders (or potentiometers) and serve as a digitizer.

this chip to be fully utilized because of its immense memory addressing capabilities. At the maximum rates, an 80 MHz-bandwidth video monitor is required.

At the present time the uPD 7220/GDC costs between $50 and $100, while the 256K × 16-bit memory array and the 80 MHz monitor would cost nearly $2000!

GRAPHICS INPUT DEVICES

A major bottleneck in any graphics system is getting the data into the computer. For example, to show a line drawing of an airplane on a graphics display, at least the endpoints of each line segment must be specified. One way (a crude one) to do this is to manually assign an endpoint (Fig. 14-21). Another way would be to outfit a drafting machine with equipment to allow the computer to read the position of a cursor (Fig. 14-22). Another more common way is to use a digitizer pad which can sense the position of a stylus.

Many of these digitizer pads are built with a PC board grid under the surface. A signal generated in the stylus is picked up by this grid and used to determine the position of the stylus. One such digitizer, the Talos Digi-Kit-izer is available as a kit and offers an eleven-inch by eleven-inch active surface with 0.005-inch resolution (Fig. 14-23).

Fig. 14-23. The Talos digitizer—a straightforward way to digitize a drawing.

All of the previous methods allow you to translate a drawing on paper into vectors which can be stored in memory. In order to draw directly on the display device (no paper original) several other types of equipment can be used. One common item is the joystick (Fig. 14-24). In Fig. 14-25 a bottom view illustrates the operation.

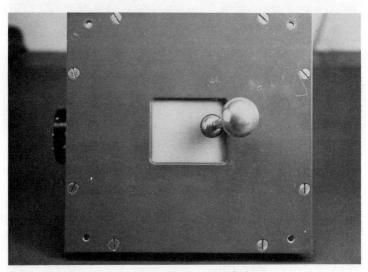

Fig. 14-24. Joysticks are popular graphics input devices.

As the stick is moved the two potentiometers are moved, resulting in a unique pair of resistance values for each stick position. These resistances can be translated into coordinates through the use of an analog-to-digital converter, which we will discuss in the next chapter.

If the computer converts the stick position into screen coordinates and draws a cursor at that position (Fig. 14-26), then all that is needed to draw figures is some way to specify the current input mode (draw, no draw, erase) which can conveniently be done with the keyboard. In a similar manner, all cursor movement can be done through the use of pushbuttons. The keypad on the Heathkit H-19 terminal (Fig. 14-27) can be used for this purpose when in the proper mode, or a system of keys can be built. (A pair of potentiometers could be used to move the cursor, but they would be very inconvenient to use.)

Many commercial graphics devices have light pens built in. A light pen is simply a stylus with photodiode or phototransistor in the tip. A switch is often mounted in the stylus to tell the computer when the user wants the pen to be active. In use, the light pen is pressed against the display screen and a signal is generated when the area of screen under the pen is lighted by the electron beam drawing the picture.

Fig. 14-25. The rear view of this joystick illustrates how it works. Moving the stick moves the potentiometer.

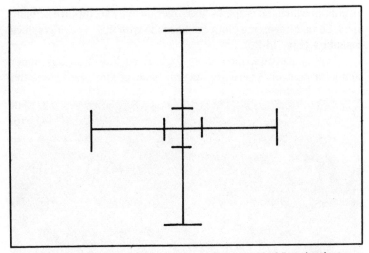

Fig. 14-26. A prominent graphics cursor makes control of line drawing on a display device easier.

The light pen can be used in two modes. The simpler mode is to use it as a replacement for the keyboard; when a menu of functions is displayed, instead of keying in your response you point to it with the light pen. The light-pen hardware reports the position of the pen to the computer and the computer determines which choice you made.

In a graphics display the pen can be used for drawing. Touching the pen to the screen, and activating it, tells the computer to find the pen position. When the pen is found (Fig. 14-28) its position can be followed and lines drawn on the display.

OTHER GRAPHICS DEVICES

Simple graphics can often be performed with equipment mainly devoted to other uses. The Heathkit H-19 terminal, for instance, has a graphics mode which uses a special extra character set. This character set consists of 33 graphics characters; and the reverse-video mode effectively doubles this. The H-19 graphics character set, in both normal and reverse video, is shown in Fig. 14-29. The H-19 pictured, by the way, has the Heath fabric anti-glare screen installed—a very good idea, at $20.00.

Many printers have a graphics mode; some have character sets, and some (like the Integral Data Systems Printers) have dot-graphics capability. In the case of the IDS-440 printer, graphics mode allows the computer to drive the print wires individually. The printer allows you to drive all seven wires but, because of the manner in which the graphics lines overlap, only six bits are actually used. Some interesting plots can be made with this type of graphics capability (Fig. 14-30).

Digital plotters, mentioned earlier, do line drawings under computer control. There are several types of plotters: One is the

Fig. 14-27. The H-19 terminal has a set of cursor control keys. This keypad can produce special (alternate mode) data if necessary.

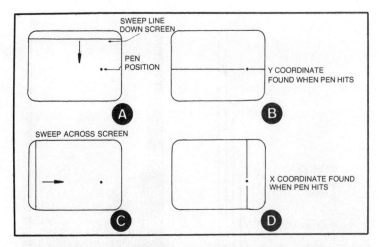

Fig. 14-28. Light pen operation: When the switch in the tip of the pen turns on (the pen has been pressed against the screen) a horizontal line (A) is swept down the screen. When the pen *hits* (produces a signal) the vertical position of the line is recorded. (B). A vertical line is swept across the screen (C). When the pen hits, the horizontal position of the line is recorded (D).

drum plotter; the plotter paper is wrapped around a drum and the pen carriage is moved along the length of the drum. The plotter shown in Fig. 14-31 is manufactured by Strobe Incorporated and offers good precision at a reasonable price. Another type is the

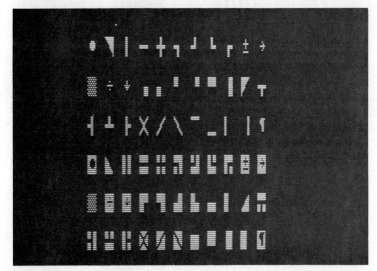

Fig. 14-29. The H-19 graphics character set is illustrated, both in normal and reverse video mode.

213

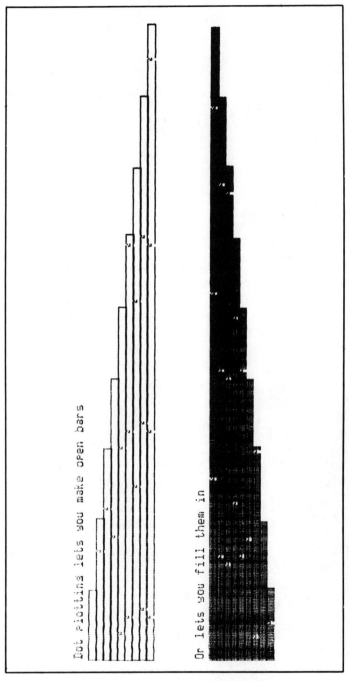

Fig. 14-30. Dot-plotting allows for some sophisticated graphics.

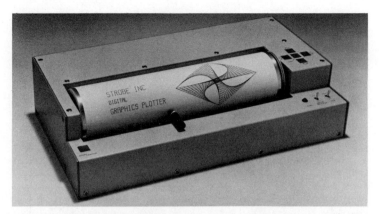

Fig. 14-31. The STROBE Model 100 is an example of a drum plotter. The paper wraps around the drum, and moves with it. The pen runs across the front of the drum. (Courtesy of STROBE, Inc.)

flat-bed plotter, as shown in Fig. 14-32 it takes a single sheet of paper and moves the pen assembly on two sets of guides.

The pen-motion assembly can be wire-driven (Fig. 14-33) or lead-screw driven (Fig. 14-34). Some plotters work like the drum

Fig. 14-32. The Houston Instruments DMP-2 is an example of a flat-bed plotter. The paper is held on the platen and the pen moves over it. (Courtesy of Instruments & Systems Division, Bausch & Lomb.)

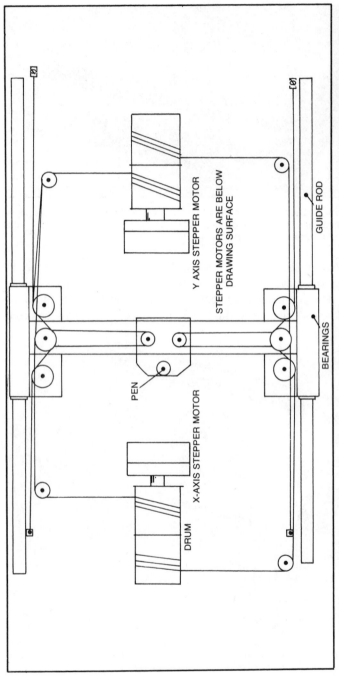

Fig. 14-33. Flat-bed plotters can be cable driven, where the pen carriage moves using a cable wrapped around a drum and driven by a stepping motor.

216

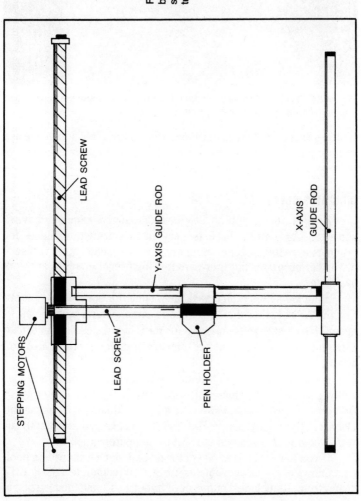

Fig. 14-34. Flat-bed plotters can also be lead-screw driven. The lead screw (a high-helix threaded rod) is turned directly by a stepping motor.

STEPPING MOTORS

LEAD SCREW

LEAD SCREW

Y-AXIS GUIDE ROD

PEN HOLDER

X-AXIS GUIDE ROD

217

Fig. 14-35. This Zeta Research plotter moves the paper under the pen through the use of a pair of sprocketed drums.

plotters except that the paper moves on rollers. This allows the use of nearly unlimited lengths of paper. One example of this type of plotter is made by Zeta Research (Fig. 14-35).

GRAPHICS SOFTWARE

Any of the graphics devices discussed require driving software. As a rule, there is very little software available for graphics in S-100 systems. Every hardware manufacturer will supply driver programs but there are few high-level graphics systems available.

Sublogic sells graphic packages, some for specific computers like the APPLE II or the TRS-80, and some general-purpose packages. Matrox also sells software for their boards, as do Cambridge Design Labs and Solon. Manufacturers of digital plotters also sell software.

If you are seriously interested in computer graphics and especially in writing graphics software, buy a copy of *Principles of Interactive Computer Graphics* (2nd ed.) by William M. Newman and Robert F. Sproull (McGraw-Hill, 1973). It is expensive ($30.00) but well worth it to a serious student of computer graphics.

If you have a plotter or vector display device there is a book containing tables of coordinates for a very complete set of 1377 characters. It includes numerous "typefaces" and many special symbols. This book (which was priced at $3.00 several years ago) is a National Bureau of Standards Publication: NBS SPECIAL PUBLICATION 424, *A Contribution to Computer Typesetting Techniques: Table of Coordinates for Hershey's Repertory of Occidental Type Fonts and Graphics Symbols*, by Norman M. Wolcott and Joseph Hilsonrath, April 1976. Order from Superintendent of Documents, U.S. Government Printing Office, Washington, D.C. 20402—SD Catalog No. C13.10:424. And yes, there *is* a Hershey's set of oriental symbols, too!

15 Contacting the Outside World

The computer's world is digital. Everything it senses is either *on* or *off*, a *one* or a *zero*. Some features of the surrounding world could easily be connected to the computer because they are basically digital. For instance, a security system for a house may need to know if the door is locked. It either *is* or it *isn't*—there is no in-between.

The signals presented by the sensor must be conditioned to levels that are compatible with the circuitry of the computer. Many other things you would like the computer to control are also digital in nature. For example, turning the garage lights on and off under computer control merely requires conversion of the low-power, low-voltage signal coming out of the computer to one that is suitable for the task. The computer serves as the "brain" of the system; and the interface to the outside world serves as the "muscle" to do the job.

Unfortunately, much of the world is not so simple. You need to know more than yes/no data—you need to know "how much". For instance, an electronic thermometer might output a voltage that is proportional to the temperature. Because this temperature changes smoothly, so does the voltage. This continuous change must be translated into a number that the computer can accept. In this case the voltage measured can never be converted *exactly* to a number. It is converted in jumps or steps.

To illustrate this, suppose you were to construct an electronic thermometer of the type discussed above. You could build a comparator for the output that would tell you (with a voltage level) whether the temperature was above or below a certain point (Fig. 15-1). This would give you one bit of information. Adding two more comparators (Fig. 15-2) would give you the ability to sense four states: greater than 75%, between 50% and 75%, between 25% and 50%, and below 25% of the maximum temperature. This would give you two bits of information. You can add bits in this manner until the error in the measurement (the space between points) is as small as necessary. It can never be *exact*, just within a certain percentage of the real value.

In contrast, you might want to have the computer put out an analog-like signal. In this case the digital word (the number) produced by the computer must be translated to a voltage.

If you want to communicate with another computer using the telephone, then your signals must be translated into sound at the transmitting end and from sound to digital at the other. All of these cases require the use of some type of digital-to-analog conversion circuit.

DIGITAL-TO-ANALOG CONVERTERS

As its name implies, this converter will change a digital word (a number in the computer) to an analog signal (a voltage or current). Some digital-to-analog converters (also written as D/A converters or DACs) convert to voltage and some to current. Commonly they are eight, ten, twelve, or sixteen bits wide. The more bits used, the more precise the output signal will be.

The simplest of these converters uses just resistors, weighting the bit inputs by the resistance used. Figure 15-3 illustrates

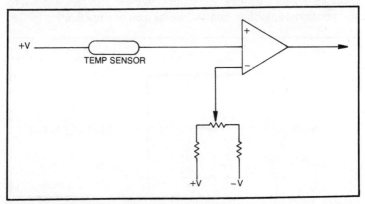

Fig. 15-1. A two-state temperature sensor.

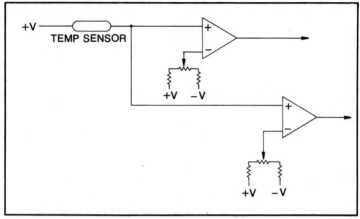

Fig. 15-2. A four-state temperature sensor.

such a converter used for three bits of TTL input. This is, however, a crude and generally unsatisfactory way to make a D/A converter.

Most applications of D/A converters make use of commercial converter chips. One of these is the Motorola MC1408. This is available as the 1408L6, a converter with six-bit accuracy, the 1408L7 with seven-bit accuracy, and the 1408L8 having eight-bit accuracy. One important factor that must be considered in choosing D/A converters is how long a time elapses between the points at which the digital word is input to the computer and the output settles. The 1408 family has a typical settling time of 300 ns.

The uses of D/A converters are many. Any time that you need to control a voltage with the computer you could use a D/A converter. One application suggested in the Motorola literature is a programmable gain amplifier. Here the converter provides a signal to an operational amplifier, controlling its gain or amplification factor.

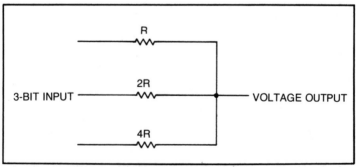

Fig. 15-3. A simple resistor DAC.

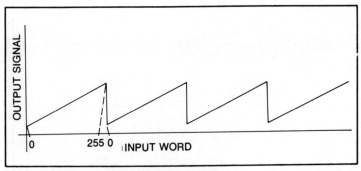

Fig. 15-4. Sawtooth wave produced by a DAC.

Another popular use for D/A converters is the generation of waves. Stepping through the possible codes in a linear fashion would produce a sawtooth wave (Fig. 15-4). If the input data is increased in a linear ramp from minimum to maximum and then immediately decreased in the same manner, a triangle wave is produced (Fig. 15-5). Ramping in a non-linear fashion can produce sinewaves (Fig. 15-6). Complex waveforms can also be generated by outputting data from a table in memory to the converter.

An eight-bit converter like the 1408L8 is one of the simplest devices to interface to the S-100 bus. The data coming into the port should be latched so the output does not change unpredictably during write cycles. This interface is illustrated in Fig. 15-7.

ANALOG-TO-DIGITAL CONVERTERS

The simplest analog-to-digital (A/D) converter is the Schmidt trigger gate. It has built-in threshold levels to determine when to

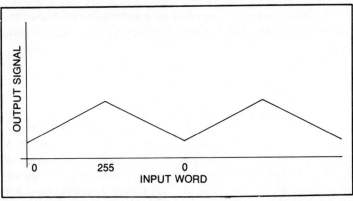

Fig. 15-5. Ramp produced by a DAC.

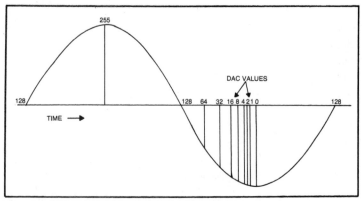

Fig. 15-6. Sinewave produced by a DAC.

change states. The low-to-high transition will not occur until the input signal voltage crosses the upper threshold voltage, and the high-to-low transition will not occur until its threshold voltage is crossed (Fig. 15-8).

At the heart of many A/D converters is a D/A converter. A design for a simple A/D converter is shown in Fig. 15-9. In this converter all the decision making is done by the microprocessor. The input analog signal and the signal generated by the D/A converter are fed to a comparator IC. The comparator changes state when the voltages on its input change sign relative to each other. That is, if it outputs a logic 0 when input A is larger than input B, then it will output a logic 1 when input A is smaller than input B. The computer sends digital words to the D/A converter until changing the least significant D/A bit changes the state of the comparator input. Obtaining the proper value can be approached in several ways. The easiest is to start with a word of zero and increment it until the correct point is found. This method will always work, but it is quite slow.

A faster way would be to execute a binary search. This involves sending a number halfway through the range to the converter and checking the polarity of the comparator signal. If this number was too small you would send a number that is three-quarters of the range and check again. If the original number was too large you would send the converter a number corresponding to one-quarter of the range and check again. You would continue this process of checking and halving the remaining range until the proper value was determined (Fig. 15-10). This method usually requires only a few tries to find the proper level.

224

To save a lot of work for the processor, converters with this binary search strategy implemented in hardware have been developed. It is possible to purchase a successive approximation register (the binary search strategy) and add a DAC to build your own converter, but it hardly seems worthwhile considering the many integrated circuits that are available.

As an example, Teledyne Semiconductor makes a set of similar A/D converters with varying precision. Their 8700, 8701 and 8702 converters are eight-, ten-, and twelve-bit devices, respectively. The 8703, 8704, and 8705 are also eight-, ten-, or twelve-bit converters respectively, but they have three-state outputs. These converters are quite simple to use, requiring only a reference voltage and several passive parts (resistors and capacitors).

There is an important factor in deciding which A/D converter to buy—the conversion time. These converters are slow, taking (for the ten-bit) at least 5 ms for each conversion. This means that only about two hundred conversions per second can be accomplished. While this rate would be more than satisfactory for converting joystick data, it is much too slow to use for the digitization of music because the maximum frequency that can be handled is 100Hz! These converters are described as being *charge-balancing* converters, a tip-off that this type may be relatively slow.

Another type is the dual-slope A/D converter. This is commonly used in digital voltmeters and integrates the input signal for a fixed time period and then integrates the reference signal (of opposite polarity) back down to zero. The amount of time it takes to reach zero is the output digital word. This type also tends to be slow.

An example of a much faster successive approximation converter is the Analog Devices 7572 eight-bit device. It has a conversion time of fifteen microseconds. This corresponds to a conversion frequency of about 60 kHz. The highest-frequency sinewave that you can sample with this is therefore about 30 kHz.

A/D converters have two difficulties which must be addressed. One is economic—converters cost from about $12.00 to well over $200. System costs can mount rapidly if there are many analog inputs to be digitized. This problem can, however, be surmounted through the use of an analog multiplexer. This device, illustrated in Fig. 15-11, serves as an electronic "rotary switch", for selecting one of several input signals. Use of a multiplexer allows one expensive A/D converter to handle inputs from several channels. This can significantly decrease the total cost of the conversion system. In

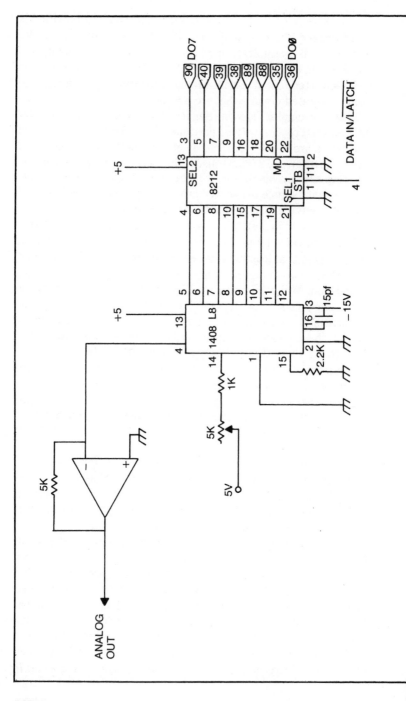

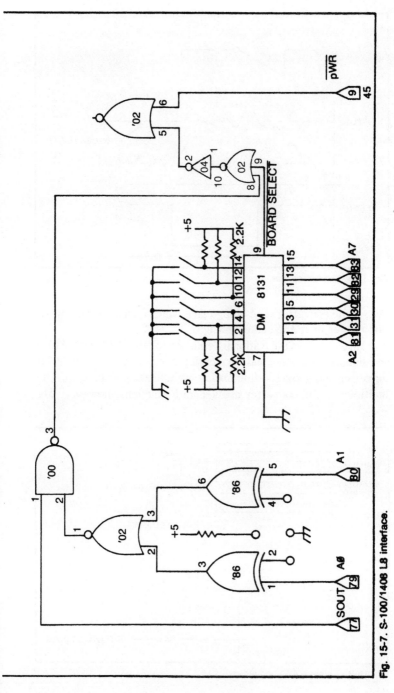

Fig. 15-7. S-100/1408 L8 interface.

227

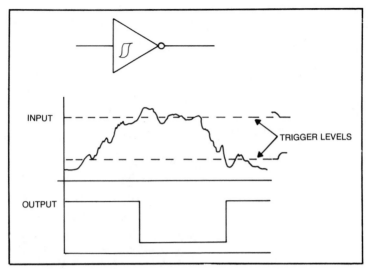

Fig. 15-8. Schmidt trigger.

fact, some converters are being made which include a multiplexer and converter in the same package.

An example is the National Semiconductor's ADC 0816. With a one hundred microsecond conversion time, this is an eight-bit converter and a sixteen-line analog multiplexer on one chip. The multiplexer and converter are separate functions, however. The

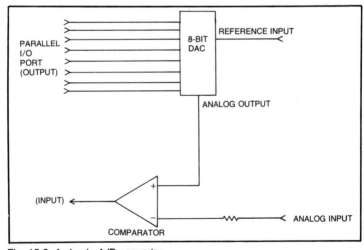

Fig. 15-9. A simple A/D converter.

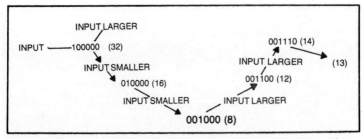

Fig. 15-10. Binary search as done by the successive approximation register.

multiplexer output and the comparator input can be, and commonly are, linked together.

The second problem that must be confronted with A/D converters is that of providing a constant input during conversions. A rapidly changing input signal can cause errors. For instance, if the input voltage to a successive approximation converter changes faster than the converter can cycle, errors will result (Fig. 15-12). In this case a sample-and-hold circuit is needed. This circuit, shown in Fig. 15-13, "remembers" the input voltage with a capacitor. The field-effect transistor serves as a switch. Normally it is open, allowing the signal to charge the capacitor. As the signal varies the capacitor charge will also vary. When the circuit is put into "hold" mode the switch is opened. The input to the operational amplifier comes from the charge stored on the capacitor. Since the input impedance of the op-amp is very high, little current is used. The sample-and-hold can hold its sampled signal for an amount of time which is dependent upon the leakage of the capacitor. Figure 15-14

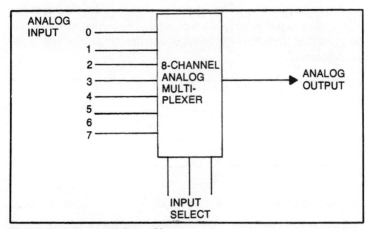

Fig. 15-11. Analog multiplexer chip.

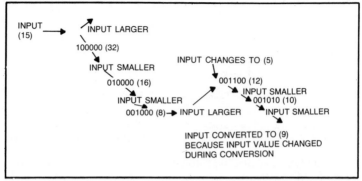

INPUT
(15)

INPUT LARGER

100000 (32)

INPUT SMALLER

010000 (16)

INPUT CHANGES TO (5)

001100 (12)

INPUT SMALLER

INPUT SMALLER

001010 (10)

001000 (8) → INPUT LARGER

INPUT SMALLER

INPUT CONVERTED TO (9)
BECAUSE INPUT VALUE CHANGED
DURING CONVERSION

Fig. 15-12. Changing input to a successive approximation converter can cause errors.

illustrates the output of a sample-and-hold circuit for a sinewave input as it is switched back and forth between sample and hold modes.

There are other ways to make these conversions but for normal use the monolithic converters are the easiest and most straightforward. Where the ultimate in performance is required, *hybrid* converters can be used. These consist of several different types of parts, on different chips, combined into one device. They are designed to exploit the best features of each different type of part included, but they are very expensive.

DIGITAL SWITCHES

In turning things on and off with the computer, the main problem encountered is that of power. The logic levels are generally too low in power to be used directly. The computer also has to be protected from the high voltages and line noise common to the outside world.

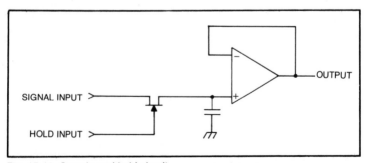

SIGNAL INPUT

HOLD INPUT

OUTPUT

Fig. 15-13. Sample-and-hold circuit.

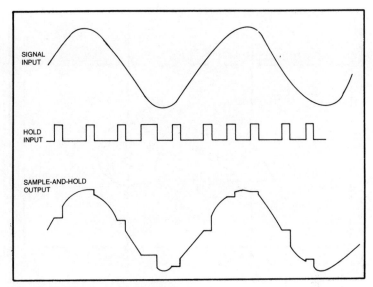

Fig. 15-14. Sample-and-hold output.

One way to accomplish this is with a 5V reed relay. The reed relay will take very little current to switch, and can be driven from a TTL gate. One difficulty with this type of relay is its low contact-current rating. If larger amounts of power are to be switched than the relay contacts can handle, then the relay must be cascaded with another relay of higher current rating (Fig. 15-15).

A good device for both controlling outside equipment and isolating the computer is the optical isolater. A simple optical

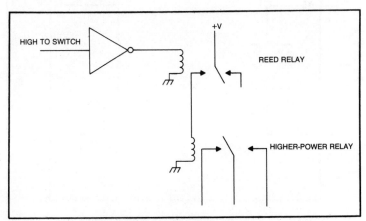

Fig. 15-15. Cascaded relays to handle higher power.

231

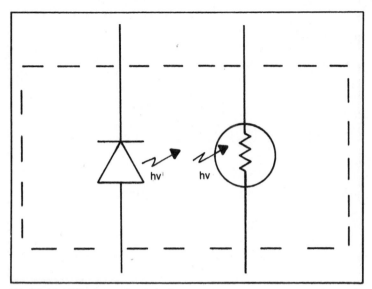

Fig. 15-16. LED/photocell opto-isolator.

isolater could use a Light-emitting diode (LED) and a photocell (Fig. 15-16). When the LED is turned on, the light from the LED striking the photocell changes its resistance and the comparator will switch. This is really not a very satisfactory method because

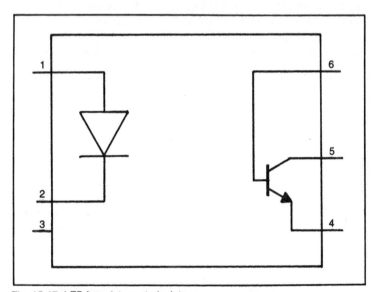

Fig. 15-17. LED/transistor opto-isolator.

the photocell requires a lot of external circuitry, is slow, and is not very sensitive.

An easier way would be to use an LED and a photo transistor. (A photo transistor is a "normal" transistor that can be controlled by shining light on it.) This is more satisfactory than using a photocell but still is not convenient. These devices have been combined into a six-pin DIP package so both the LED and the photo transistor are convenient to use (Fig. 15-17).

The photo transistor can also be used to drive another transistor if the current requirements are too high for the isolator transistor to handle (Fig. 15-18). The optical isolator will isolate the computer from a voltage differential of over one thousand volts because there is no electrical connection between the LED and the transistor. The connection is made by light.

Opto-isolators can also be obtained with photo SCRs (Fig. 15-19) and photo TRIACs (Fig. 15-20). SCRs and TRIACs are

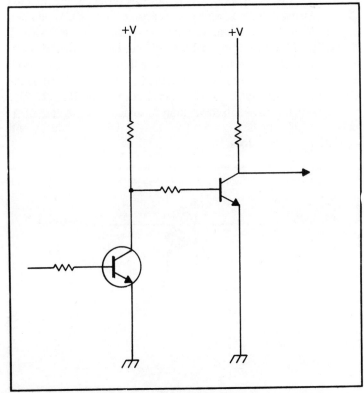

Fig. 15-18. Cascaded transistors for higher power.

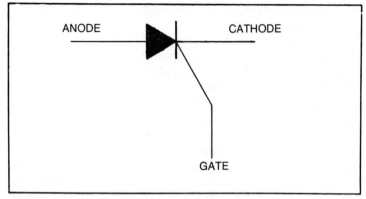

Fig. 15-19. Silicon-controlled rectifier (SCR).

special electronic switches. They have input and output terminals and a gate terminal. The SCR will not conduct at all until it is turned on with a signal at its gate. When the SCR turns on, it acts like a diode, passing current in only one direction. The TRIAC will pass current in either direction. The one drawback to these devices is that they will not turn off until the voltage through them drops to zero. With a dc voltage across them, once they turn on they stay on. With an ac voltage they stay on until the first time the signal passes through zero volts *after* the gate signal is removed (Fig. 15-21).

The SCR is useful in controlling dc signals or ac signals where only one polarity is needed. The TRIAC will pass dc or both polarities of an ac signal.

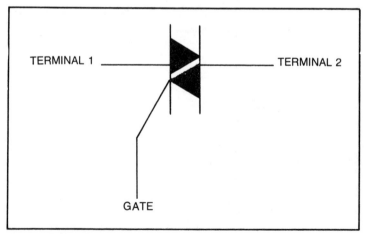

Fig. 15-20. TRIAC.

234

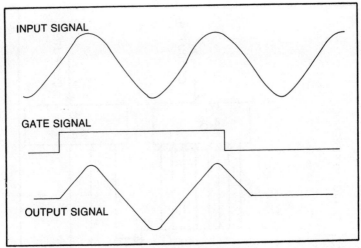

INPUT SIGNAL

GATE SIGNAL

OUTPUT SIGNAL

Fig. 15-21. SCRs or TRIACs shut off when load passes through zero volts.

MUSIC AND OTHER NOISE

"Computer music" involves three basic areas. One is the sampling of sound by the computer to allow study of the frequencies that it contains. This is an area of great interest in the field of speech analysis and synthesis. Sampling is useful if you need specific quantitative data about music (the frequency spectrum of an instrument, perhaps). Analysis of the sampled data is the second area. This tends to be numerical analysis. It doesn't make too much difference whether the data was sampled or generated in the computer. The third and most popular area is the generation of sound. This allows the computer to generate sound and music "to order". We have already discussed the basic building blocks that are necessary to sample and generate sounds—the A/D and D/A converters.

Sampling is usually done with a microphone, amplifier, and an analog-to-digital converter (Fig. 15-22). The microphone convert the sound to a voltage which is eventually converted to a digital word. During our discussion of these converters, the maximum frequency that a converter could sample was mentioned—it was always one-half the conversion frequency of the device. The reason for this relationship is one of the basic principles of signal analysis.

This principle, the Nyquist Theorem, states that the highest frequency that can be directly observed is one-half of the sample frequency. Further, any frequency higher than the Nyquist limit will reappear ("fold into") in the spectrum observed. Figure 15-23 illustrates this point.

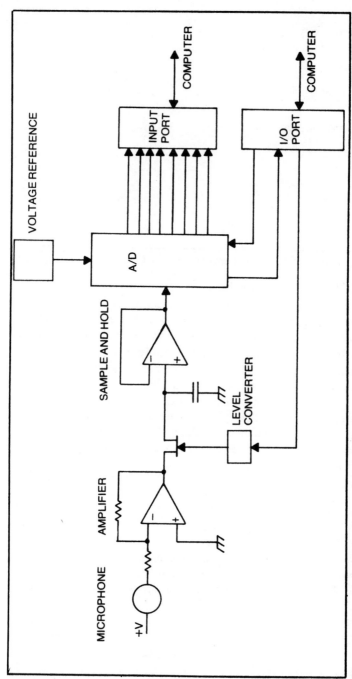

Fig. 15-22. Block diagram of microphone sampling system.

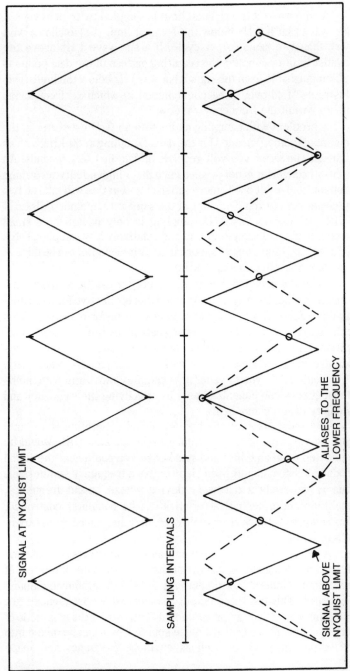

SIGNAL AT NYQUIST LIMIT

SAMPLING INTERVALS

ALIASES TO THE LOWER FREQUENCY

SIGNAL ABOVE NYQUIST LIMIT

Fig. 15-23. Foldover occurs with frequencies higher than the Nyquist limit.

A sine wave at the Nyquist limit is sampled twice per cycle. A sine wave that is J Hz below the Nyquist limit is also shown with more than two samples per cycle. If a sinewave J Hz above the Nyquist limit is sampled, the resulting pattern of the data points is indistinguishable from the signal that was J Hz below the limit. This illustrates "fold-over", the phenomenon in which *all* frequencies end up within the frequency window.

A problem with sampling audio with an A/D converter is the amount of memory needed for the data. Sampling at 60 kHz with an eight-bit converter you will get 64K of data in 1.024 seconds! An eight-bit converter is not precise enough for high fidelity recording; a ten- or twelve-bit one is more satisfactory but this will take up two bytes per conversion. Sampling at the same rate, memory fills up at 0.512 sec. Continuous A/D sampling is only useful for a small computer if small sampling time and relatively low sampling rates are used. A/D sampling of speech input, for example, can be done at low sampling rates (about 4 kHz).

Once the sampled data is in memory it can be analyzed in a number of different ways. One method that is effective for determining the frequencies in a signal is Fourier transform analysis. This technique is a method for converting data in the time domain (signal *vs* time) into data in the frequency domain (signal *vs* frequency). One can also generate time-domain data from frequency-domain data. This would allow you to generate a complex waveform with multiple frequency components simply by specifying the frequency and intensity of the components.

The most common method for sound generation is to build *wave tables* in memory for output to a DAC. This DAC would be connected to an amplifier and speaker so you could hear the sound produced. The computer can also control a frequency synthesizer. This is generally a hardware device whose output frequency, amplitude and other characteristics can be computer controlled. This requires some fairly complex circuitry and can be quite expensive to build.

A better way to generate music and sound effects is to use one of the chips designed especially for that purpose. One of the best of these is the General Instruments AY-3-8910 Programmable Sound Generator. This has three output channels whose frequencies are programmable. It allows programmed control over the amplitude of each channel. There is also a noise source which can be mixed into the output channels, as well as envelope frequency and shape control. The AY-3-8910 also includes two eight-bit bidirectional parallel ports which can be used for almost any application. The function of the channel frequency programming is obvious, as is that of the amplitude control. The programmable envelope allows an additional "template" to be superimposed over the channel frequency (Fig. 15-24). A table of musical notes is available for use with this chip. The clock frequency that is typically used is one-half the colorburst frequency, allowing the clock oscillator to be cheaply and easily made (Fig. 15-25).

Ackerman Digital Systems has an S-100 card available which uses two AY-3-8910s (Fig. 15-26). The data manual for this device includes a fairly complete S-100 interface.

The DAC used in the AY-3-8910 programmable sound generator chip is somewhat different from the DACs we discussed earlier. In a "normal" DAC linearity is a highly-prized feature. The voltage change produced by the converter should be the same no matter what the input data is (Fig. 15-27). Unfortunately, the human ear is not a linear device. DACs which more exactly match the sensitivity of the ear act in a logarithmic fashion (Fig. 15-28). The sensitivity increases as the output voltage approaches zero. This results in a response that matches the response of human hearing, allowing better sound quality from a converter of fairly low resolution.

The sound generated by these devices can be used for the production of music, the synthesis of speech, and as sound effects for games.

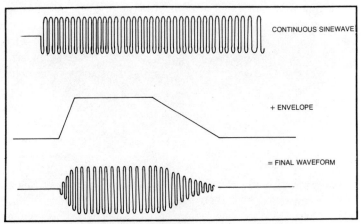

Fig. 15-24. An envelope-can be superimposed on the basic signal.

239

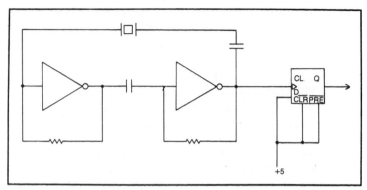

Fig. 15-25. A simple clock oscillator.

MODEMS AND INTERSYSTEM COMMUNICATIONS

The transfer of data between two computers can be quite a challenge. Passing diskettes around is a good way to make such a transfer if the computers involved are compatible. Incompatible media (one computer with 8-inch diskettes and one with 5¼-inch diskettes, for instance) or different equipment (a Z-80 and a 6502, perhaps) complicate things. In these cases, port-to-port transfer is an answer. The most compatible medium of communication between computers is a serial link. The serial format (start bit, data, stop bits) is nearly universal. Two computers would be connected as shown in Fig. 15-29.

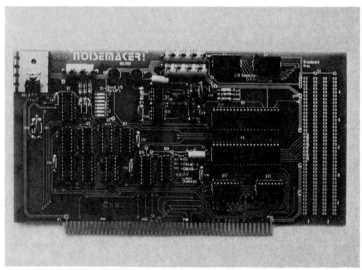

Fig. 15-26. S-100 noise card. (Courtesy of Aclcerman Digital Systems.)

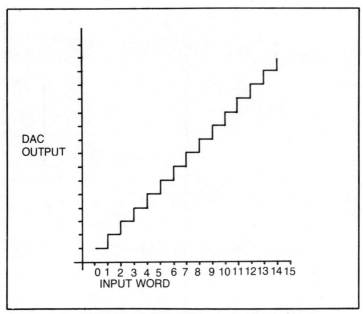

Fig. 15-27. Most D/A converters are built to supply a linear change.

It may, however, be impossible to physically link the computers together. If some distance separates them, the most practical means of communication uses the telephone. The problem then arises of how to arrange the communication. You can't just wire your RS-232 port into the phone line—it wouldn't work and "Ma Bell" wouldn't appreciate it. The phone system is designed for the transmission of low-frequency, voice-grade audio signals. Bandwidth (the range of frequencies which can be accepted) is limited to that necessary to transmit voice with reasonable quality.

The trick, then, is to translate digital data, in the form of RS-232 voltage levels, into some type of audio signal that is acceptable to the telephone system. Four standard frequencies have been defined. Four were necessary because both ends might be trying to transmit at the same time. Each end of the conversation has a pair of frequencies, one for mark and one for space. Each end of the conversation transmits its assigned frequencies and receives the others. The originate-mode end (the end that originated the call, usually) uses 1270 Hz and 1070 Hz for *mark* and *space*, respectively. The answer-mode end (normally the computer which answers the phone) transmits at 2225 Hz and 2025 Hz for *mark* and *space*, respectively.

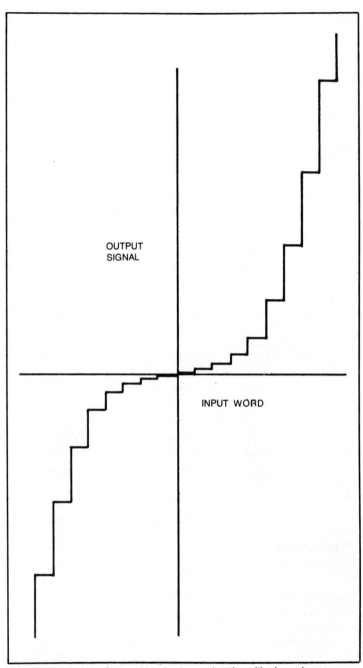

OUTPUT
SIGNAL

INPUT WORD

Fig. 15-28. Some DACs used for music supply a logarithmic scale.

242

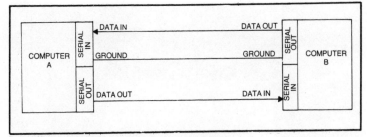

Fig. 15-29. A serial link between two computers.

The originate and answer terminology came from the way in which modems are normally used. You call up a timesharing computer. Your modem is set for *originate* mode. The computer that answers the phone is set up for *answer* mode. When two small computers communicate it doesn't really matter which mode the answering or calling computer is in as long as one is in answer and the other in originate mode.

Fig. 15-30. An acoustic coupling modem.

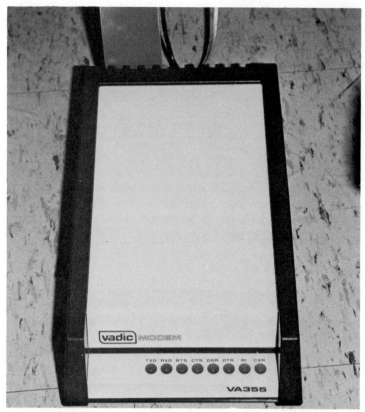

Fig. 15-31. A direct-connect modem.

The hardware used to translate between RS-232 data and the audio frequencies is a MODEM (MOdulator-DEModulator). Modems are available in several styles. Many of them are set up to be acoustically coupled (Fig. 15-30). They take a standard telephone handset, and the data is transferred acoustically, using a microphone and speaker. This is a convenient type of modem to have if you are not sure what type of telephone equipment is available, although acoustic coupling is not as efficient as direct connection to the phone system. The direct-connect modem (Fig. 15-31) eliminates the acoustic link. It requires a telephone jack for the modem.

Some modems are designed to connect to a Data Access box (DAA) which can be rented from the telephone company. Most of the new direct-connect modems contain an FCC-approved coupler to the phone line, so do not require the extra equipment. Many direct-connect modems have originate/answer/autoanswer mode.

They have the capability of automatically answering the telephone, allowing the use of your computer as a "dial-up" system that can be run remotely. There are also direct-connect modems available that plug into the S-100 bus and allow automatic dialing under computer control.

The other part of the intersystem communication story is software. There is software available in the CP/M Users Group libraries that is designed for just this purpose.

Construction

The advantages of building your own computer are many. To design, build, and debug a piece of additional equipment for it can also be most rewarding. You learn a lot about hardware (and software) in the design of a circuit. You are able to have equipment in your computer that you can't buy commercially anywhere. You can save a substantial amount of money by building instead of buying your equipment. You can often build onto one board the desired features of several commercial boards, leaving out capabilities that you don't want. Finally, it feels nice to successfully complete a project and be able to show it off as something you built yourself.

The only real disadvantage to building things at home is that you must be prepared to support them. You will have to repair the item if it doesn't work (after getting it working in the first place) and write support software for the equipment that you design yourself.

TOOLS AND EQUIPMENT

The first, and most important, thing to have is a good place to work. Any large flat table will do but it is best to have something that you don't have to worry about. If you use the kitchen table, cover it with newspapers to keep it from being damaged by hot solder and sharp tools. If possible, find a spot that you can use throughout the construction.

The area where you work should be well lighted. An overhead fluorescent lamp or a bright incandescent lamp can be used, but be

246

sure to diffuse the light. My work station has an incandescent bulb in a reflector, but pointed at the wall to reduce the glare (Fig. 16-1).

You will also need a good soldering iron. Most board manufacturers recommend a 25-watt iron. You will want a very fine tip on the iron because the solder joints that you will make are fairly small. A large tip will tend to cause solder bridges—places where a blob of solder shorts two pads together. You may sometimes need a larger iron if you try to solder heavy wires or very large PC board pads.

One way around having to buy more than one soldering iron is to get one with interchangeable heat elements. The Ungar irons, for instance, have replaceable cords, handles, heat cartridges, and tips (Fig. 16-2). You will also need fine ROSIN CORE (ONLY!!) solder. Use ONLY rosin core solder—acid core solder will corrode the thin copper pads on PC boards, leaving you with an unrepairable mess. Another handy item to have is a tip-cleaning sponge. This, (Fig. 16-3) is a sponge and holder used for cleaning the tip of your soldering iron. The damp sponge is very effective in removing old solder and used flux, and should be used constantly when you use the iron.

Other necessary tools include a set of small screwdrivers, a small pair of wire cutters, needlenose pliers, and a set of wire strippers (Fig. 16-4). One of the most useful tools that you can have is a pair of hemostats (Fig. 16-5). These tools, originally surgical instruments, have been enthusiastically adopted by modelmakers, electronic hobbyists, and others who need a lockable clamp. Their

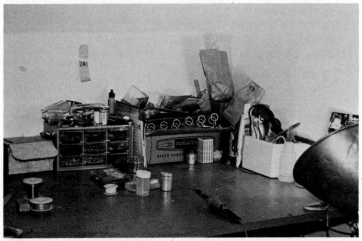

Fig. 16-1. A well-lighted work area is a must if you do much construction work.

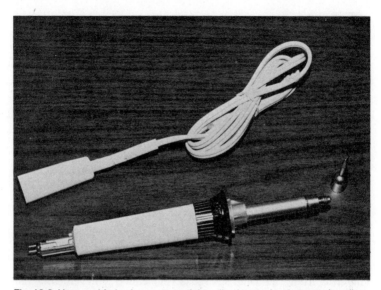

Fig. 16-2. Ungar soldering irons are modular, allowing cords, elements, handles, and tips to be changed.

real utility lies in their use as an extra hand, to hold and clamp things while you work on them.

The IC puller (Fig. 16-6) is a very useful tool for coercing an integrated circuit (IC) out of its socket. The alternatives, prying

Fig. 16-3. A soldering iron tip sponge can keep the iron clean. The sponge should be damp but not soaking wet.

248

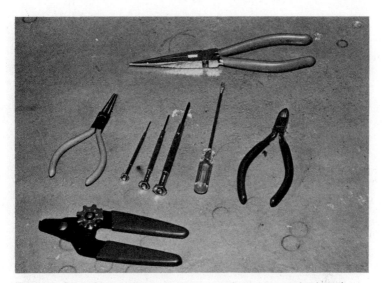

Fig. 16-4. Screwdrivers, pliers, wire cutters, and strippers are basic tools.

with a screwdriver or your fingers, invites bending pins or worse. Prying out an IC with your fingers often results in it popping out of the socket, sticking its pins into your finger, and leaving you with a row of little holes on 0.10-inch centers. You will sometimes need to cut insulation or peel up pads on printed circuit boards. For these uses a small modeling knife like the X-acto No. 1 is good. You do

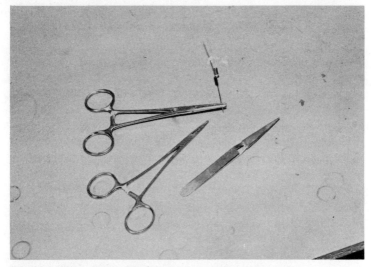

Fig. 16-5. Hemostats and fine forceps are indispensable tools.

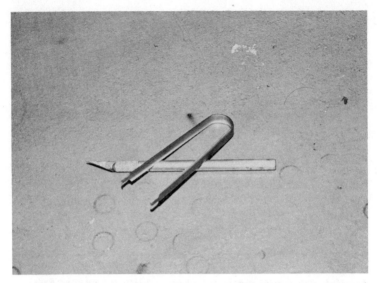

Fig. 16-6. IC pullers save ICs (and fingers!). An X-acto knife also comes in handy.

have to be careful not to overstress the blades because they *will* break. There are other tools that are needed for specialized uses. These we will discuss as we get to the areas where we use them.

BOARD-LEVEL CONSTRUCTION

Designing and building circuit boards for use in your computer does not generally require heavy tools, but there are some specialized tools required, depending upon the construction technique. There are several different ways in which to construct boards for your computer and the techniques for handling them differ, as discussed in the following sections.

Printed Circuit Board Assembly

Assembling a printed circuit board is one of the easiest ways to add capability to your computer. When you purchase a PC card for your computer, whether as a bareboard or as part of a kit, someone else has done all the design work on the circuitry and the layout work on the printed circuit. All that you need to do is buy the parts and solder them in the right places.

Whenever you build a PC board you should use sockets for each IC on the board. Socketing the integrated circuits makes it easy to remove an IC if it becomes defective. Some kits include

250

sockets for all the ICs, but some include sockets only for the expensive MOS chips so these can be more easily replaced, and some don't include any sockets at all. Since MOS devices are sensitive to static electricity care must be taken never to handle such devices unless you are "grounded". You should keep such chips in pads made from the black conductive foam (Fig. 16-7) or in aluminum foil. *Be sure to touch the board and the foam just before handling the chip to allow any static charge to dissipate.*

You should *ALWAYS* use sockets for MOS devices. Any IC is difficult to remove if it is soldered down, so there is no point in soldering down chips that you may subsequently damage and have to replace. Some manufacturers solder down TTL chips in their assembled products to save money. This is not too inconvenient as long as the boards are well tested.

Cheap sockets that corrode are worse than no sockets at all because they will make intermittent contact. The best sockets have gold-plated screw-machine pins (Fig. 16-8). These sockets are quite expensive, so most people use less costly ones. Some have wide spring contacts to grab the face of an IC pin (Fig. 16-9). These are available with either gold- or tin-plated contacts.

Most PC cards are at least solder plated to make soldering easier (Fig. 16-10). More often, with new boards, the traces will be covered by a plastic solder mask. This mask allows the solder to

Fig. 16-7. Black conductive foam protects MOS parts from damage by static electricity.

251

Fig. 16-8. Screw-machine sockets are very reliable but quite expensive.

stick only in the holes, where it is supposed to. Solder masking reduces the tendency to make solder bridges. Most solder-masking boards have also been silkscreened to identify the locations of the parts.

There are some parts that should *not* be put in sockets. Any-place on the board that uses a DIP switch (Fig. 16-11) shouldn't get a

Fig. 16-9. Spring-contact sockets are reliable and inexpensive.

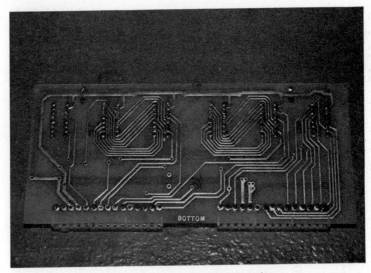

Fig. 16-10. A solder-plated board makes soldering easier.

socket. DIP switches do not seat well in sockets and should be soldered down. Transistors are also normally soldered straight to the board.

Commercial printed-circuit boards are the easiest way to add capabilities to your system. Your chances of the circuit working

Fig. 16-11. DIP switches should not be socketed.

right are much higher than with a board that you have designed and wired yourself. Most bareboards cost in the area of $30.00 to $80.00 apiece. You can make a substantial cost savings by finding sockets and parts wherever they are the cheapest.

Wire-Wrapping

One-of-a-kind or prototype boards are often wire-wrapped. Wire-wrapping is a technique making use of sharp cornered square posts and fine (#28-30) wire. The stripped wire is tightly wrapped around the post. The post cuts into the wire at the corners providing a secure, gas-tight seal. These wrapped connections make use of special long-tail (wire-wrap) sockets. These sockets are more expensive than the solder-tab sockets used with PC boards. Some cost reduction can be effected by getting wire-wrap sockets whose pins are tin-plated, with a gold inlay where the pin contacts the IC lead.

The greatest difficulty encountered in wire-wrapping a board is keeping track of where the wires go. Two things can aid you in this. One is to "call out" all of the pin numbers on the schematic diagram (Fig. 16-12). The other is to build a wiring list from the schematic (Fig. 16-13). This list should cover every connection that you will make. As each connection is made it is crossed off the list. If you wire without such a list, using only a schematic diagram, you should have a copy of the diagram so you can cross off each connection as it is made.

Power-supply connections should be wired first, before any of the signal lines are added. Also, different colors of wire should be used to show the difference between power, data, address, and control lines. I also use a separate color for repairs or modifications. Don't "daisy chain" power supplies using wire-wrap wire! The wire gauge is so small that it may have trouble delivering enough current to supply a lot of circuits (Fig. 16-14). There are two basic schemes for wire-wrapping a board. These are discussed next.

Normal Wrapping. The usual method of wire-wrapping uses standard wire-wrap sockets in a prototype board. A number of companies offer prototype boards for use on the S-100 bus. Vector Electronics makes a wide range of such boards. Three of their S-100 prototypes are especially suitable for wire-wrapping. The 8800V (Fig. 16-15) distributes power and ground over the board. The pattern that is used (Fig. 16-16) allows easy connection to the grid and to decoupling capacitors. This board also has space for four different voltage regulators, making it especially suitable for projects needing multiple voltages. The one disadvantage is that there

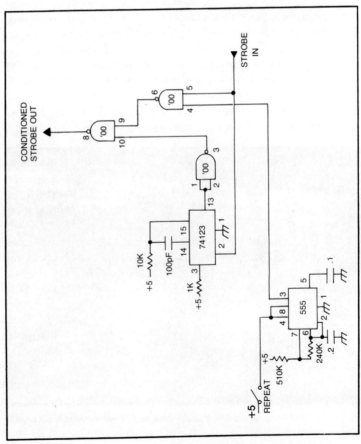

Fig. 16-12. A schematic diagram complete with pin numbers is easy to wire from.

```
STROBE IN   to 7400 pin 5 to 74123 pin 2

74123 pin 1 to GND
74123 pin 3 to 1K pull up
74123 pin 13 to 7400 pins 1,2
74123 pin 14 to 100pF timing capacitor (+)
74123 pin 15 to 100pF timing capacitor (-) and 10K pull up

555 pin 1 to GND
555 pin 2 to 555 pin 6 to .2 timing capacitor (+) to 240K resistor end A
555 pin 3 to 7400 pin 4
555 pin 4,8 to +5V through REPEAT switch
555 pin 5 to .1 capacitor (+)
555 pin 7 to 240K resistor end B to 510K pull up
--------- .2 and .1 capacitors (-) end to GND --------

7400 pin 3 to 7400 pin 10
7400 pin 6 to 7400 pin 9
7400 pin 8 to CONDITIONED STROBE OUT
```

Fig. 16-13. A wiring list makes wire wrapping easier.

is no convenient place for connections along the top of the board. The Vector 8804 is very similar to the 8800V except that the power distribution buses run horizontally. There is room for only two voltage regulators but there are provisions for connectors along the top. The Vector 8801-1 board (Fig. 16-17) has no foil pattern at all. A set of goldplated contact figures is provided for connection to the bus, and two holes are provided to bolt down voltage regulators. Other than this, the board is uncommitted.

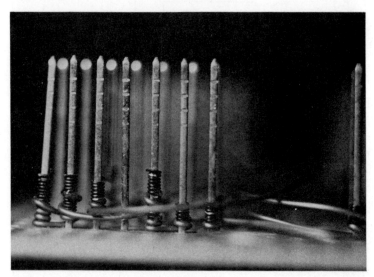

Fig. 16-14. Wire-wrap wire is thin, so daisy-chaining power supplies is not a good idea.

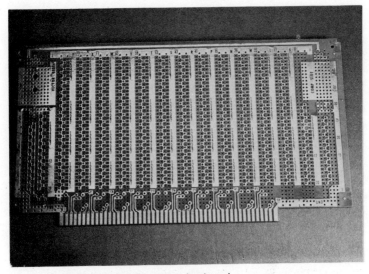

Fig. 16-15. The Vector 8800V prototyping board.

Wire-wrapping presents some problems involving bus connections and connections to discrete parts. You often find that you need to have a wire wrapped to a post at one end and soldered down to something at the other. There are several ways around this prob-

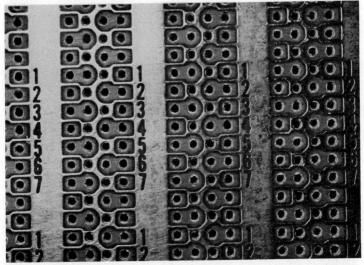

Fig. 16-16. The distributed power and ground patterns on the Vector 8800V board.

257

Fig. 16-17. The Vector 8801-1 board is completely uncommitted.

lem. The easiest way to make connections to the bus is to insert a Vector wrap post into the hole in the pad. When they are inserted, these posts provide a wire-wrap pin for the connection to the pad (Fig. 16-18). Inserting these pins is easier, of course, with the correct tools—most builders use the hand installing tools made by

Fig. 16-18. Vector wrap posts make wire-wrapped connection to PC traces easy.

Fig. 16-19. The Vector T46-4-9 pin is ideal for making wrapped connections.

Vector. There are different tools for the different pins. The most useful pin for inserting into bus pads is the T46-4-9 pin (Fig. 16-19).

Connections to discrete components offer a similar problem. One easy way to handle discrete components is to solder them to a DIP header (an Augat 16-pin DIP header is shown in Fig. 16-20).

Fig. 16-20. These op-amps are soldered to an Augat 16-pin DIP header which plugs into a 16-pin socket.

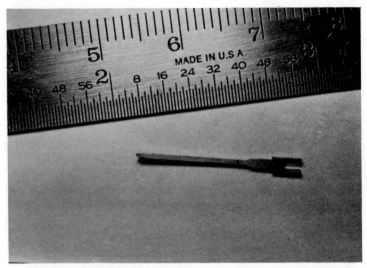

Fig. 16-21. The Vector T44 and T46 pins allow wrapped connections on one side of the card and soldered connections to the other.

The header then plugs into a socket like an IC. If only one capacitor or resistor is needed you can use one of the wrap posts, designed for soldering components, such as the Vector T44- and T46-series pins (Fig. 16-21). When using any wire-wrap post or socket in a hole in the PC foil the pin must be soldered to both sides of the foil as most holes in prototype boards are not plated through. (There is no electrical connection through the board.)

One of the difficulties with wire-wrapping is that you are working on the back of the board. This reverses the pin numbering on the IC sockets. (Pin 1 is in the upper right hand corner of the socket when viewed from the back.) It is also difficult to tell which socket is which from the back. For this reason OK Machine and Tool Corporation sells Wrap-IDs, which are preprinted plastic labels designed to fit over the pins of a wire-wrap socket (Fig. 16-22). They are numbered and provide a space to write on.

The last detail that must be attended before wrapping begins is to connect power and ground to each chip. It was mentioned earlier that the connections should not be daisy-chained with wire-wrap wire. An ideal way to avoid this if you are using the Vector prototype boards with power and ground planes is to use the Vector bus links. These are little metal things which slide over the pins of a wire-wrap socket and solder down to the foil on the PC board (Fig. 16-23).

Fig. 16-22. OK Machine & Tool Wrap-IDs help you keep track of which IC and which pin are which.

Wire-wrapping is often done with a hand-wrapping tool. These are available from several suppliers including Vector Electronics, OK Machine and Tool Corporation and Radio Shack. The tool that is sold by Radio Shack seems to be the same as the OK tool. The OK

Fig. 16-23. Vector bus links simplify connection to power and ground traces.

Fig. 16-24. To make a wire-wrapped connection, first measure the wire.

tool (and its Radio Shack clone) is a combination wrap/unwrap tool and wire stripper.

There are two styles of wire-wrapped connection, the standard and the modified wrap. The modified wrap adds a turn of insulated wire at the start of the connection. This extra turn can act as a strain relief. (All of the illustrations here show modified wrap connections.)

There are five steps involved in making a wire-wrapped connection:

1. Measure the length of wire that is needed. Be sure to allow an extra inch at each end for the wrapped connections (Fig. 16-24).
2. Strip 1 inch of insulation at each end (Fig. 16-25).
3. Load the wrap tool by sliding the wire into the tip. The wire goes through the edge hole and into the groove—not into the big hole at the center (Fig. 16-26).
4. Push the tool over the wrap post. The post fits into the large hole in the center of the tool (Fig. 16-27).
5. Turn the tool clockwise to wrap. Do not press down on it. Continue to turn until the wire is gone (Fig. 16-28).

The completed connection should look like Fig. 16-29. If it didn't work, unwrap the joint by using the unwrap end of the tool (the short end) and turning counterclockwise (Fig. 16-30).

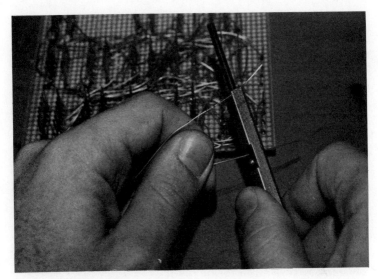

Fig. 16-25. Strip the wire.

Two of the greatest problems involved in using the standard wire-wrap tools are the time and effort it takes to measure, strip and, load the wire, and the effort needed to daisy-chain wires. The stripping difficulty can be avoided to some extent by using pre-stripped wire.

Fig. 16-26. Load the tool.

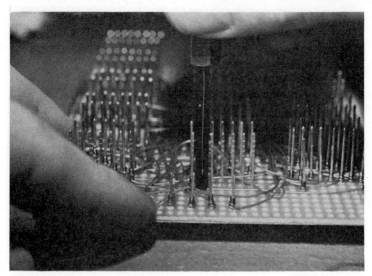

Fig. 16-27. Place the tool on the post.

Another way around both of these problems involves the use of one of the special wire-wrapping tools. The "Just Wrap" by OK Machine and Tool carries a special wire-wrap wire. Stripping is avoided by simply wrapping the wire around the post. The insulation is very soft, and the sharp edges of the post push it aside,

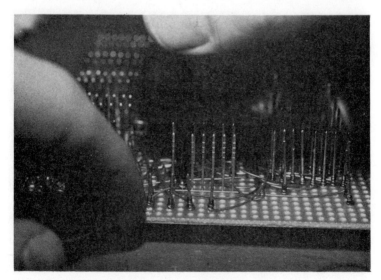

Fig. 16-28. Wrap the wire by turning the tool clockwise.

Fig. 16-29. The completed connection should look like this.

making the connection. The difficulty with this is that you must be careful not to pull the wire too tightly against other sharp edges or corners as this may cut the insulation in undesired places.

Another tool similar in concept is the Vector Slit-n-Wrap tool. This (Fig. 16-31) uses special 28-gauge wire. The tool contains a

Fig. 16-30. If you made the wrong connections or a bad wrap, unwrap the connection by using the unwrap end of the tool and turning counterclockwise.

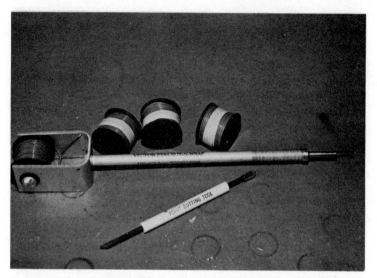

Fig. 16-31. The Vector Slit-n-Wrap tool uses 28 gauge wire with special insulation.

slitting blade in the tip; as you wrap the wire, the insulation is first slit. A metal-to-metal contact is made without having to displace the insulation. The wrapped connections are larger, but only one (Fig. 16-32) is needed to daisy chain a number of connections.

The drawback to these special tools is cost. The modified wrap tool costs about $9.00, while the Just Wrap is about $16.00 and the Slit-n-Wrap about $40.00. The wire for the standard tool is about $3.00 for 100 feet; for the Just Wrap it costs about $3.50 for 50 feet, and the Slit-n-Wrap wire sells for around $5.50 for two 50-foot spools.

The process of wiring with the Slit-n-Wrap tool is simple:

1. Grasp the end of the wire with a pair of hemostats, or your fingers if you are cheap (Fig. 16-33).
2. Place the tool over the post (Fig. 16-34).
3. Turn the tool about seven turns *clockwise* (Fig. 16-35).
4. Move it to the next post (Fig. 16-36).

These special tools may seem costly but they do allow you to make two or three times as many connections per hour as the standard tool.

Frontside Wirewrapping. The one disadvantage to wire-wrapping in an S-100 system is the amount of space that it takes up. With the typical board-to-board spacing, a board built up with

Fig. 16-32. The Slit-n-Wrap makes daisy-chaining easy.

wire-wrap sockets effectively prevents the use of the bus socket behind it because the wire-wrap pins stick out so far. A technique used on prototype boards for the DEC LSI 11 is to put the wrap pins on the front of the board. You can do the same thing using one of the

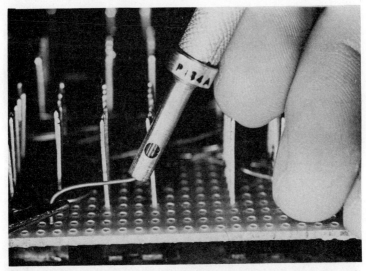

Fig. 16-33. To make a Slit-n-Wrap connection grab the end of the wire with a pair of hemostats.

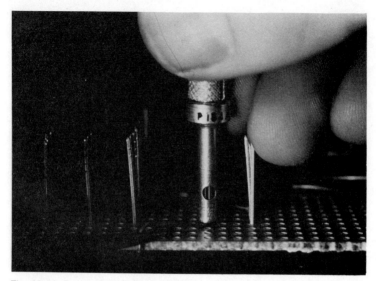

Fig. 16-34. Put the tool on the post.

Vector S-100 prototype boards, the Vector 8802-1. This is a "pad per two hole" board, meaning that a pair of holes shares one copper pad (Fig. 16-37). It is necessary to use such a board because each wire-wrapping pin must be connected to the corresponding socket pin.

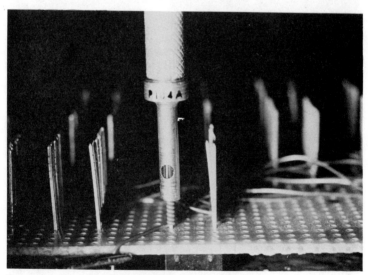

Fig. 16-35. Wrap the connection by turning clockwise.

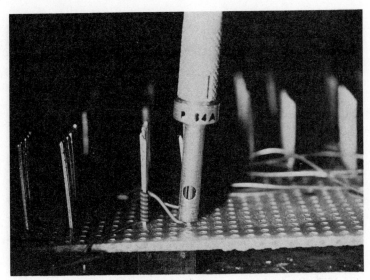

Fig. 16-36. Move the tool to the next post.

There are two ways to do this. One is to use the Vector wrap posts and solder-tail IC sockets (Fig. 16-38); the second is to use wire-wrap sockets. To use a wire-wrap socket you must first insert the socket from the back of the board leaving at least a ⅛-inch space between the socket and board. The pins must be in the outermost

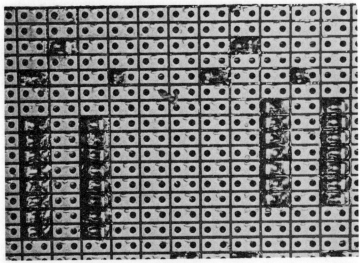

Fig. 16-37. A pad per two-hole board pattern.

Fig. 16-38. Front-side wire-wrapping requires a solder-tab socket and wrap posts.

holes on the pads! (Fig. 16-39). Solder down the row that is in position and cut the pins close to the board, freeing the socket (Fig. 16-40). Do the same for the pins on the other side. Now insert the socket from the front and solder it down (Fig. 16-41). If you did it right, you will have a socket with wire-wrap pins on the outside. After the sockets and pins are installed, wire the board as if it were a normal wire-wrap board.

Wiring with the Wiring Pencil. The Vector wiring pencil is a tool something like the Slit-N-Wrap which feeds tiny (#36) wire from a spool. This wire has a special solder-through insulation. In use, you wrap it onto the pins of a solder-tail socket (Fig. 16-42) and solder the wire in place, using a soldering iron with a tip temperature of 750° F or hotter. The insulation degrades rapidly at this temperature leaving the copper wire exposed. The soldering iron must, in the my experience, really be 750° F or higher. The insulation isn't bothered by a cooler iron.

It is imperative, however, that one other accessory be used. The wires are fragile and difficult to route unless the Vector P179 wire spacers are used (Fig. 16-43). It cannot be overemphasized how important these spacers are to this operation. My experience with the wiring pencil includes construction of an I/O board without the spacers, disassembly of the board, and then reassembly with spacers!

270

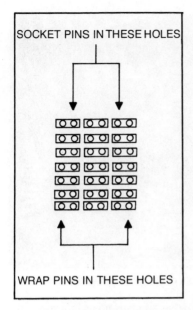

SOCKET PINS IN THESE HOLES

Fig. 16-39. Be sure to put the wrap posts in the outermost set of holes.

WRAP PINS IN THESE HOLES

Nearly any prototype board can be used with the wiring pencil. The major advantage of this pencil is its low profile on the back of the board. The pencil really comes into its own for wiring things like unencoded keyboards, where wires must be daisy-chained among many pins but wire-wrapping can't be used.

Fig. 16-40. Cut the socket away from the pins.

Fig. 16-41. Put the socket onto the front of the board and solder.

Point-to-Point Wiring. Wiring point-to-point is really only suitable for small and relatively uncomplicated circuits. It requires at least a pad per two hole (and better a pad per three hole) prototyping board. The California Computer Systems pad per three hole board is suitable for this type of wiring.

Fig. 16-42. Wrap the wiring-pencil wire around the pin and solder it down. The insulation melts off at 750°F or higher.

Point-to-point wiring involves connecting parts in the circuit with standard insulated hookup wire soldered to the pads. This method is also low profile but it is quite slow.

Homemade Printed-Circuit Boards

It is possible to build your own printed circuit boards at home. The typical method requires creating the artwork two- or four-times lifesize (Fig. 16-44), making or having negatives made, and exposing a photo-resist coated board to light through the negative. The exposed board is often developed in a solvent such as toluene and etched in ferric chloride solution.

If you start with bare copper-clad board, then the board will have to be trimmed when it is finished. Some manufacturers (Vector, for one, with their 8800R2 board) supply S-100-size copper-clad boards with the connector fingers already made and protected with a plastic coating. The Vector board is coated with positive photo resist. This produces the required pattern when exposed using the original positive artwork rather than a negative.

The major difficulty with making PC boards in this manner is in keeping registration between the two sides of the board. Homemaking two-sided PC boards is not something to enter into lightly. The yield is not fantastic, sometimes requiring two or three tries to get one good board. The board must be drilled (a time-consuming task)

Fig. 16-43. Plastic wire-spacers are essential when using the wiring pencil.

273

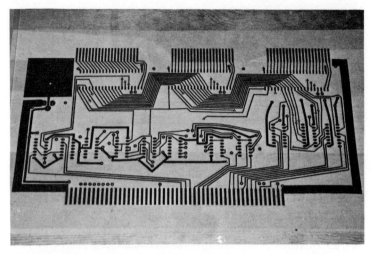

Fig. 16-44. The artwork for most PC boards starts out four times life size.

and jumpers inserted. The jumpers are necessary because your holes won't be plated through the board.

It is, however, quite feasible to build good single-sided boards at home. One easy method is to use etchant resistant patterns and build the artwork right on the board. This is only advisable for single-usage boards. If you need more than one, you must go to some kind of photographic technique.

SYSTEM-LEVEL CONSTRUCTION

Construction at this level requires different techniques from construction at the board level. You will be involved more with the physical development of the system.

Building the system enclosure can be separated into two inter-related parts. The first, building the power supply, involves most of the electrical work in the system. The second, building the enclosure, concerns the physical construction of the computer. These two parts should be carefully coordinated because the power supply must be able to service everything in the system, and the enclosure must support the power supply and provide a means to carry away the heat that it generates.

A Power Supply Construction

A power supply has fairly simple requirements. It must be supplied sufficient primary ac current to generate the necessary voltages. It must protect the computer from noise and transients on the ac power line and must prevent radiation of noise back into the power line. It must be firmly mounted and able to dissipate the heat generated in the system. It must provide some protection for the rest of the computer system.

The first requirement is easy to fulfill. A heavy gauge three-wire grounded line cord and a 2 A slow-blow fuse will supply ample current for any normal home computer. Protection from and of the power line can be obtained through the use of an ac line filter (Fig. 16-45). This filter is rated at ten amps, far in excess of the requirements of the computer. *Because grounding and fusing of the computer is so important, you should review the discussion in Chapter 10.*

Power supplies are usually built onto the frame of the computer or, on occasion, built on an aluminum sheet bolted to the frame of the computer. This would allow the power supply to be upgraded by simply unbolting the old supply and installing the new one. Frame mounting also helps the components to dissipate heat.

There are several practical considerations in building power supplies. The power switches used in small computers usually are fairly small. To switch the currents used in a computer power supply, good design requires the use of an ac contactor. A contactor is a high-power ac relay. Switching the contactor requires only a small amount of power. The low-power signal from the switch activates the contactor which carries the high current (Fig. 16-46).

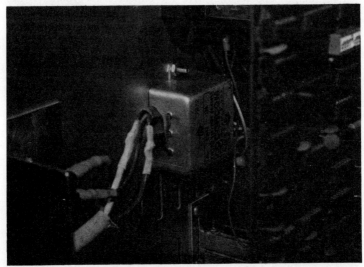

Fig. 16-45. An ac line filter installed in the author's computer just after the fuse.

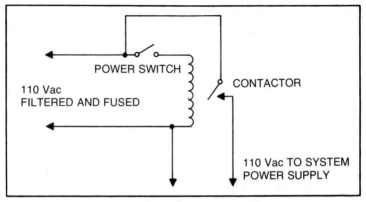

Fig. 16-46. A contactor is used to switch higher power than the power switch can take.

Protecting the system is often accomplished with fuses. A regulated power supply for a floppy disk drive feeds the TTL circuitry in the drive directly. This circuitry would be damaged if a regulator failed and allowed high voltage into the drive. To protect the drives against such a failure, the computer should be equipped with overvoltage protection.

Lambda manufactures overvoltage protectors that can be included in any power supply. These devices have a positive terminal and a negative terminal. The positive terminal is connected to the voltage output and the negative is connected to ground. If the positive terminal gets higher than $+5.6V$ the protector turns on, shorting to ground. This is designed to blow the power supply fuse or current-limit the supply (Fig. 16-47).

Some 16K dynamic memories require the power supply to be cycled up and down. This can be done by making use of the RC time constant of the S-100 16V power supply. Another way would involve the use of a one-second time-delay relay that connects the $+8V$ and $+16V$ supplies one second after the power comes up; another relay sits across the $-16V$ supply and disconnects the other supplies if the $-16V$ supply drops (Fig. 16-48).

Any wires that carry 110Vac (to the disk drives or fan, for instance) should be twisted together to minimize the amount of 60 Hz interference.

Mechanical Construction

The physical enclosure of the computer has several jobs to do. It must provide mechanical stability and protection for the com-

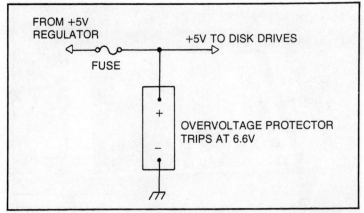

Fig. 16-47. Overvoltage protectors guard against voltage-regulator failure.

puter. It also must contain any high-frequency noise generated by the computer to prevent interference with television and radio receivers. It must, finally, route cooling air to the places that need it.

Enclosures can be built from scratch or purchased. If you buy an enclosure you can usually spend a fair amount of money for it, but it will easily accommodate the motherboard and power supplies. General-purpose enclosures can often be purchased as surplus. My computer is housed in an enclosure, purchased for about $50.00 through a surplus electronics house. Such a cabinet often needs internal mechanical work before it is suitable for use as a home for your computer. Figure 16-49 shows an enclosure with internal

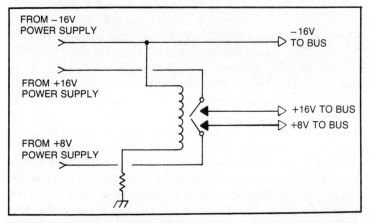

Fig. 16-48. System dc supplies can be shut off with a relay if the −16V supply is lost.

Fig. 16-49. Internal aluminum crosspieces were installed to support the disks and power supply.

aluminum crosspieces installed as supports for the disk drives and power supply.

This enclosure is a tabletop rack-mount enclosure, meaning that it is designed to accept standard 19-inch relay-rack-mountable equipment. The card cage (Fig. 16-50) used is a Vector Electronics CCK100 S-100-size card cage. The motherboard mounted in it is an SSM 15-slot board. Resting on top of the cage (and bolted to it) are three 4-inch fans used to provide air flow over the cards.

A completely home-brew cabinet can also be constructed. There are many ways to build such an enclosure but all share some features. They should all be constructed of metal in order to contain rf noise. One way to construct such an enclosure is with a set of aluminum rails. These rails, along with a heavy-gauge aluminum front and back panel provide the mechanical framework of the computer. Aluminum sheet can then be used to form the sides and bottom. Somewhere, often in the back panel, a hole is drilled in order to provide ventilation for a fan. The entire computer, in fact, could be mounted in a standard relay rack. It would not be as nice looking, but it is efficient and easy to do. The usual way to lay out the components for the enclosure is to gather all of the parts in one place and attempt to fit it all together. You should eventually come up with a result that you like, and then construction can begin.

COMPUTER KITS

There are only a handful of "kit computers" left. The major source for these is Heath Company. The Heathkit H-8 and H-89 computers are both 8080/Z-80 non-S-100 computers. The Heathkit H-19 terminal is an emulation of the DEC VT-52 with some additional features. It is an-easy-to-build (about three or four evenings) kit that provides you with a high quality terminal for a relatively low price.

Several single-board computers are available as kits, but these require a power supply, disk drives, and a terminal in order to work. Few, if any, manufacturers (other than Heath) provide entire computers in kit form. Building the computer yourself will usually result in a more versatile system.

MISCELLANEOUS CONSTRUCTION TECHNIQUES

This section is mainly devoted to the little tricks that are useful to know about when you're building things.

Getting Sockets Flush With the Board

When you are using sockets on a board—especially when you use a lot of them—it is sometimes difficult to get them all down flat on the surface of the board. To get all of your sockets on right, use the following procedure:

Fig. 16-50. The card cage bolts into the back of the enclosure.

279

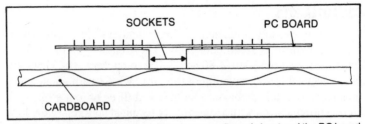

Fig. 16-51. Sandwich the sockets between a cardboard sheet and the PC board to hold them in when you flip it over.

1. Put a row (or two) of sockets into the board.
2. Place a piece of cardboard, a magazine, or anything stiff over the sockets. While pressing down on the cardboard to hold the sockets in, flip the board over so that it rests on the table, upside down. The cardboard should be on the table, then the sockets, then the board (Fig. 16-51).
3. Solder two diagonally opposite pins on each socket (Fig. 16-52). The sockets should be held to the board with two pins.
4. While pressing the socket to the board, reheat the soldered pins one at a time (Fig. 16-53). As the solder melts, the socket should snap into place.

Eliminating DIP Switches

DIP (dual-inline-package) switches tend to be expensive and, for many things, are not frequently used. For instance, I/O port selection is seldom changed so the convenience of a DIP switch is really not necessary. You can replace it by soldering-in wire-wrap pins. The easiest way is by using the same method that you use to make front side wire-wrap positions using wire-wrap sockets. Stick the socket through the board, using the DIP switch mounting holes, leaving enough room to cut the pins. Solder them in. Cut the pins and wire-wrap the connections (Fig. 16-54).

Soldering in Three-Terminal Regulators

When soldering in a three-terminal regulator, remember to do two things:

1. Coat the back of the regulator with heat-sink compound before you bolt it down. The compound increases the conduction of heat into the heatsink (Fig. 16-55).
2. Solder the leads to *both* sides of the board (Fig. 16-56). This will minimize power distribution problems.

280

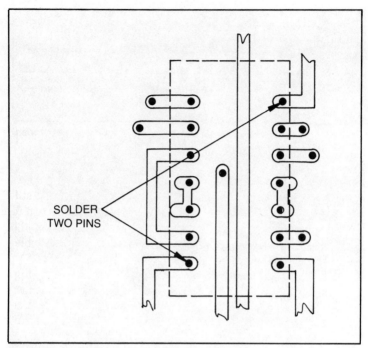

SOLDER
TWO PINS

Fig. 16-52. Solder diagonally opposite pins.

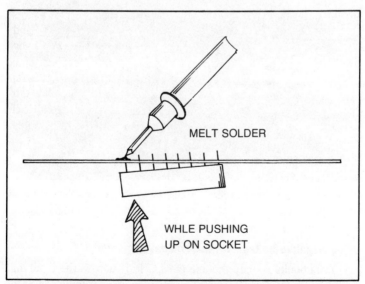

MELT SOLDER

WHLE PUSHING
UP ON SOCKET

Fig. 16-53. Melt the solder on the soldered-in pins while pushing the socket into the board. The socket will snap in flush with the board. Solder the rest of the pins.

Fig. 16-54. DIP switches can often be replaced by wire-wrapping and wrapped jumpers.

Using Negative-Voltage Three-Terminal Regulator

Data books specify the use of capacitors across the input and output sides of three-terminal negative-voltage regulators (Fig. 16-57). While the books specify values for aluminum-electrolyte

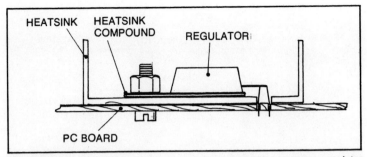

Fig. 16-55. Heatsink compound increases heat conduction between regulator and heatsink.

capacitors, experience has convinced me to use *only* tantalum capacitors, as anything else seems to oscillate.

Removing Sockets

If you find a problem either with or under a socket you will want to remove it. With many sockets, you can pry the body off of the board, leaving the pins which can be removed individually (Fig. 16-58).

Removing Soldered-in ICs

Assuming that you want to remove the IC *without* destroying the board (and don't care about destroying the IC) do the following: Cut using sharp, fine-tip wire-cutters) the leads off the IC. When the body of the IC is free, remove it and unsolder the pins individually.

Opening Solder-Clogged Holes on the PC Board

Opening holes filled with solder on a pc board can be a trick. Here are some things to try:

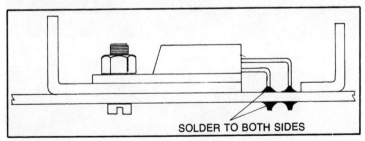

Fig. 16-56. For best power distribution, solder the regulators to both sides of the PC board.

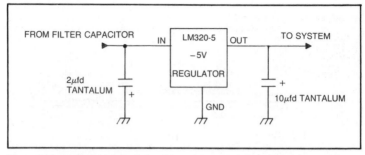

Fig. 16-57. Negative-voltage regulators *require* tantalum capacitors.

1. Heat the hole with a soldering iron and try to suck out the solder using a desoldering bulb (Fig. 16-59) or a "solder-sucker" tool.

2. Do the same, but use the desoldering tool on the opposite side of the board from the soldering iron.

3. Heat the hole and push a wire (a cut resistor lead) into the hole. When it sticks, heat the wire and push it in farther. You should eventually take the solder out of the hole by coating the wire with it.

4. Heat the hole and use the desoldering bulb to *blow* the solder out. Watch for the splatter and check the board carefully for blobs of solder.

Fig. 16-58. To remove a socket, first remove the body and unsolder each pin individually.

Fig. 16-59. A desoldering bulb can be used to remove solder when removing parts.

5. Use a desoldering wick which removes the solder by capillary action.

6. If you have a difficult time melting the solder in the hole add a little more at the tip of the iron. The improved heat conduction may allow you to get it all out.

Improving Heatsinks

If the blades of some heatsinks are turned slightly, they will work better (Fig. 16-60).

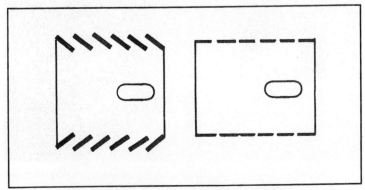

Fig. 16-60. Twisting heatsink blades can increase their efficiency.

FIGURING YOUR POWER NEEDS

To plan for your power needs you should account for each board that you intend to use in the system. Figure out how much power these boards will require and plan the power supply to have a current rating at least 50% greater. Power requirements for each card can generally be found in the manual. If not, assume approximately one ampere per regulator.

When it Doesn't Work

Anyone who builds a computer and nearly anyone who buys a computer will eventually have trouble with it. The trouble may be minor (e.g., a bad disk) or major, requiring replacement of parts. The computer, if designed well, can be *very* reliable, especially considering its complexity. The correction of problems with the computer is much easier if you have been able to define the nature of the problem. The more precisely that the nature can be defined, the easier the difficulty will be to locate and correct. There are basically two types of errors that a computer can make—"soft" errors and "hard" errors. These are discussed in this chapter.

SOFT ERRORS

A soft error is a transient problem with the computer. This is not really the same as an intermittent problem. An intermittent error is a hard error that occurs only once in a while under a certain set of conditions.

In comparison to other devices, large memory chips suffer from relatively frequent soft errors. In 64K RAM chips the alpha-induced soft error is common. An alpha particle, released from a radioactive atom in the ceramic, for example, can strike one of the storage cells and change the information held in it. When that cell is read there will be an error caused by that data being wrong. This is a soft error because if the correct data is written to the "bad" cell it will read correctly and continue to read correctly. There is nothing wrong with the bit cell, it just encountered conditions which corrupted the data.

A glitch in the power line can also cause a soft error. Losing the ac power supply for a few cycles can cause the computer to crash. When the system is brought up again it will stay up, there is nothing wrong with it. Soft errors are usually *not* repeatable.

HARD ERRORS

A hard error is a repeatable error caused by a part failure. If a memory chip develops an address-line short, then this is a hard error. A scratched diskette will always have a data error at the point of the scratch. Hard errors do not always mean that there is a hardware problem. You can have hard errors that are the result of, for instance, having a dip switch set incorrectly.

The worst kind of hard error is an intermittent error. The best way to handle an intermittent is to live with the problem, if possible, until it fails completely. One of the more common types of intermittent problems is the thermal intermittent. If an error disappears after the system warms up, or if the system works until it warms up, then you probably have a thermal intermittent. This might be a bad connection in (or around) a chip which makes contact only after the part heats up. In this case the error would disappear after the system has run for a while.

Once you determine which parts are suspect you can use a canned refrigerant to cool the part. If the circuit stops working after you have used the freeze spray you may have found the problem. You can also heat parts with a small heat gun or soldering iron to see if it fails when it warms up.

Unless it is caused by a bad solder joint, always replace an intermittent part. Thermal intermittent parts tend to get worse with time, and you will just end up replacing it eventually.

DIAGNOSIS

The most difficult part of repairing any trouble you might have is figuring out what the problem is. The easiest way to diagnose a problem with the computer is to have it tell you itself what is wrong. As an example of this, my system was having problems reading and writing on diskette B. Nothing obvious was wrong and no headway was being made toward solving the problem until a version of the operating system was generated that dumped the status bytes from the disk controller when an error occurred. With this new information the fault was isolated to a particular circuit and the problem was fixed within a half hour.

Memory-testing programs are good for determining whether a memory problem exists. If these programs can be used they will normally tell you the addresses at which the errors occurred and the data written and read from that location.

The program will not run, however, if it resides in memory that is bad. This is where the monitor in PROM comes in very handy. If the monitor will run you can use its Dump and Examine commands to inspect memory. Make sure that all the memory that should be there *is* there, and check for obvious errors. Check especially in the areas that the operating system needs, as an error there will ensure that the system will not run.

IF THE MONITOR WON'T RUN

If you can't get the monitor to come up at all you may have a real problem. Here is a set of steps to take at this point:

1. Check the fuses. Check *all* the fuses—110Vac, +8, +16, −16, etc.

2. Check the terminal. Switch the terminal offline and type. If you get what you type, then the terminal is probably OK.

3. Convert to a minimum system. Take out everything except what is actually needed to make the system run. Especially remove all unneeded I/O boards. If the system works, then the problem is in one of the other boards that you removed. Put them in one at a time until you find the one that fouls things up. If the minimum system won't run, make sure that all of the boards are seated well on the bus.

4. Check each board for bent-over pins. An IC with a leg folded under will not make contact in the socket and can cause major problems.

5. Check the power supplies. With a voltmeter check the power supplies on the bus. If these are OK, check the supplies on each board. If you find a regulator getting hot and putting out practically no voltage then you have a short circuit.

6. Check all dip switches.

7. You didn't put the boards in *backwards*, did you?

8. At this point, the best thing to do is to test each board individually on another system to see if it works.

BOARD SWAPS

If you are lucky enough to have access to another system using the same boards, swap boards between the two systems, one at a time. If the board from your system was good the other system should work and yours still wouldn't. If yours will work with the borrowed board, and the other system will not work with your board, then you've found the problem. (This is where belonging to a computer club comes in handy—you'll have friends with whom you can do this swapping!) *Before* you board swap, however, try to make sure that there is nothing in your system that will damage the swapped-in boards.

DIAGNOSIS ON THE BOARD LEVEL

After you've determined which board has the problem you can begin to diagnose it at the board level. The most important tool needed to do this is a good schematic diagram.

Check the board visually, looking for bent IC pins and the like. The next step is to put it in the system on an extender board. This board has PC fingers at one end that plug into the backplane and a bus socket at the other. It is used to elevate the board that you are working on over the top of the others so you can get at it.

At this point you have to go looking for signals. A voltmeter isn't too useful because it can't follow the changes in a high-speed signal. To properly see high-speed signals you need special equipment—a digital logic probe (Fig. 17-1) or an oscilloscope (Fig. 17-2).

The logic probe can respond to very-high-speed signals and will show you the state (high or low) of the signal that you are examining. The oscilloscope will let you see the signal *vs* time. A dual-trace oscilloscope allows you to see two signals at once so that you can look at their timing relative to one another. What you want to do is ensure that all the signals that must be present *are* present.

For instance, on a board with an EPROM, check the Chip Select or Output Enable signal to the EPROM. If this signal is OK, there is probably no reason to look at the signals that generate it. If they weren't right, then the select signal couldn't be.

Look especially for clock signals, and the status and strobe signals from the bus. What you are searching for is an important signal that is not getting through. If a board doesn't do anything at all and the power supplies are OK, find the board-select signal. Any memory or I/O board will have a select signal available somewhere. If the board-select signal is present, then all of the address decoding circuitry is probably working. Next, look for the data buffer enable signals. The bus signal pDBIN should cause the Data-In buffers to be enabled if the board is selected. Next, make sure that the I/O or memory chip on the board that is to be accessed is getting all of its read, write, and select signals. If everything seems to be working up to the memory or I/O chip, then you can chip-swap.

CHIP SWAP

Chip-swapping involves replacing each suspect IC with one

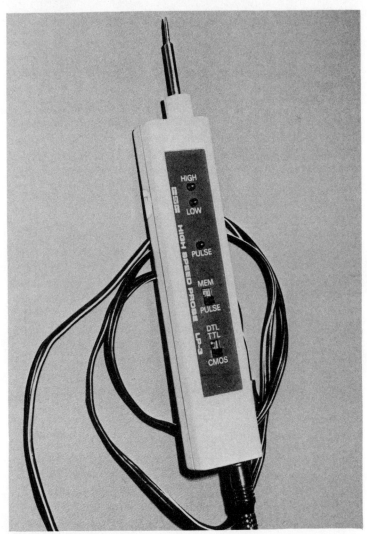

Fig. 17-1. Digital logic probe.

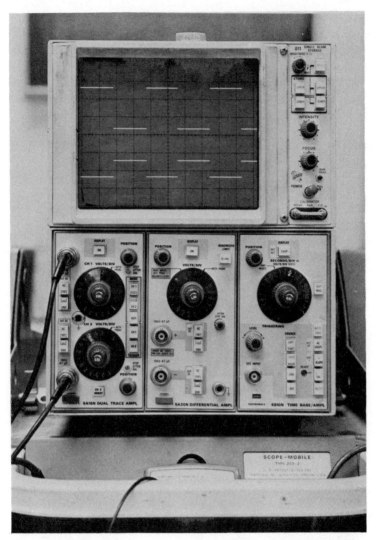

Fig. 17-2. Oscilloscope.

that is known to be good. This method is only practical if all of the chips are in sockets. Each swapped chip should be marked, perhaps with a piece of tape, so that you can keep track of what has been changed. When you really get stuck, you can swap-out all of the chips on the board. Chip-swapping will often not find the problem if more than one chip is defective. This usually occurs only in extreme conditions, or when one chip takes another with it when it goes.

STILL WON'T WORK

First, make sure that all of the signals are actually getting to all of the places that they should be. If a signal makes it only part way to where it is going (you can follow the signal along the PC traces) you have either a cracked trace or a bad plated-through hole.

You can locate the fault with an ohmmeter. Bad plated-through holes are treated by putting a wire through them (a clipped resistor lead is good) and soldering it to the pads on both sides of the board. Cracked traces can be jumpered over with wire-wrap wire soldered into the holes.

You will also need to know if things are happening at the right *time*. You can do this with a dual-trace oscilloscope, but access to a logic analyzer (Fig. 17-3) will allow you to see several signals at once.

My system was found to be turning on the data buffers, at one time, on the CPU board when they should have been off, and turning them off when they should have been on. The problem was traced (using a logic analyzer) to a defective NAND gate. One input was zero, the other had a signal on it, and the inversion of that signal was on the output. The output of a NAND gate with an input zero is *always one*. Replacing the defective chip fixed the board.

AS LAST RESORT

When things still won't work, and nothing much seems to be

Fig. 17-3. A logic analyzer being used to debug a system.

wrong, then it is time to gather together the manuals on all of the boards involved. Have the boards ever worked together before? If so, there is certainly a problem on one or the other. If not, you have to carefully examine the schematics on each board to find out if a signal that one board wants isn't being generated by another. Check especially for:

PHANTOM*	pin 67 normally
REFRESH*	often pin 66
pWAIT	not on the standard, old bus pin 27

Not all boards look at the PHANTOM* line. This can be a real problem if something else on the bus is trying to PHANTOM* that board.

The pWAIT signal was removed from the standard proposal for some reason. It was a response signal by the CPU that told the rest of the system that it was in a wait state. It was of only limited validity, normally being generated by gating XRDY* and PRDY* together, but many boards need it.

REFRESH* is a signal usually only available on Z-80 CPU cards. Since it is common and easy to generate (the CPU does it all itself), most boards put it on the bus or make it available as an option. One Z-80 card that doesn't is the Godbout CPU-Z. For whatever reason (Godbout makes only static RAM cards) the signal isn't on the bus. If you want it you have to jumper to one of the unused gates on the board.

The other pitfall is a board that isn't designed well, or was designed before the standard. The SD Sales Expandoram II is an example of a board that was designed before the standard. It uses the edges of status lines to derive some of its timing and will work only with a Z-80 CPU using unlatched status. The board works fine when you get it running, however.

One other bus pin has been changed. Pin 53 *was* SSWDSB* and is *now* ground. Grounding this pin on a system using the SSWDSB* signal will cause it to disable the CPU's data bus buffer!

Once you find the error, write down what you found. It may be of help on a later problem. If you can't locate the problem, write down all the symptoms. This will help whoever works on it, whether a friend you can con into helping you or a commercial repair place (at $35/hour or worse!).

Glossary

access time—Amount of time required for a memory chip to make its data available.

address—Location of an element of memory.

A/D conversion—Conversion of an analog voltage to a digital word.

alphanumeric—Alphabetic letters (A-Z) and numbers (0-9), including punctuation symbols as on a typewriter keyboard.

applications program—Program used by the operator of the system, in contrast to a system program.

ASCII character—An 8-bit code for alphanumerics with 128 binary patterns using 7 binary digits (**A**merican **S**tandard **C**ode for **I**nformation **I**nterchange).

backplane(motherboard)—Board into which component boards plug.

binary—Base two number system, using 0 and 1.

bits and bytes
  bit—A single binary digit.
  byte—Group of eight bits; 1024 bytes is 1K.
  megabyte—One million bytes.
  baud rate—Speed of a serial communication in bits per second; one bit per second is one baud.

bootstrap—The use of one technique to help in the start of another.

buffer—Software: temporary storage area; hardware: a device used to increase the current drive of a signal.

bug—Something causing a malfunction in either hardware or software.

bus—Wires or electronic pathway connecting a large number of devices.

Bi-directional Bus—Data to and from the processor uses the same set of wires.

Uni-directional bus—Data to the bus and data from it use different sets of wires.

S-100 Bus—Bus based on 100-pin connector.

chip—Specifically the square of silicon with the circuitry on it in an IC, but often used to refer to the whole packaged IC.

clock—A repetitive signal used for timing.

console—Normally the main control terminal of a computer.

crt display—A TV-like display using a cathode ray tube (CRT).

D/A conversion—Conversion of a digital word to an analog voltage or element.

debug—removing errors from either hardware or software.

disk—Device allowing storage of large amounts of data.

disk drive—Hardware device used for mass storage; data is stored on disk coated with magnetic material.

disk controller—Circuit card used to control disk drive.

diskette (floppy disk)—Disk storage using data stored on mylar disks coated with magnetic material; they are commonly 5¼ inches or 8 inches in diameter.

Hard disk—Disk made of an aluminum platen coated with magnetic medium.

digital—Data in binary digits; represented as numbers rather than voltages or currents.

file—Sequence of records that are logically related.

flowchart—Diagram of logic and program flow.

frontpanel—Part of computer that lets user talk directly to it.

handshaking—Interface design where computer sends signal and waits until interface sends one back.

hardcopy—Anything printed.

hardware—Equipment.

IEEE standard—A proposed standard for the S-100 bus.

instructions set—The specific instructions that the microprocessor is able to execute.

interface—Circuitry allowing different devices to be connected to system.

interrupt—A signal to the computer that stops the program because of some condition that must be serviced.

    maskable—Interrupt that can be disabled by the processor.

    nonmaskable—Interrupt that cannot be disabled by the processor.

I/O—Input-output

    I/O ports—Connections to computer for sending data to or from (in or out).

    parallel I/O—I/O that transfers all 8 bits at a time.

    serial I/O—I/O that transfers data one bit after another.

languages—Aids in writing programs; these are all discussed fully in Chapter 11.

    assembler—Language using instructions that can be directly translated to microprocessor instructions.

    BASIC—Beginners Allpurpose Symbolic Instruction Code.

    COBOL—COommon Business Oriented Language

    FORTRAN—FORmula TRANslator

    Pascal—A language named after mathematician, Blaise Pascal; designed for the teaching of structured programming.

line printer—Printer that prints a whole line at a time.

memory—Elements in the computer that retain the instructions.

    dynamic memory—Type that does not retain memory unless "refreshed" (a process of restoring information that fades).

    static memory—Retains data indefinitely.

    high memory—Address near the top end of memory; addresses near FFFF.

    low memory—Address near the bottom end of memory; addresses near 0000.

    RAM—Random access memory; any word in memory can be directly addressed in any order or at random.

    ROM—Read only memory; permanently programmed memory, also normally random access.

    PROM—Programmable ROM; can be programmed by the user rather than at the factory.

EPROM—Erasable programmable ROM.
EEPROM—Electricially erasable programmable ROM.

mnemonics—Group of letters or characters grouped to assist user in remembering phrase.
modem—**MO**dulator/**DEM**odulator; used for digital communications over phone lines.

NOP—No-operation instructions; has no effect on computer operation, sometimes used to conserve space for future use.

op code—Operation code.

program—A set of instructions to the computer.
Examples:
compiler—A program which converts high-level language to machine code for computer.
monitor (software)—A basic frontpanel replacement program. (In hardware, a monitor as a TV-like display device.)
source code—A program in its original form, before compilation.

routine—Piece of a program.
service routine—A routine that serves an I/O device.
support routine—Any type of routine that supports a device or feature of the computer.
subroutine—A routine that is called when needed; may be called many times instead of duplicating the code.
register—Special memory location within the processor.

software—Programs or routines; as opposed to hardware, which is equipment.

terminal—An I/O device connected to computer in order to communicate with it; could be keyboard and video display.

Winchester drive—drive using special sealed disks and light heads.

Appendix A
Suppliers

IC MANUFACTURERS

Advanced Micro Devices
901 Thompson Place
Sunnyvale, CA 94086

Analog Devices
Route 1 Industrial Park
Norwood, MA 02062

Fairchild
464 Ellis Street
Mountain View, CA 94042

General Instrument
600 West John Street
Hicksville, NY 11802

Intel
3065 Bowers Avenue
Santa Clara, CA 95051

Mos Technology
950 Rittenhouse Road
Norristown, PA 19401

Mostek
1215 West Crosby Road
Carrollton, TX 75006

Motorola
5005 East McDowell Road
Phoenix, AZ 85008

NEC
3120 Central Expressway
Santa Clara, CA 95051

National Semiconductor
2900 Semiconductor Drive
Santa Clara, CA 95051

RCA
P.O. Box 3200
Somerville, NJ 08876

Texas Instruments
P.O. Box 225012
Dallas, TX 75222

Teledyne Crystalonics
147 Sherman Street
Cambridge, MA 02140

TRW
P.O. Box 1125
Redondo Beach, CA 90278

Western Digital
3128 Red Hill Avenue
Newport Beach, CA 92663

Zilog
10340 Bubb Road
Cupertino, CA 95014

HARDWARE: BOARDS

Ackerman Digital Systems
110 North York Road #208
Elmhurst, IL 60126

John Bell Engineering
P.O. Box 338
Redwood, CA 94064

California Computer Systems
250 Caribbean Drive
Sunnyvale, CA 94086

Cromemco
280 Bernardo Avenue
Mountain View, CA 94040

Digital Research of Texas
P.O. Box 401565
Garland, TX 75040

Bill Godbout Electronics
P.O. Box 2355, Oakland Airport
Oakland, CA 94614

Heath
Benton Harbor, MI 49022

Ithaca Intersystems
1650 Hanshaw Road
Ithaca, NY 14850

Logical Devices
781 West Oakland Park
    Boulevard
Ft. Lauderdale, FL 33311

Morrow Designs
5221 Central Avenue
Richmond, CA 94804

Sierra Data Systems
1800 East Shaw Avenue #164
Fresno, CA 98710

SSM Microcomputer
2190 Paragon Drive
San Jose, CA 95131

Teletek
9767F Business Park Drive
Sacramento, CA 95827

Vector Electronics
12460 Gladstone Avenue
Sylmar, CA 91342

W W Components
1771 Junction Avenue
San Jose, CA 95112

HARDWARE: COMPUTERS

Atari, Inc.
1265 Borregas Avenue
P.O. Box 427
Sunnyvale, CA 94086

Cromemco
See Hardware: Boards

Digital Equipment
Parker Street
Maynard, MA 01754

Exidy, Inc.
Data Products Division
390 Java Drive
Sunnyvale, CA 94086

IBM
General Systems Division
5775 Glenridge Drive, NE
Atlanta, GA 30301

Ithaca Intersystems
See Hardware: Boards

Ohio Scientific
1333 South Chillicothe Road
Aurora, Ohio 44202

Quasar Data Products
10330 Brecksville Road
Cleveland, OH 44141

Southwest Technical Products
219 West Rhapsody Avenue
San Antonio, TX 78216

HARDWARE: PRINTERS

Diablo Systems
24500 Industrial Boulevard
Hayward, CA 94545

Digital Equipment
See Hardware: Computers

Integral Data Systems
Milford, NH 03055

SOFTWARE

B & D SOFTWARE
c/o Lifeboat Associates
1651 Third Avenue
New York, NY 10028

The Code Works
P.O. Box 550
Goleta, CA 93116

CompuView Products
1955 Pauline Boulevard, #200
Ann Arbor, MI 48103

CP/M Users Group
1651 Third Avenue
New York, NY 10028

Digital Research
P.O. Box 579
Pacific Grove, CA 93950

Microsoft Consumer Products
400 18th Avenue NE
Bellevue, WA 98004

M T Microsystems
1562 King's Cross Drive
Cardiff, CA 92007

Sorcim
405 Aldo Avenue
Santa Clara, CA 95050

Supersoft
P.O. Box 1628
Champaign, IL 61820

Tiny C Associates
P.O. Box 269
Holmden, NJ 07733

Whitesmiths Ltd.
P.O. Box 1132, Ansonia Station
New York, NY 10023

GRAPHICS

Bausch & Lomb (formerly
Houston Instrument)
Instruments &
Systems Division
P.O. Box 15720
Austin, TX 78761

Cambridge Development Lab
36 Pleasant Street
Watertown, MA 02172

Strobe, Inc.
897-5A Independence Avenue
Mountain View, CA 94043

Sublogic Communications
Corp.
713 Edgebrook Avenue
Champaign, IL 61820

Talos Systems, Inc.
7419 East Helm Drive
Scottsdale, AZ 85260

GENERAL

Computer People
20 Oak Grove Avenue
Woodacre, CA 94973

Priority One Electronics
9161-I Deering Avenue
Chatsworth, CA 91311

POWER SUPPLIES

Lambda
515 Broad Hollow Road
Melville, NY 11746

PARTS

Active Electronics
P.O. Box 1035
Framingham, MA 01701

Advanced Computer Products
P.O. Box 17329
Irvine, CA 92713

JDR Microdevices
1224 South Bascom Avenue
San Jose, CA 95128

Jameco Electronics
1355 Shoreway Road
Belmont, CA 94002

Page Digital, Inc.
1858 Evergreen Avenue
Duarte, CA 91010

TOOLS

OK Machine & Tool
3455 Conner Street
Bronx, NY 10475

Vector Electronics
See Hardware: Boards

Appendix B

ZMON 62
Monitor Program

```
F000                    ORG     0F000H
E26E =          STACK    EQU     0E26EH
                ;
                ;
                ;       ZMON 6.2
                ;
                ;
F000 C312F0             JMP     INIT      ;0F021H
F003 C310F2             JMP     CONIN     ;0F389H
F006 C305F2             JMP     CONOUT    ;0F37EH
F009 C3D4F0             JMP     PRINT     ;0F1A1H
F00C C334F2             JMP     CONSTAT   ;0F3ADH
F00F C312F0             JMP     INIT      ;0F021H
                ;
                ;       COLD START MONITOR
                ;
                INIT:            ;F021
F012 316EE2             LXI     SP,STACK        ;0E26EH
F015 CD2BF2             CALL    CLRSCR    ;0F3A4H
F018 E5                 PUSH    H
F019 2140F2             LXI     H,SOMSG   ;0F3D5H
F01C CD1BF2             CALL    OSTR      ;0F394H
F01F E1                 POP     H
F020 CDBDF0             CALL    PINIT     ;0F18AH
                ;
                ;GET A COMMAND AND PARSE IT
                ;
                PARSE:           ;F032
F023 DB01               IN      1
F025 CDCFF1             CALL    PROMPT    ;0F348H
F028 CDF2F1             CALL    CMD.      ;0F36BH
F02B FE45               CPI     'E'       ;45H
F02D CA3DF0             JZ      EXAM      ;0F070H
F030 FE4D               CPI     'M'       ;4DH
F032 CA77F0             JZ      DUMP      ;0F146H
```

303

```
                    ;       ERROR IN COMMAND
                    ;
           ERROR:           ;F067
F035 3E3F                   MVI     A,'?'    ;3FH
F037 CDFAF1                 CALL    PNT      ;0F373H
F03A C323F0                 JMP     PARSE    ;0F032H
                    ;
                    ;       EXAMINE MEMORY
                    ;
           EXAM:            ;F070
F03D CDDAF1                 CALL    EPROMPT  ;0F353H
F040 CD24F1                 CALL    LOADHL   ;0F1F0H
           EXMN:            ;F076
F043 CDE5F1                 CALL    LFCR     ;0F35EH
F046 CD2FF1                 CALL    POH      ;0F1FBH
F049 3E3A                   MVI     A,':'    ;3AH
F04B CDFAF1                 CALL    PNT      ;0F373H
F04E CDF2F1                 CALL    CMD      ;0F36BH
F051 FE20                   CPI     ' '      ;20H
F053 CA63F0                 JZ      NEXT     ;0F096H
F056 FE52                   CPI     'R'      ;52H
F058 CA67F0                 JZ      RUN      ;0F09AH
F05B FE0D                   CPI     0DH
F05D CA23F0                 JZ      PARSE    ;0F032H
F060 C368F0                 JMP     DEPOS    ;0F09BH
                    ;
                    ;       EXAMINE NEXT
                    ;
           NEXT:            ;F096
F063 23                     INX     H
F064 C343F0                 JMP     EXMN     ;0F076H
                    ;
                    ;       RUN
                    ;
           RUN:             ;F09A
F067 E9                     PCHL
                    ;
                    ;       DEPOSIT
                    ;
           DEPOS:           ;F09B
F068 CD86F1                 CALL    MORE     ;0F252H
F06B 77                     MOV     M,A
F06C CDC7F1                 CALL    SPACE    ;0F340H
F06F 7E                     MOV     A,M
F070 CD4FF1                 CALL    PHCHAR   ;0F21BH
F073 23                     INX     H
F074 C343F0                 JMP     EXMN     ;0F076H
                    ;
                    ;
                    ;       DUMP MEMORY
                    ;
           DUMP:            ;F146
F077 CDDAF1                 CALL    EPROMPT  ;0F353H
F07A CD06F1                 CALL    BOUND    ;0F1D2H
F07D CD2BF2                 CALL    CLRSCR   ;0F3A4H
F080 0618       D0:         MVI     B,18H    ;SET B FOR 24 LINES ON A SCREEN
F082 CDE5F1     D1:         CALL    LFCR     ;0F35EH
F085 0E10                   MVI     C,10H    ;SET C FOR 16 BYTES ACROSS
                    ;
                    ;       PRINT ADDRESS STARTING THIS LINE
                    ;
```

```
F087 7C              MOV     A,H
F088 CD4FF1          CALL    PHCHAR   ;0F21BH
F08B 7D              MOV     A,L
F08C CD4FF1          CALL    PHCHAR   ;0F21BH
              ;
F08F CDC7F1          CALL    SPACE    ;0F340H
          PNTBYTE:                    ;F161
F092 7E              MOV     A,M      ;GET THE BYTE FROM MEMORY
F093 CD4FF1          CALL    PHCHAR   ;AND PRINT IT
F096 CDC7F1          CALL    SPACE    ;AND A SPACE
              ;
              ;       ARE WE DONE
              ;
F099 7C              MOV     A,H
F09A BA              CMP     D
F09B C2A3F0          JNZ     KEEPON   ;NOT DONE
F09E 7D              MOV     A,L
F09F BB              CMP     E
F0A0 CA23F0          JZ      PARSE    ;DONE
              ;
F0A3 23      KEEPON: INX     H
F0A4 0D              DCR     C
F0A5 CAB1F0          JZ      LINEDONE        ;THIS LINE DONE
              ;
              ;       IS HE BEATING ON THE KEYBOARD?
              ;
F0A8 DB00            IN      0
F0AA 0F              RRC
F0AB D223F0          JNC     PARSE    ;0F032H
              ;
F0AE C392F0          JMP     PNTBYTE  ;0F161H
              ;
          LINEDONE:                   ;F180
F0B1 05              DCR     B
F0B2 C282F0          JNZ     D1       ;
F0B5 CDF2F1          CALL    CMD
F0B8 0610            MVI     B,10H
F0BA C380F0          JMP     DO
              ;
              ;       INIT PRINTER
              ;
          PINIT:                      ;F18A
F0BD 3E00            MVI     A,0
F0BF D3C0            OUT     0C0H     ;SET UP
F0C1 D3C2            OUT     0C2H     ;DDRS
F0C3 D3C1            OUT     0C1H     ;INPUT
F0C5 2F              CMA
F0C6 D3C3            OUT     0C3H     ;OUTPUT
F0C8 3E3D            MVI     A,'='    ;3DH
F0CA D3C0            OUT     0C0H
F0CC 3E3D            MVI     A,'='    ;3DH
F0CE D3C2            OUT     0C2H
F0D0 CDF7F0          CALL    STAT     ;0F1C3H
F0D3 C9              RET
              ;
              ;       PRINT A CHARACTER
              ;
          PRINT:                      ;F1A1
F0D4 C5              PUSH    B
F0D5 0664            MVI     B,64H    ;RETRY COUNT
F0D7 05      PNT1:   DCR     B
```

305

```
FOD8 CAFOFO          JZ      FAULT    ;0F1BDH
FODB DBC2            IN      OC2H
                     BIT     7,A
FODD CB7F
                     JRZ     PNT1
FODF 28F6
FOE1 C1              POP     B        ;28H
FOE2 79              MOV     A,C
FOE3 D3C3            OUT     OC3H
FOE5 3E34            MVI     A,'4'    ;34H
FOE7 D3C2            OUT     OC2H
FOE9 3E3C            MVI     A,'<'    ;3CH
FOEB D3C2            OUT     OC2H
FOED DBC3            IN      OC3H
FOEF C9              RET
            FAULT:            ;F1BD
FOF0 C1              POP     B
FOF1 CDF7F0          CALL    STAT     ;0F1C3H
FOF4 C3D4F0          JMP     PRINT
            ;
FOF7 DBC3   STAT:    IN      OC3H
                     BIT     3,A
FOF9 CB5F
FOFB C0              RNZ
FOFC 214CF2          LXI     H,PFMSG  ;0F3E1H
FOFF CD1BF2          CALL    OSTR     ;0F394H
F102 CD10F2          CALL    CONIN    ;0F389H
F105 C9              RET
            ;
            BOUND:            ;F1D2
F106 CD24F1          CALL    LOADHL   ;0F1F0H
F109 CDC7F1          CALL    SPACE    ;0F340H
F10C 3E54            MVI     A,'T'    ;54H
F10E CDFAF1          CALL    PNT      ;0F373H
F111 3E4F            MVI     A,'O'    ;4FH
F113 CDFAF1          CALL    PNT      ;0F373H
F116 CDC7F1          CALL    SPACE    ;0F340H
F119 E5              PUSH    H
F11A CD24F1          CALL    LOADHL   ;0F1F0H
F11D 54              MOV     D,H
F11E 5D              MOV     E,L
F11F E1              POP     H
F120 CDE5F1          CALL    LFCR     ;0F35EH
F123 C9              RET
            ;
            LOADHL:           ;F1F0
F124 F5              PUSH    PSW
F125 CD78F1          CALL    TOBIN    ;0F244H
F128 67              MOV     H,A
F129 CD78F1          CALL    TOBIN    ;0F244H
F12C 6F              MOV     L,A
F12D F1              POP     PSW
F12E C9              RET
            ;
            ;       PRINT HL THE : THEN MEMORY CONTENTS
            ;
            POH:              ;F1FB
F12F F5              PUSH    PSW
F130 CD3DF1          CALL    POH1     ;0F209H
F133 3E3A            MVI     A,':'    ;3AH
F135 CDFAF1          CALL    PNT      ;0F373H
```

```
F138 CD48F1                CALL    POH2      ;0F214H
F13B F1                    POP     PSW
F13C C9                    RET
               ;
               ;           PRINT HL IN HEX-ASCII
               ;
               POH1:                 ;F209
F13D F5                    PUSH    PSW
F13E 7C                    MOV     A,H
F13F CD4FF1                CALL    PHCHAR    ;0F21BH
F142 7D                    MOV     A,L
F143 CD4FF1                CALL    PHCHAR    ;0F21BH
F146 F1                    POP     PSW
F147 C9                    RET
               ;
               ;           PRINTS M POINTED AT BY HL IN HEX-ASCII
               ;
               POH2:                 ;F214
F148 F5                    PUSH    PSW
F149 7E                    MOV     A,M
F14A CD4FF1                CALL    PHCHAR    ;0F21BH
F14D F1                    POP     PSW
F14E C9                    RET
               ;
               ;           CONVERTS BINARY VALUE IN A TO HEX-ASCII
               ;           AND PRINTS IT
               ;
               PHCHAR:               ;F21B
F14F C5                    PUSH    B
F150 CD5DF1                CALL    BHCONV    ;0F229H
F153 78                    MOV     A,B
F154 CDFAF1                CALL    PNT       ;0F373H
F157 79                    MOV     A,C
F158 CDFAF1                CALL    PNT       ;0F373H
F15B C1                    POP     B
F15C C9                    RET
               ;
               ;           CONVERTS BYTE IN ACCUM TO TWO
               ;           HEX-ASCII DIGITS IN BC
               ;
               BHCONV:               ;F229
F15D E5                    PUSH    H
F15E 6F                    MOV     L,A
F15F 1F                    RAR
F160 1F                    RAR
F161 1F                    RAR
F162 1F                    RAR
F163 CD6EF1                CALL    BIN1      ;0F23AH
F166 47                    MOV     B,A
F167 7D                    MOV     A,L
F168 CD6EF1                CALL    BIN1      ;0F23AH
F16B 4F                    MOV     C,A
F16C E1                    POP     H
F16D C9                    RET
               ;
               ;           CONVERT THE BOTTOM NYBBLE OF THE BYTE IN A
               ;
               BIN1:                 ;F23A
F16E E60F                  ANI     0FH
F170 C630                  ADI     '0'       ;30H
F172 FE3A                  CPI     ':'       ;3AH
```

307

```
F174 D8                    RC
F175 C607                  ADI     7
F177 C9                    RET
                    ;
                    ;          CONVERT UP TO 4 HEX DIGITS TO BINARY
                    ;
                    TOBIN:            ;F244
F178 CD09F2                CALL    INECHO  ;0F382H
F17B FE0D                  CPI     0DH
F17D C286F1                JNZ     MORE    ;0F252H
F180 316EE2                LXI     SP,STACK          ;0E26EH
F183 C323F0                JMP     PARSE   ;0F032H
                    MORE:             ;F252
F186 E5                    PUSH    H
F187 210000                LXI     H,0
F18A CDA3F1                CALL    CHECK   ;0F26FH
F18D CDBFF1                CALL    ATOB    ;0F28BH
F190 87                    ADD     A
F191 87                    ADD     A
F192 87                    ADD     A
F193 87                    ADD     A
F194 6F                    MOV     L,A
F195 CD09F2                CALL    INECHO  ;0F382H
F198 CDA3F1                CALL    CHECK   ;0F26FH
F19B CDBFF1                CALL    ATOB    ;0F28BH
F19E E60F                  ANI     0FH
F1A0 B5                    ORA     L
F1A1 E1                    POP     H
F1A2 C9                    RET
                    ;
                    ;          CHECK FOR LEGAL HEX-ASCII IN A
                    ;          RETURN TO COMMAND MODE IF NOT
                    ;
                    CHECK:            ;F26F
F1A3 FE30                  CPI     '0'     ;30H
F1A5 DAB9F1                JC      CHERROR ;0F285H
F1A8 FE41                  CPI     'A'     ;41H
F1AA DAB3F1                JC      NUMBER  ;0F27FH
F1AD FE47                  CPI     'G'     ;47H
F1AF D2B9F1                JNC     CHERROR ;0F285H
F1B2 C9                    RET
                    NUMBER:           ;F27F
F1B3 FE3A                  CPI     ':'     ;3AH
F1B5 D2B9F1                JNC     CHERROR ;0F285H
F1B8 C9                    RET
                    CHERROR:          ;F285
F1B9 316EE2                LXI     SP,STACK          ;0E26EH
F1BC C335F0                JMP     ERROR   ;0F067H
                    ;
                    ;          CONVERT ASCII DIGIT TO BINARY
                    ;
                    ATOB:             ;F28B
F1BF D630                  SUI     '0'     ;30H
F1C1 FE0A                  CPI     0AH
F1C3 D8                    RC
F1C4 D607                  SUI     7
F1C6 C9                    RET
                    ;
                    ;          PRINT AN ASCII SPACE
                    ;
                    SPACE:            ;F340
F1C7 F5                    PUSH    PSW
```

308

```
F1C8 3E20              MVI     A,' '     ;20H
F1CA CDFAF1            CALL    PNT       ;0F373H
F1CD F1                POP     PSW
F1CE C9                RET
            ;
            ;       PRINT MONITOR PROMPT
            ;
            PROMPT:              ;F348
F1CF F5                PUSH    PSW
F1D0 CDE5F1            CALL    LFCR      ;0F35EH
F1D3 3E3A              MVI     A,':'     ;3AH
F1D5 CDFAF1            CALL    PNT       ;0F373H
F1D8 F1                POP     PSW
F1D9 C9                RET
            ;
            ;       PRINT THE > PROMPT
            ;
            EPROMPT:                    ;F353
F1DA F5                PUSH    PSW
F1DB CDE5F1            CALL    LFCR      ;0F35EH
F1DE 3E3E              MVI     A,'>'     ;3EH
F1E0 CDFAF1            CALL    PNT       ;0F373H
F1E3 F1                POP     PSW
F1E4 C9                RET
            ;
            ;       PRINT LF,CR
            ;
            LFCR:                ;F35E
F1E5 F5                PUSH    PSW
F1E6 3E0A              MVI     A,0AH
F1E8 CDFAF1            CALL    PNT       ;0F373H
F1EB 3E0D              MVI     A,0DH
F1ED CDFAF1            CALL    PNT       ;0F373H
F1F0 F1                POP     PSW
F1F1 C9                RET
            ;
            ;       INPUT ROUTINE THAT RETURNS TO THE
            ;       MONITOR ON A CR - ECHOS CHARACTER
            ;
            CMD:                 ;F36B
F1F2 CD10F2            CALL    CONIN     ;0F389H
F1F5 FE0D              CPI     0DH
F1F7 CA23F0            JZ      PARSE     ;0F032H
            ;
            ;       PRINT TO THE CONSOLE
            ;
            PNT:                 ;F373
F1FA F5                PUSH    PSW
            PRDY:                ;F374
F1FB DB00              IN      0
F1FD 07                RLC
F1FE DAFBF1            JC      PRDY      ;0F374H
F201 F1                POP     PSW
F202 D301              OUT     1
F204 C9                RET
            ;
            ;       CONSOLE OUT - CP/M COMPATABLE
            ;
            CONOUT:              ;F37E
F205 79                MOV     A,C
F206 C3FAF1            JMP     PNT       ;0F373H
```

309

```
                    ;
                    ;       GET CHAR FROM CONSOLE AND ECHO IT
                    ;
                    INECHO:         ;F382
F209 CD10F2             CALL    CONIN   ;0F389H
F20C CDFAF1             CALL    PNT     ;0F373H
F20F C9                 RET
                    ;
                    ;       CONSOLE IN
                    ;
                    CONIN:          ;F389
F210 DB00               IN      0
F212 0F                 RRC
F213 DA10F2             JC      CONIN   ;0F389H
F216 DB01               IN      1
F218 E67F               ANI     7FH
F21A C9                 RET
                    ;
                    ;       STRING PRINTER
                    ;       PRINTS TILL A BYTE OF FF IS FOUND
                    ;
                    OSTR:           ;F394
F21B F5                 PUSH    PSW
F21C 7E         OST1:   MOV     A,M
F21D FEFF               CPI     0FFH
F21F CA29F2             JZ      OST2    ;0F3A2H
F222 CDFAF1             CALL    PNT     ;0F373H
F225 23                 INX     H
F226 C31CF2             JMP     OST1    ;0F395H
F229 F1         OST2:   POP     PSW
F22A C9                 RET
                    ;
                    ;       CLEAR THE TERMINAL SCREEN
                    ;
                    CLRSCR:         ;F3A4
F22B E5                 PUSH    H
F22C 213DF2             LXI     H,CLRMSG        ;0F3D2H
F22F CD1BF2             CALL    OSTR    ;0F394H
F232 E1                 POP     H
F233 C9                 RET
                    ;
                    ;       GET CONSOLE STATUS CP/M COMPATABLE
                    ;
                    CONSTAT:            ;F3AD
F234 DB00               IN      0
F236 0F                 RRC
F237 3E00               MVI     A,0
F239 D8                 RC
F23A 3EFF               MVI     A,0FFH
F23C C9                 RET
                    ;
                    CLRMSG:         ;F3D2
F23D 1B45FF            DB      1BH,'E',0FFH
                    SOMSG:          ;F3D5
F240 5A2D4D4F4E        DB      'Z-MON  V5L3',0FFH
                    PFMSG:          ;F3E1
F24C 0D0A464155        DB      0DH,0AH,'FAULT',0FFH
                    ;
F254                    END
```

Index

Edited by Roland Phelps